IAN 'MACCA' McNAMARA

AUSTRALIA ALL OVER

Why I Live Where I Live

IAN 'MACCA' McNAMARA

AUSTRALIA ALL OVER

Why I Live Where I Live

ABC
Books

Published by ABC Books for the
Australian Broadcasting Corporation
GPO Box 9994 Sydney NSW 2001

First published October 2005

National Library of Australia
Cataloguing-in-Publication data

McNamara, Ian.
 Why I live where I live.

ISBN 0 7333 1599 2.

1. Dwellings – Social aspects – Australia. 2. Australia –
Social conditions. 3. Australia – Social life and customs.
I. Australian Broadcasting Corporation. II. Title.
III.Title : Australia all over (Radio program).

392. 360994

Design, illustrations and typesetting by Helen Semmler
Editorial coordination by Neil Conning & Associates
Text keyboarding by Paul Conroy
Interview transcribing by Helen Beard
Cover picture by Kevin Killey
Project management by Richard Smart Publishing
Colour reproduction by PageSet, Victoria
Printed and bound by Ligare, NSW

5 4 3 2 1

For the people, again

And to the memory of

Dawn Webb, Gilbert Bennion and Eric Kroll

ACKNOWLEDGEMENTS

This is the fifth book based on *Australia All Over* and, just like the program, each one takes a lot of research and dedication from the team that's put most of them together. Nothing, of course, would happen without my producer Lee Kelly, who somehow manages to find the time to hunt through files for great material and at the same time make sure we go to air every Sunday. Nerida Reeves, too, has been a great help chasing up facts and seemingly impossible-to-find place names. Sadly, Dawn Webb, who did such a wonderful job transcribing interviews for the first four books, succumbed to cancer in 2004. She's much missed. Happily Helen Beard has seamlessly taken over the transcribing role. Helen Semmler has once again unerringly captured and transferred the program's essence to book form with her design and drawings, and Neil Conning ensured a calm and smooth flow over all editorial matters, with keyboarding assistance from Paul Conroy. Finally, Kevin Killey always takes great cover shots, and he's again made me look good. So, once more team, thanks very much.

The pictures in the book come from listeners and letter writers. Some of them are so good they are having a second run, having been used in previous books as well. Apologies to anyone whose picture's been used without a credit; sometimes they arrive without an owner's name.

So, here are the second-time-arounders: Ron and Gladys Bone page 81, Pauline and Richard Ayton page 135, Alf Garrard (on a bike) and Toby Bunion (on a horse) page 121, Andrew Rankin page 151, and Jessica Kirkham page 159.

The first-timers, with new pictures between pictures 96 and 97, are: Heather Hastings (also page 15), Casey, Lance and Marlene Fairlie, Ben Cuthbertson (also page 69), Margaret McKeachie (also page 53), Robin Tiffen, Denise Kennedy, Bev Gellie, Graeme and Deidre Brown, Mary D, Shirley Mealey, Jenny and Bob Chambers, Penny Murphy, B. J. Marshall, Bill Scott, Desley McDonagh, Wilma and Ken McCubbin, Jenny Weyman, Sue and Steve Shepherd, Yvonne Shirley, Brian 'Rowdy' McDowell, and Irene Shanks. Other new ones were supplied by Tony Hosworthy page 47, and the Finlay Family page 115.

As I've said before, many thanks happy snappers all!

Lastly, a special bow to Roy Heuir for allowing us to use the house at Ravenswood, Queensland, on the book's front cover, and also thanks to ABC local radio marketing for the lovely (says Lee) picture of me on the chapter opening pages.

Neil's helper, Crosby

CONTENTS

Macca wrote a song to celebrate Why I Live Where I Live, and here are the words. Almost every Sunday morning it can be heard right around Australia, and overseas. So, sing along as you enjoy the book.

WHY I LIVE WHERE I LIVE

I love my little house
In this sleepy country town
She's living on an island
They're sailing right around

It's our home among the gum trees
And if you've got the time
I'll tell you why I live where I live

We're on our hobby farm
We bought a church complete with pews
We're down-sizing to a unit
In the city, stunning views
Whether shed or shack or caravan
Or outback way you choose

I'll tell you why I live where I live
I'll tell you why I live where I live

Introduction

'Ian, sometimes the contributions to your Why I Live Where I Live segment are just too good to be true, mate . . . I have doubts about some of those who write from their "pristine hideaways" and watch "glistening dawns and radiant sunsets".'

That's my mate Russell, surveyor and cynic, commenting on Why I Live Where I Live, which has been the most popular segment on the program over the last twenty years. And it is just that, people from 'all over' telling us about their 'neck of the woods'.

It's true that not a lot write and say, 'I live in ... and it stinks.' Why would they? However, I do remember one woman grizzling about the place she lived in, saying, 'this place (name withheld to protect the innocent) would be a good place to hold a funeral'!

I think the segment provides a window on Australia, if you like a personal perspective, and as such enriches our knowledge of the country we call home. I also suspect it satisfies that inquisitive part of our nature: wondering about the 'other man's grass'.

Of course some contributions are a bit over the top: 'my little piece of heaven' or 'we call it purgatory – the closest thing to heaven', and the perennial, 'it's God's country, Macca'. But mostly we get wonderful insights into places, and especially people.

For instance, here's some classic, tongue-in-cheek Australian from Eric Williamson, Lawson, NSW:

We live in a place where the washing won't dry
And the pile of wet clothes is as high as the sky
It's hard to tell whether they're wet or just cold
Till you see they're all covered in fungus and mould

We live in a place full of drizzle and sleet
Where the ground is so wet that we're growing web feet
And you can't mow the lawn but that isn't a loss
Because all of the yard is just covered in moss

We live in a place where the fog is so thick
That you feel your way round with the aid of a stick
And the clouds and the mist that roll over the hills
Never seem to do much for our colds and our chills

We live where the easterlies bring in the smog
And the northerlies stir it and mix it with fog

Then the westerlies blow like an Antarctic gale
And the southerlies follow with thunder and hail

But now and again when we see the sun shine
And the wind dies away and the weather is fine
We remember why this was a good place to choose
We live here because of the wonderful views

What Australians do when they write in is not just describe a house, suburb or city, the bush or a country town, living on the road, an island or overseas; it's more an explanation to the rest of us of what this thing called Australia really is and the effect it has on them. And I can see listeners nod their heads as realisation dawns on them as well. Take this incisive contribution from Rod Milne.

A part of your show that fascinates me is Why I Live Where I Live. Half the time I can only listen in quiet envy as people describe their remarkable and fortunate residential circumstances. There are so many of us that seem to live in cities through no real sense of choice, out of work or even a lack of work. There are also family ties that keep us living in places that are not the first or even eighth choice, and I would count myself amongst those. While my physical presence may be at a bus stop in Adelaide Street at 3.00 p.m. in Brisbane, my heart definitely lies elsewhere: watching the sun rise on the wheat belt gums of Wyalkatchem, walking a windswept beach at Esperance under a Roaring Forties sky, or driving along a road at twilight through the paddocks of the Eyre Peninsula. Australia is a highly urbanised country, but for me the Big Sky is what the place is all about.

Rod was at North Tamborine when he wrote that some years ago. He may have moved on, and that's another interesting strand to the letters. People who keep moving or, as June Osborne from Loxton said, 'You have to keep on the move otherwise you'll corrode up and be useless.'

The reason that people move or stay goes part of the way to understanding the human condition. Most of us don't choose where we live, we're just there, always were. But we like to read of the couple in the caravan, the bloke on the forty-fifth floor, to think 'How can they live out there, solar power, no running water?' I love the reasons and I love the 'love of country' evinced.

Frances once wrote indignantly, 'I don't know if these letters are real or if you just make some of them up. I can't believe there are so many happy, contented people sitting on verandas all around the country looking out at green paddocks and flowering fruit trees to the blue hills beyond . . . life's just not like that.' Frances was possibly a bit jaundiced at the time because her engineer husband had been retrenched, again, so it was off to somewhere else, yet another mining town, for a new life.

Getting back to my mate Russell, who by the way lives in Canberra and loves it, here's his poem 'Why I Live Where I Live'. It's not in the footsteps of Dorothea Mackellar talking of love of a sunburnt country but . . .

I live where I live
because
two or three mornings a week

an old black cat
comes to my back door — of glass
as I breakfast alone

He looks in
I give him milk in a plastic plate
He lets me scratch behind his ears
then
he goes.

. . . and that's why I love the letters and poems sent in to Why I Live. They reflect a diversity of outlook, seeing the world from a particular perspective and enriching us all. I wish I could show you the thousands of letters I've received over the years. It makes me feel so proud — no, that's not the right word. My mum used to say 'aren't they wonderful' when she helped me get through the mail, and that's a better description.

Australia and its people are wonderful, and although I can only fit a fraction of the letters into this book, there's enough of them here to make you smile as you read and wonder about the people and places. You'll find them all here, the stay putters, the gypsies, the drifters, farmers, runners, ringers, adventurers, all ages from kids to golden oldies. I suppose each letter goes a little way towards revealing the mosaic of the country we call home. As I write I'm leafing through letters from the mid-1980s when the segment first started. I've included a few of them because their philosophy and love of the place is timeless and deserves to live on in this 'kleenex world'. In one of them a lady says, 'Ian, during the week I live in this small unit but on Sundays I live where I like.' And I sometimes think that's a more satisfying place.

Why I Live Where I Live is not really about where you live but more a state of mind; it's a window on Australia from the perspective of everyday folk like you or me. I suppose you can 'practise contentment', as Gilbert Bennion said, anywhere; some need hustle and bustle while others space and quiet. Whatever, each individual story builds the mosaic.

This year marks the twentieth I've been presenting *Australia All Over* in its current form, a live broadcast right round Australia. Before 1985 it was a live or pre-recorded regional program. It's a great privilege to be associated with it because it's given me the opportunity to meet wonderful people, to see this great country and share it with listeners. And it's no coincidence that the listeners appreciate the importance of a national radio network.

Thanks to everyone who's written, faxed, phoned, emailed or even thought about contributing. It's what makes a great community, a great country and a great radio program. Like Australia, it's yours, enjoy it!

Finally, here are two contributions from over the years that I particularly remember. See how much they tell about the people and the land they live in.

Firstly, Bob Moon from Townsville, Queensland.

This is a variation on Why I Live Where I Live — Why I'm Glad I Grew Up Where I Did.

There might not appear to be anything special about growing up during the 1930s and 1940s in Waverley, a suburb of Sydney. What is important for me is that I grew up about 100 yards from Waverley Cemetery, only fifty yards if you were prepared to climb the fence, as we generally were.

I think we learned a lot about Australian history and tradition in an interesting and eccentric sort of way at the cemetery, or the cemo as we knew it. There we looked at the grave of the poet and writer Roderick Quinn (I hadn't been aware that he lived in nearby Paddington until I heard your program) and saw the impressive grave of Henry Kendall. And in a typically unadorned grave in an obscure place we found Henry Lawson.

But it wasn't just poets we met at the cemo. We also admired 'the governor's grave' – I forget which governor it was – an impressive plot guarded by metal lions and a chain fence, and learnt that even the 'great' are mortal. At the cemo gates there was a soldier's memorial and each year a ceremony was held to remember the fallen in the Great War, in particular the Australians lost in France.

Another monument, in fact the biggest in the cemo, was in memory of the Irish patriots who died during the 1916 Easter uprising in Dublin. We were intrigued by the heroes' names listed on the back of the monument – not that they were described as 'heroes' to us kids. Our family, being English, Welsh and also protestant, weren't enthusiastic about Irish Catholics so they certainly didn't regard them as heroes. But even if the story we learnt was biased at least we became aware that history is a struggle and conflicts of beliefs.

There is another important aspect of Australian culture I first encountered at the cemo. The cemetery ends at the edge a cliff which then drops a couple of hundred feet to the sea. Just beside the cemetery and tucked into the cliffs was a huge cave, and on Sunday mornings we'd see men of all ages and types picking their way along the narrow cliff-face track towards it. Not all of them went into the cave; there were always five or six standing idly around, yarning and smoking. The curve of the cliff allowed us to look into the cave and see the men standing in a circle. Their heads would go up and down and then there'd be a muffled roar. This went on time after time. Two-up! Since then I've seen it played at some ritzy casinos around Australia, but with none of the mateship, intensity and authenticity on display in that sandy-floored cave on bright Sunday mornings, with the sea surging over the rocks below.

There was excitement for us as well as one morning there was a police raid. The cave was a huge trap and there were only two choices, either walk up into the hands of the police or scramble down a rough track and take to the water. And that's what some of the braver gamblers did. Luckily it was a calm day, but even so, once in the water it was almost impossible to get back to the rocks, and the nearest beach, Bronte, was a very long way off even for good swimmers. So, we watched the scuffling police and players at the top of the cliff, and below heads bobbing up and down in the surf. This is Australia, so it wasn't the Mounties or the Cavalry to the rescue but the lifesavers! In those traditional, heavy wooden surfboats they rounded the headland and picked up the swimmers. If I remember correctly no-one was drowned, no-one was fined too heavily, and they all lived to play another day!

Where else but in Waverley Cemetery could a kid get such an introduction to Australia?

And here's the late Eric Kroll from Biloela, Queensland, who was at a one-teacher school in Springsure, Queensland, when he wrote this some years ago.

I live where I live because that's where I have been put. I teach at Tresswell state school. It is situated 1,000 kilometres north-west of the nearest ABC Shop (Brisbane). After school hours the population is one man and a dog. The dog is mine and is called Bunji. One half of the twain lives in the dog box and the other half lives in the garage.

My friends told me when I was sent here that in two weeks I'd be talking to myself. I got the dog so that if the Inspector asked me if I'd started talking to myself I'd say, 'No.'

Since I arrived at my dog box I have had three visitors:
1. A friend.
2. A bloke who was lost, and
3. A drunk.

The pace never slackens off.

Bunji keeps me from going insane, despite what my analyst says. He doesn't even believe I can colour in the skin on the inside of the dog's ear with a paintbrush. And that's why I live where I live.

Yours in stability

PS I can have the radio up as loud as I like. The dog doesn't object.

Oh, I didn't tell you why I live where I live. When I was a kid we had blue wrens, some little – I think they're called red-capped robins – and eastern spinebills in our garden. I'll soon move back to that house where I grew up, and I hope that by planting many native shrubs and bushes I'll be able to attract the birds back to the suburb, a place they've long since disappeared from.

A garden with frogs, blue-tongue lizards and blue wrens – food for the soul.

And that's why I live where I live.

Talk to you Sunday,

Macca

1 – The Big Smoke

To each his own, but Gillean Wootten, then of Beauty Point, Tasmania, summed it up this way:

As I lie exhausted in the bed every Sunday morning listening to other people's ideas of paradise (bird calls, fluffy lambs in spring, wattle blooms bursting into life) I wish I could hear the thunder of never-ending traffic, only had window boxes to garden and was just two minutes from the deli.

Bob Dever,
Worongary,
Queensland

I lived in Balmain in the heart of Sydney all my life. I worked for Telstra for forty years, starting off as a telegram-boy and working my way up to middle management. When finally given the big package, my wife and I bought a motorhome and hit the wallaby for two wonderful years, all the time searching for a place to settle down away from the rat race. We found our little niche, so I'd like to share our good fortune with you and your listeners in a little poem I wrote that I called 'Town'n'Country'.

TOWN'N'COUNTRY

I'd like to tell you why I live where I live
And I reckon it'll make you pretty jealous
'Cause we've got the very best of both worlds
All within a five-kilometre radius.

We live in the hinterland at the back of the Gold Coast
In a little log cabin amongst the gum trees
Just a couple of private acres where we can please ourselves
Each evening we cop a lovely sea breeze.

As the population explodes down on the Coast
It brings us all the conveniences of a city
It's up to us to choose between the hustle and the bustle
Or the peace and quiet of our secluded valley.

The low-maintenance native gardens fed by a bore
Surround a patio where we spend a lot of time
There's a dam and a pond fed by a waterfall
And enough firewood to last us a lifetime.

The open log fire is inside and a firepit outside
A focal point for music, poetry and yarn-spinning
This pleasant area acts as a conservation pit
Where we indulge ourselves, playing and singing.

I've got a big boy's shed for big boy's toys
And a swimming pool to keep hangovers at bay
There are no neighbours close enough to disturb the peace
And a separate granny flat where our friends love to stay.

We hand-feed the resident possums, kookaburras and lorikeets
And are regularly visited by king parrots, galahs and a hare
Add to this ducks, rosellas and butcherbirds
Who give us a pleasure we have not experienced elsewhere.

We are lucky to be ringed by National Parks and glorious beaches
With all sports catered for at our front door
The weather is certainly kind to rheumatic joints
While the fresh air just adds to the score.

The whole area has a quaint village atmosphere
Whereas the locals are very friendly and nice
They are there to support you if ever you need them
It's no wonder they call this place paradise.

I'm writing this on return from 'duty' in a lovely public garden. It's a most pleasant duty as its setting is a wonderful scene of sandstone paths, taking you past waterfalls, ferns, rows of colourful annuals, large mossy rocks, a summerhouse and pergola, azaleas, blossom trees, myriads of camellia bushes and native trees, all merging into bushland. A haven for birds small and large. The crisp, melodious calls of the butcherbird, lyrebird and whipbird can often be heard. A peaceful bit of heaven on earth, just five minutes from a bustling CBD!

My own garden is confined to a fairly large patio which also gives me much joy. Not quite room for 'a swimming pool and a pony' but big enough for some horticultural pursuits. With the northerly aspect, I can grow a variety of plants and have set up a worm farm. In my eagerness and ignorance, I soon discovered quite a few of the inmates running away from home, but after reading the book and starting over again with the survivors, they appear to be thriving! A 180-degree view of surrounding bushland and lovely old homes and gardens allows for viewing the rich gold of a sunset, and sometimes simultaneously a huge, silver full moon rising in the east. Early mornings I often see a stream of white mist along Old Man's Valley.

I have several uninvited visitors, most of them welcome. They include white cockatoos (surprisingly well-behaved) who come for the birdseed, and rainbow lorikeets (not so welcome – noisy, messy and who demand sweeter treats). There's an occasional visit from a brilliant king parrot, magpie, and the not welcome noisy miners and feral pigeons. Tiny skinks scamper up the warm brick wall and bask in the sunshine. A couple of surprise visitors have been a pair of tree frogs, quite tame, which took up temporary residence under my dark green patio umbrella, mistaking it for a tree! A rustling noise one evening revealed that an owl (I think boobook), often the only sound heard at night, made the same mistake! I've even seen a brush turkey and an echidna walking along the nature strip (and I was quite sober!).

I consider myself very blessed to live among such beauty of nature, yet so close to all necessary amenities.

A well-behaved cockatoo

✏
Barbara Wood,
Hornsby,
New South Wales

I am at my small holiday house at beautiful Victor Harbor, just one hour's drive from Adelaide. Lovely white beaches, nice weather, Granite Island, horse tram, Sunday Maccas, and whales usually from June to October. I live just ten minutes from the GPO in Adelaide. A lovely quiet area with plenty of parks and big trees. Lots of birds – kookaburras sometimes sit on my clothes line – flocks of galahs and sulphur crested cockatoos make sure we don't get any almonds and very few apples. I have orange and black monarch butterflies breeding in my garden. We have the best public transport – buses and trains – and excellent medical services. On

✏
Aileen Lancaster,
Kingswood,
South Australia

February the first we went on the Ghan from Darwin on the first anniversary trip – excellent. Weather was good, no rain. We stopped at Alice Springs, Katherine and Darwin. Please bring your show to Adelaide or Victor Harbor soon. Very best wishes for the twentieth anniversary.

Beryl Mullard,
Morisset,
New South Wales

I live on a quarter-acre block of land opposite a busy railway line and on the main street in Morisset. The traffic is constant and the trains go chug, chug, chugging along, all night and all day. These sounds have become just familiar background music to my answer over a period of forty years. When I wake up each morning, I see birds sitting on or running up and down the branches of my jacaranda tree. The eagle-eyed kookaburra is a constant visitor. At the rear of my home is a profusion of green and brilliant colour. Two very large macadamia trees dominate smaller growth of grevillea and bottlebrush trees. Honeyeaters are always flitting around with a myriad of other feathered friends. Bird-baths and water bowls provide a place for them to drink and have a splash. I have not seen a snail for years as the blue-tongue lizards and skinks find them appetising. You would hardly think my little bit of paradise could exist with trains, buses, trucks and cars circling all around, but it really is a tranquil and comforting place. Friends and town folk are special and are the very best you would find anywhere. The exquisite feeling of experiencing the beautiful sunsets on almost every evening, combined with all those other bonuses I have just related to you, make my place the reason Why I Live Where I Live.

Pamela Reid,
Middle Park,
Victoria

I bought a single-fronted Victorian terrace in Middle Park twenty-four years ago. Sixteen feet and six inches wide and nestled amidst a row of similar cottages in a very narrow street, the neighbourhood is as charming now as it was then. We don't have gardens in Middle Park, we have very small courtyards. But I tell my friends that we have 'the best backyard'.

I walk along the beach daily, never tiring of the ever-changing morning light. Today as I walked I was listening to your program, hearing how other Australians love where they live. It was cold and crisp, but the sky was clear, and Port Phillip Bay was a glistening blue mirror. Plenty of seagulls, occasionally disturbed by dogs, jubilant in their Sunday morning romps. As I wandered along the Upper Esplanade, I nodded 'good morning' to the stall holders setting up for their Sunday market trade. People flock into St Kilda from all over Melbourne to enjoy this lively part of the city.

It was quiet on Acland Street. Too early for the locals or visitors. Just the occasional person rugged up in 'winter woollies' sipping a coffee and reading the newspaper. And the delicious smells from the variety of cake shops! I bought some just-baked pastries for the family's breakfast and quickened my pace on the walk home.

How's that for a backyard!

Jackie Turner,
Glebe,
New South Wales

I live in the city because I love it. I get a homely feeling whenever I am down on the docks looking at the water and the boats.

On my way home from work I love the smell of food cooking on Glebe Point

Road, and the general hustle and bustle of people going out for dinner. I like to be amongst crowds of people going about their business in a disciplined way, always keeping to the left. People are great, don't ya know?

The sound of sirens thrills me to bits. Recently I travelled in an ambulance with the siren going; it was very exciting. I felt so elated and young again. We went through a red light and turned left in front of lines of traffic!

However, being a towney doesn't exclude trees and birds from my passionate feelings. I can't tell you how delighted I felt when I woke up to hear on the news that the Lord Mayor of Sydney was trying to save the magnificent trees in the Domain. It really offended me to hear that they were going to be removed whilst there was still life in them.

A part of your show that fascinates me is Why I Live Where I Live. Half the time I can only listen on in quiet envy to others as they describe their remarkable and fortunate residential circumstances. There are so many of us that seem to live in cities through no real sense of choice, out of work or even a lack of work. There are also family ties that keep us living in places that are not the first or even eighth choice, and I would count myself amongst those. While my physical presence may be at a bus stop in Adelaide Street at 3.00 pm in Brisbane, my heart definitely lies elsewhere: watching the sun rise on the wheat belt gums of Wyalkatchem, walking along a windswept beach at Esperance under a Roaring Forties sky, or driving along a long road through the paddocks of the Eyre Peninsula. Australia is a highly urbanised country, but for me the Big Sky is what the place is all about. Tim Winton once described the Australian coast line as a great big veranda, and I understand what he means.

Rod Milne,
North Tamborine,
Queensland

However, it is getting harder and harder for city-dwellers to get out in the true bush. Twenty-five years ago train travel in Australia was cheap, now much of the country is not served by train and it costs the proverbial arm and leg to get there. If I had my way I'd be travelling Australia in a campervan tomorrow with no deadlines and commitments! I know a number of urbanites who are a bit dismissive of your show, but I and many others welcome it as an opportunity to link again to the heartland of the country, where life doesn't revolve around national basketball, cable TV, mobile phones, fast food and rap music. Keep up the connection, Ian!

I'm a city 'kid' (now forty) born and bred. I live in Bondi in Sydney, probably Australia's most densely populated area, and absolutely love living there. But I still appreciate country life and what it offers, largely due to the amount of time I spent in Grenfell as a kid in the sixties and seventies.

Margaret Dennis,
Bondi,
New South Wales

I grew up in a small, 'single parent' family in suburban Sydney. Mum had to work full-time to pay the bills and during school holidays we often stayed with family and friends. The best of these holidays were always the ones on the Grenfell wheat and sheep farm of my mother's best friends, 'aunty' Kath and 'uncle' Barry.

As city kids we were a bit of a novelty to the locals which, of course, we loved. But Grenfell and farm life was a whole new world to us. It gave us an appreciation

Rabbit in the spotlight

of a way of life very different to our own, of wide open spaces, a beautiful country-side, and open, warm, down-to-earth and hard-working people. It was an invaluable experience, one to which many city kids never have access. When you're a kid you don't realise its significance and it's only when you grow up that you value it and realise it was very special. Your program from Grenfell reminded me of that.

Memories of those chilly, sunny mornings which dawned into beautiful days under a cloudless blue sky; sitting on the back of the big red Massey Ferguson tractor while my 'uncle' prepared the paddock for the next wheat crop; learning to ride horses and motor bikes under the tutorage of my country 'cousins'; collecting wood for the ever-burning wood fire in the house; shooting rabbits by spotlight in the forest; caring for tiny motherless lambs; guinea pig races and mice plagues; taking my 'uncle's' battered Ford over to the back paddock to do 'wheelies' in the dust – beyond sight of the house!; dressing-up and trooping into town for mass on a Sunday; fresh home-cooked cakes (seemingly) daily; shared family meals around a huge kitchen table; and shared baths in what was often dust-filled dam water during years of drought (traumatic for a city girl!).

We don't get up to Grenfell much these days. But I thank Grenfell (and my second family on the farm at 'Sunnyside') for those great memories and for the things I learnt there. As I said to my 'aunty' Kath a few years ago – much to her amusement – if I ever have a nervous breakdown from big city living I'll be up to Grenfell like a shot.

PS Love your program. You have plenty of fans amongst us cappuccino-drinking city folk!

Brian Bohan,
Geelong,
Victoria

I live in a one-bedroom unit in a block of ten in North Geelong because it's what I can afford and it's close enough to Melbourne to allow me to commute there to work. But it's far enough away to allow me to enjoy one of the better things about Melbourne – being one of the roads away from there!

Over the years I have been able to learn the art of patience and self-control when dealing with my fellow tenants, but the boot has sometimes been on the other foot when I have come home from my football club celebrating a win, so I suppose we have to get on with it and smile!

When it starts getting me down I just turn the clock back to December 1969 when I moved to Melbourne to do my apprenticeship. At sixteen going on seventeen I thought I knew the lot. What a wake up call! From mum and dad, grandad, eight brothers and sisters and a couple of cats and dogs to Mrs D's Boarding House.

She was a kind, caring, friendly and helpful landlady supervising anywhere from between thirty and forty all-male boarders, ranging from kids just out of St Vincent's boys home to others from country Victoria, all the way though to elderly pensioners with nowhere else to go.

Geelong is the gateway to the Victorian western districts with the great fresh water lakes' fishing, what bliss, and the Great Ocean Road with the best surf, swimming and fishing beaches. Again what bliss, and all those other touristy things. It's where I'm allowed to live the way I like: to watch, listen, read, talk to and be with whoever I want. My little unit is and will for the time being anyway remain my home.

2 - Go Bush

One of the first contributions to Why I Live came from Lindsay Lee Yabsley on her property near Girilambone, NSW:

To us this place is the most beautiful on earth. There is something about a western property that is hard to define – you love it or hate it. Those dust storms and winds, wretched mosquitoes, not being able to get out when it really rains, sloshing around in the black soil. You forget all that when, after a drought, you smell the first drops of rain, see the grass grow almost overnight, and take time to watch the glorious sunsets. You just get caught up with optimism and a sense of excitement.

Margaret Armitage,
Briagolong,
Victoria

*I just can't work under
these conditions*

I left a comfortable suburban home in the eastern suburbs of Melbourne, a home in which many happy years had passed, a home where a family matured and grew into adulthood, a home from where a demanding career was pursued, enjoyed and completed.

We decided to 'go bush'. We discussed the plan with anyone and everyone. We bored people. We made people look at our photographs. We asked advice, constantly. When with friends we talked of nothing else. From our friends came a variety of responses: 'Will there be clubs you can join?'; 'Country people are different, you know'; 'What on earth will you do?'; and sometimes, 'I wish I could do that.'

Well, we did it, we moved to an 'alternative' home made of bush poles and mudbrick in the foothills south of the Divide, beyond Briagolong. In doing it we have learned so much about ourselves, our capabilities, our limitations, others around us, our world, and above all about friendship and caring.

We have met challenges large and small. We have dealt with leaking taps, bull ants in the kitchen, a refrigerator that wouldn't light, a bat on the curtains (all on the same night); we have tracked down and fixed a major water leak from our precious tank supplies (500 litres daily!); we have learned how the copper pipe connections work behind the bathroom basin (I am a receptionist, not a plumber!); we disposed of no less than nine little mice caught in our trap, one after the other, one memorable night (there was a nest under the cooker); I now know that writing poetry while baking bread means the fire will go out, and the bread will sink; we have learned that we can do things ourselves without waiting for someone to do it for us; Colin has faced an eight-foot goanna near the washing line; I have grown and actually eaten my own vegetables; we have made mud bricks and built with them (I defy anyone to knock down my wall in a hundred years!); we have felt the kindness and friendliness of the articulate and talented people who live as we are living, and we are content.

How can I describe the life I am now privileged to live? How can I find words that will wrap around what is mine? Beauty and peace are within my grasp – all the time – whenever I reach for those priceless things, they are there.

Let me tell you about my forest, my peaceful, restful places. There is an air of ageless timelessness. The floor is littered with leaves and twigs, and I know that above, among and beneath these layers life is busy, hurrying and scurrying, surviving, adapting, doing all the things that always must be done. Living here, where I live, are all the creatures who should be here, and we are all getting quite used to one another.

We are some distance from shops, hospitals and cinemas and our contacts with people have reduced somewhat, but our power and warmth are free as the air, and we never sit at traffic lights! We can see the mountains all around us, and feel what they say. The lifestyle we have chosen for this part of our lives is not for everyone, but it does great things for the soul, and for family relationships!

Here there is no noise, no fumes or trash, no brash insincerity, no falsehood, no contrivance or connivance. Do I miss hi-tech, modern, brightly glinting metallic parts of life? Do I miss daily rush and daily wear? No, I do not. My life is certainly less convenient, and I perform many tasks the old way, but my body is healthier, my mind more content than before, both for the obvious reasons, and for obscure ones like accepting a challenge when it may generally be considered time to leave challenges alone!

Our friends from before are as important to us as ever, and we will continue to be enthusiastic and active members of our old groups from our position on the outer. What we have gained we are anxious to share, and anyone who would like to visit us, for whatever reason, for whatever term, is welcome always.

If anyone reading or hearing my small account is considering a major change – nowadays the term is 'change of direction' – I would encourage a thorough investigation of all aspects, a serious assessment of situations, and then PLUNGE!

I left Sydney to retire to the Sunshine Coast three years ago after forty years of working in our biggest capital city. The quiet and fresh air here are pure bliss. Each morning I wake to the rustle of the wind in the trees and the songs of myriads of birds. There are parrots of all hues and sizes, bush minors, butcherbirds, magpies, peewees, swamp pheasants, crows, plovers, ibis, cranes, kookaburras, black and white cockatoos, wood ducks and many others.

Maroochy River is a rural suburb about eight minutes from Bli Bli and ten minutes from Yandina. My property is in an acreage estate on top of the Bli Bli Range which is surrounded by cane fields and an occasional patch of bush. It would have to be one of the most beautiful areas I have seen, a vista across the cane fields and Maroochy River to the ocean, stretching from Mt Coolum to Maroochydore. We have all modern facilities such as hospitals, an aerodrome with flights to southern capitals, and modern shopping centres. Our climate is great. At present, like everywhere else, we are in need of rain, especially the farmers and those of us dependent on rain water for our tanks.

As my greatest passion in life is painting, I was lucky enough to find a home with an area suitable for a studio. To the west of the house is a yard of native trees and shrubs, fruit trees and a dam which in season is covered with yellow, blue and lipstick pink waterlilies. In the distance Mt Ninderry stands sentinel above all. At present a lot of the native trees are in blossom and the air is filled with the hum of bees.

Unfortunately last year I was smitten with rheumatoid arthritis and am somewhat limited in my painting but am still utterly determined to resume my great love no matter how much it costs physically. Last year in my darkest hours of this dreadful disease one of my greatest joys was being able to look out of my windows at the wonderful bush scenery around me and listen to the song of the birds. It restored my faith. So, you can see why I'm glad I found this place and why I am happy to live where I live.

➥ Gaye Lee,
Maroochy River,
Queensland

The reason I live here is much more than the town's locality and seasonally changing climate and beautiful landscape. It's the people, because that's what a town is, the community. When things go wrong and disaster strikes the community pulls together for the good of each other. This is where you have a name, an address, a family, a history, where your neighbours and shopkeepers know your name and

➥ Deborah Rutter,
Canowindra,
New South Wales

sincerely ask, 'How are you today?' If you need groceries delivered or you're not well enough to go to the shops, they'll deliver your order to your home, no extra charge. Where the doctors, hospital, medical, community, pharmacy, nursing, health and home care staff know your name and respectfully treat you as an individual. The police become involved with the community, encouraging its development. Creative and sporting groups support and encourage personal development. Where churches respect the beliefs and customs of others in the community. The schools strive to encourage their students to reach their full potential in a safe and friendly environment. The backbone of Canowindra are the volunteers, the many who give seeking nothing in return. When you walk down the street you'll meet someone to say hello to, or a wave of recognition.

The night sky is radiant with stars, clear, pretending to be within reach. To wake in the morning to hear the birds calling, singing of the earth's wonder and bounty. Today in the distance a solitary flutist practised 'Silent Night'. I'm unsure which warmed me the most, the morning spring sunshine promising a fresh clear day or the sweet, innocent symphony of the solitary flutist.

This is why I live where I live.

Sue Robinson,
Trentham,
Victoria

I live where I live because it reminds me of what life is all about — away from the urgency of the city, the traffic snarls and road rage, where you can still leave your keys in the car and the house unlocked. The locals have time to talk and show genuine concern for each other without invading your privacy. There is a true sense of community: a community that mobilised to stop destruction of our local native forest, a community that twice in recent times threw a benefit for someone's uninsured house that burnt down, providing clothing, furniture, funds and promises of assistance with rebuilding. True community!

And my modest patch? I look out onto the towering gums in the forest, kookaburras on the fence posts, over one hundred species of birds in the garden, flocks of cockatoos and galahs overhead. There's a paddock full of kangaroos opposite, koalas and possums grunting at night, and the occasional visit from an echidna or wombat. The air is so fresh, mornings crisp, nights cool and starry, and snow at times to delight. Seasons are distinct — winter refreshingly cold, spring full of brilliant bulbs and blossom, summers mild and dry and autumn trees spectacular. To me, this is heaven on earth — and only an hour from Melbourne.

Margaret Marion,
South Caulfield
Victoria

While listening to this segment Why I Live Where I Live I thought of the old collection of rhymes my mother collected using the names of places in Australia. Old names are an important indication of the history of an area and its pioneers. My street was named after the family who ran a dairy on the hill overlooking Port Phillip Bay. I come from the goldfields area of Victoria and the street was named after an ancestor. However, for no reason newcomers have changed the spelling so no-one will know the importance of my family to the area. City people need to know about our great country.

But soon the Coleraine pelted down
No Hattah coat had he
Not even a Tempy-rary roof
So drenched he soon Wilby.

Let people have their motors
Equestrian he'd Thoona be
For on his nag, he often says
The Moyhu ride, the Moyhu see.

Two donkeys that Braeside by side
Annoyed him after dark
To stop them all in vain he tried
His dog no Mooroolbark.

I thought you and your listeners might be interested in hearing about our experiences moving from the city to the bush. We used to live on the northern beaches in Sydney, which is a beautiful part of the world, but the pressures of a high mortgage, the stresses of trying to get to work on time through the traffic, and Stuart's asthma in the city, led us to make a country change almost two years ago. We moved to the Coffs Harbour area and it was the best thing we ever did.

We exchanged white cockatoos for black cockatoos, mynah birds for rosellas (the birds on the Arnott's biscuit tin), pigeons for ducks, water birds and the glorious spoonbills. We see horses and cows every day, hear the owls at night and the back garden is full of blue wrens and an almost unlimited variety of other birds. Instead of an alarm clock the kookaburras wake me every morning (if the ducks don't get in first) to beautiful clean air. Our water is crystal clear tank water.

The country is beautiful. You don't really see much from the highway, but go west and it rapidly changes. Where we are, just south of Coffs, there are dams, ponds, streams and bridges. The waterlilies are rampant and we have tiny green tree frogs in the roses at the front of our veranda. On warm evenings we have dinner out there and have no need for music. The creek in front of the house is full of frogs: first of all you hear the maestro revving up his orchestra, then the full frog chorus fills the air! This and the waft of orange jasmine makes for a very romantic setting. When it rains the little tree frogs jump from leaf to leaf in the roses, and when it rains a lot the mist comes down from the mountains. The Great Dividing Range comes down to the sea at Coffs and we are nestled in the base of one of the mountains.

Every day becomes an adventure. It is no longer 'go to work, come home, go to work, come home'. Just getting the paper can be an adventure and there are some great characters in the area. The plumber is as dry as an outback drought, Danny the builder regales us with endless stories about gold-mining in the hills, and absolutely everyone has either bought or sold a cow to Russell Crowe or worked on his property!

Stuart became seriously ill with a tumour in his bowel, but we have had the most wonderful medical care. Terrific doctors, terrific staff and a terrific hospital,

Diana Wallace,
Coffs Harbour,
New South Wales

all ten minutes from home. He needed chemo every Friday – no problems, the hospital sent transport for him and I pick him up after work. All of this and it didn't cost us one penny. The doctors and hospitals waived any gap fees so there was no additional stress. It would not have been possible in Sydney.

Everything here is an easy ten minutes away; Coffs itself, the beaches, the airport, the racecourse and beautiful Sawtell, which is full of cafes and restaurants. I email my friends each week with tales from the country and they love it. I thought I would share this with you as I know a lot of the people in Sydney have the same thoughts and I would like them to know it is all worth it. It wasn't easy for us to move: I had to give up a wonderful job and the security that provided, and finding work here was not easy. But perseverance pays off. If you don't have to work, all the better. There are wonderful golf courses, fishing, beaches, riding, crafts – you name it. Anything will grow in the garden, and our starfruit tree is so laden with fruit that I am feeding them to the horse on the property behind us.

Rod, Central Coast, New South Wales

Morning, Macca. This is Rod from the central coast. I'd just like you to stop calling us fellas 'Old Blokes'! I'm sixty-five and my wife's not far below me. We've just bought acreage here and I'm digging postholes, building a chook run and digging vegetable patches. I've never worked so hard in my life!

So, you're not down at the beach with the dolphins.

No way! You have to remember that it's us old blokes who hold this country together while the young blokes are out there partying and having a good time.

Is this a career move or fun thing?

It's something I dreamed about all my life and I wouldn't change it for quids. I should have done it when I was forty. It's a lifestyle you can't appreciate until you've done it. You can have your city residential blocks, doesn't matter whether they're quarter acres or 400 square metres, this beats them all.

Well, I'm not sure about the posthole digging!

I tell you what, I get into bed at night, my legs are tired and my back's aching and I think to myself Gee, I've really done a good day's work. I've really achieved something trying to keep the foxes out and the ducks in. It's a good life.

Well Rod, I was going to say I'll see you at the beach. But I won't, will I! Good luck.

Rod again, Central Coast, New South Wales

The last time I spoke to him, Rod was farming on the central coast of NSW. Here he is again.

Rod, are you still doing your farming?

The chook run

No. Sadly we had two burglaries on the property. One was a major one and my wife had a heart attack after it. Then we both had knee operations. While we loved going up to the chook house and getting the fresh eggs, and growing our own zucchinis and garlic, we just sold up. We couldn't find another place on the central coast so we came back to Sydney.

There you go. There's the whole circle of why I live where I live. When you rang before, I thought, I wonder why they left the big smoke? How long were you there, about five years?

Only a few years. The burglary was what really upset us. We'd virtually rebuilt the house. We had an old timber house, pulled everything off it and rebuilt over the old frame, and added on to it. It was a lovely little home and it suited us down to the ground. Then when these mongrels got in a trashed the joint it was just soul destroying. Then we had a second burglary. We thought, my God, are we that vulnerable? We were fairly isolated. But it was a beautiful property and I'd go back there tomorrow if I was a younger man. I can't understand why people want to be sitting on 600-square-metre blocks in the city with next-door neighbours breathing down their necks.

Rod, I'm glad you rang. Now you've moved back to Sydney are you enjoying it?

No. Not totally. We'll probably move again – better than an even chance we'll move back up to the central coast. There's a lot of oldies there and it's a bit slower paced than Sydney.

And a million miles from care from the sound of things.

I listen to you all the time, Ian, and thoroughly enjoy your program. It's wonderful to hear snippets from all over Australia and all over the world. If you've got one more minute, I'll tell you a very quick story. I'm a guy who likes to throw bottles over the back of ships. Would you believe on two occasions I've actually had responses to my notes in them. The last one was from a pearl farmer up near Tahiti. His letter was absolutely beautiful. It would take too long to read it out now, but maybe some other time.

Jenny Weyman, Falls Creek, New South Wales

Good morning Jenny, where's Falls Creek? I thought it was in Victoria.

I know, it's tricky isn't. We're actually ten minutes south of Nowra, just on the turn-off to Jervis Bay. It's a lovely place to live.

How's the weather there?

It's going to be a good day. A little bit overcast and we're just getting into the chilly autumn coastal weather. I just wanted to tell you about our straw bale house. This week 350 beautiful bales of straw arrived from Cowra. We offloaded them and put them inside our house, our frame. We're going to be rendering them and turning them into a house.

What do you render with?

We're going to use an earth render but you can also use a cement render. You end up with the most magnificent thermally excellent house!

How long will that take?

Rendering and putting the bales up will only take a couple of days, and then you have to allow the render coats to dry. All up the house has taken about two years so far. It's becoming really popular in Australia and I don't think you've covered it on your program yet.

We haven't, but we'll do it. I'll come down and have a look at the site.

I understand you're in the middle of Australia today. I can't believe that people build tiny fibro houses in Alice Springs and pop an air-conditioner on the top. Why not build a house that sustains a cool temperature without any electricity?

Jen, I'll come and see you in Falls Creek.

⬅
Jenny Weyman,
Falls Creek,
New South Wales

We started building our straw bale house in 2000 after a wait of nearly six months with council plans. We were the first straw bale house to be put forward to the Shoalhaven Council so we guessed they would not approve it in a hurry!

When I phoned last year we had just had our straw delivered. Since then it has been placed in the walls and we have nearly finished the first coat of earth/clav render.

The main reasons we built in straw were: the look and feel of a rendered wall; we could do it ourselves with little help; we wanted to cut the costs of heating and cooling over our lifetime; straw is a renewable resource that would otherwise mostly be burnt; we didn't like the idea of using materials that take enormous amounts of energy to produce, i.e. concrete; rendered straw bale is incredibly fire resistant and also will screen out nearby highway noise.

Our house is based on a shearing-shed design, skillion roof with verandah (although we had to fill in one end due to baby number four arriving). It is non-load-bearing, which means the roof is not supported by the bales. We built the walls and put on the roof before we infilled with straw bales, some cut in two, others shaped to fit the space. We have learnt a lot in the process and would definitely do some things differently second time around.

My grandparents owned a sheep property down at Bibbenluke, so the link to shearing is strong for me and I feel totally in 'love' with the design. (See the photographs between pages 96 and 97.)

🐕

⬅
Jan Harvey,
Forbes,
New South Wales

I want to tell you where our little piece of paradise will be soon. At the end of 1998 I took long service leave and during 1999 we found paradise. I know everyone tells you about their bit of paradise, but we really found it, 500 acres six kilometres from the coast bordering Deepwater National Park, which is just south of Agnes Waters and 1770 in Queensland. We will leave our four-bedroom house with two bathrooms, a walk-in robe and a walk-in pantry for living in a shed! After a couple of years my husband and I both hope he can build a home on a small part of a hill which will give us ocean views, albeit distant, on a clear day. The birds and trees are so beautiful. We are two kilometres off the road in absolute peace.

We will be off early next year to our part of paradise. We plan to grow a crop, but of course firstly we will get a vegie patch going to feed ourselves.

Andrew Prentice, Shepparton, Victoria

Meet Andrew Prentice of Prentice's Orchard. He's a fruit grower and is passionate about his job. He sponsored an Albanian bloke called Guri, and you'll meet him next.

This fruit business was first established in 1913. I'm the third generation. My grandfather planted the original orchard and my father ran it before me. We have expanded it since then.

It always seems when I do anything agricultural on the program there's a bit of a crisis. It's hard running an agricultural business isn't it.

There's no doubt it's hard work and we've seen so much change. When I first came to the orchard it was mainly canning fruit and it was going through a fairly difficult stage. We've since changed over to mostly fresh fruit and it's more technical. Growing systems have changed, as well as the way we manage irrigation. The markets are forever changing and a sudden depreciation of the dollar can affect us very quickly.

Do you sell a lot of your stuff overseas?

Yes, we sell a lot of stone fruit to Thailand and Singapore. That's been quite knocked around this year by currency.

You obviously enjoy being in the fruit business.

I do enjoy growing fruit because there's real satisfaction every year in seeing something start from nothing and then turn into beautiful fruit, particularly if you can get it into the market place and it just looks right. There can be many challenges though. We had a big frost earlier this year and it took probably thirty per cent out of the stone fruit.

So will your family continue in the fruit industry, or is there too much overseas competition?

That's a difficult one. My kids are still pretty young. It's not something you do just because it's there. You've got to do it because you love it. If either my son or daughter's interested I'd like to have them in the business. But they've got to want to do it.

We talked to the Guri the Albanian picker you sponsored

He's a great worker and his family is terrific. He's put a big effort in and it really worked out. He gave us the commitment. He's been a tremendous worker – we'd like to have more like him.

He's just a really nice bloke, his family too.

Guri and Luma, Shepparton, Victoria

Andrew Prentice sponsored Guri and his wife Luma from Albania. They came to Australia seven years ago and he is now a permanent resident. They pick pears on Andrew's orchard and are very good workers. Andrew's very pleased to have them. They have a great attitude.

Do you like living in Australia?

I very much like living in Australia. I'm lucky. I'm second time born here. It was big day the day I got my permanent residency, April 23 2003. I will never forget that day. Maybe next year I get my citizenship.

What's it like picking pears? It must be pretty tough.

I like every job here on the orchard. My life now is not so bad. Everyone works very hard. Everyone that works with me and my wife Luma is a good worker. My wife is a very fast worker. She can do everything. A good worker, a very good worker. Sometimes she's faster than me. Even when it is forty-two or forty-three degrees we never stop because it is important to get the fruit off the trees. I have to help the boss here.

Max Gregory
Red Rock,
New South Wales

Cool trumpeting broglas

I live in the little coastal village of Red Rock about forty kilometres north of Coffs Harbour and six kilometres off the Pacific Highway, so we are completely insulated from the noise of the constant stream of traffic.

I listened to the first half-hour of your program today, but then I went for a walk along some of the tracks that lead through seventy acres or more of coastal heath adjoining the village on the south side. I heard brolgas trumpeting in that direction, but couldn't sight them. Their call travels well on the still morning air.

The heath is close to its best at present. On one side of the main road it is predominately yellow and on the other side white, but mixed in with the tiny blooms are purple, mauve, blue, yellow and orange flowers. The flannel flowers will soon be out, and with this warm winter Christmas bells have bloomed since summer in a small patch that was burned. They always come out in profusion after a fire. Small honeyeaters and tits are active in the growth, and I was lucky enough to see one of the rare but shy green parrots that live there.

I strolled for a while along the boardwalk adjacent to the clean little river that flows in and out with the tide, and then went over the coastal dune to see if any whales were in view. No luck, but they will be coming past next month with their calves on the return journey to the Antarctic.

I walk most mornings and usually have a few friendly words with other residents doing the same. But this morning there wasn't a soul in sight – they must all have been listening to you! Well, the walk was almost worth missing your show for about forty minutes.

Maxine and Jack Woodhouse, Esperance

Maxine and Jack Woodhouse are farmers in Esperance. They'll tell you why they live where they live.

JACK: I was born in the city, in Adelaide, and I learnt a bit about farming on the River Murray near Walker Flat. The local farmer taught me how to shear a sheep and milk a cow when I was in primary school. I always wanted to be a farmer but didn't think it possible for a city lad. I went to an agricultural high school and agricultural college, and then I headed west because I'd heard there was land on the Ord River at Esperance. I got a job tractor driving for three months and then went contract fencing. We were known as 'the barbed wire boys'. That was forty years ago. I was allocated a block of bush west of Grass Patch and started there. In the early days the banks didn't want to know. I remember applying for a Commonwealth Bank development loan and they sent a chap out to have a look at the block. I got a report back three weeks later saying, 'Come back in about five years, sonny, and we'll see if you can grow a crop.' So I had to go shearing and contract super spreading to keep a bit of money coming in. Maxine comes from a farm closer to Perth. We got married in 1966 and have been battling away ever since.

What's life on the farm like Maxine? Do you like it? Does it have a lot of natural beauty or is it all farmland?

MAXINE: I love it because it's what I was born to. I guess we're lucky where we live now because we've developed two farms. At the second one at Cascade we've left a lot of natural bush so we have plenty of wildlife and birds we can farm amongst. It's a beautiful place. A traveller from the city came to the gate one day and asked, 'Do people really live here?'! It's a wonderful community at Cascade and a little different to other farming communities because we all started there together and are like a close family. Jack and I are getting to be the eldest ones. Maybe it's time we moved on!

I don't know about that. It sounds a lovely place.

JACK: It's a magnificent spot. I've really grown to appreciate the bush over the years. We've got echidnas around the house and kangaroos. We don't like to see too many emus because they knock over the crops, but it's lovely to see the native parrots come in.

And it's why you live where you live!

JACK: That's dead right, Macca.

Maxine: We have wonderful wildflowers as well and they're just sensational this year. That's another attraction of the area.

You're making us all want to have a look at Cascade some time.

MAXINE: I hope you do one day.

Val and Trevor Gray,
Tolmie,
Victoria

After hearing your program today I thought I would scribble you a few lines to tell you about Tolmie. We have been coming here for the last twenty-seven years. We have our house in Melbourne but we come up to check up on our steers and my husband does 'his thing', e.g. fencing and making hay. We have 112 acres up here and half of it is blackberries.

Tolmie is about twenty-two kilometres up in the mountains from Mansfield. We just had our 119th Tolmie Sports Day. One of the events is wood chopping and it was the North-East championship. It was great to see the young boys trying out this year. Also we have the Tolmie three-man challenge, married ladies race, old buffers race, kids events – sack races, egg and spoon races – potato peeling contest, horse events, and crosscut saw. To finish the day off we have a dance in the local hall. There is also the 'Star Lady of the Evening' who is rewarded with a sash. My kids always look forward to suppertime where home-cooked cakes and biscuits are consumed.

There are still a couple of pioneer families up here. One is Don Swainton who still plays tennis at eighty-one!

I just picked sixteen kilograms of blackberries so I will dehydrate some to make into roll ups; make jam; make blackberry liqueur; and I might even make the blackberry jam drops!

Well I had better close as we have to pack up and head down to another week in Melbourne. It is hard to leave the solitude. The days go quickly up here. I am looking forward to winter where we can have bonfires, Dutch oven roasts and toasted marshmallows on sticks.

OUR HOME

Priscilla Fenton,
Mount Moriac,
Victoria

From Melbourne and Sydney where we had resided
We sought a better life
To buy some land and build a farm
Where the air is sweet and the politics calm.

The city friends looked on in dismay
'These Fenton folks would rue the day'
They gave up the life of suburban rules
and took up fencing with strange-looking tools.

The Barrabool Hills where beauty sets the scene
Of rolling slopes fulfilled our dreams
Eighty acres of pastures and lake
What a start! What a break!

Each weekend, the garage in the boot
A thermos, a lunch, and off on the route
To our new land of glorious hopes
Its birds, its water, its gentle slopes.

Our shed went up and hundreds of trees
Were planted and growing beneath plastic sleeves
The house was built to face the north
It is constantly light and full of warmth.

The view down our valley has to be seen
A row of blue lakes and grass so green
We never dreamt of owning such land
And every morning when I stand
To see the frost or rain or dew
I feel refreshed and face the world anew.

They say that the kitchen is the hub of the home, well my kitchen is part of a one-room house, eleven by five metres. It contains a living area with a conversation pit, open fireplace, my office, and a reading nook – then up the spiral stairway is the mezzanine floor which is a sleeping area.

It's a pole-frame log cabin which we built ourselves, and after nearly four years we've carved out a wonderful life on our eighty acres, along with our four horses, chooks, two dogs and a cat. Like most people we live on a shoestring but with our varied talents we can make a fallen log into work of art! We're attempting to be as self-sufficient as we can, sometimes hilariously.

We cogitate often on the state of the planet which basically is why we decided to remove ourselves from the rat-race to the bush.

Sue, Russ and
Carolyn Fernandes,
Bombala,
New South Wales

Murray Everett, Barrington, New South Wales

Where are you Murray?

Just on the outskirts of Barrington on the Barrington River.

How long have you been here?

All my life: thirty-six years. I'm the third generation here. When dad got married he bought this farm. There were four of us. The girls have all moved away and I took over the farm in 2000 when deregulation started. I've taken it over and we've come into the biggest drought of the century! Not just myself, but everyone else is doing it real tough at the moment.

Do you think you'll survive?

Not on the current milk prices we're going to get for the next six months. It's going to be very touch and go. We're going from an average of nearly 38 cents per litre during the winter and now they've cut it back to 26.5. I might average out about 31 cents.

What could you do if you weren't dairying? Could you use this country for anything else, like beef cattle?

Yes. The bigger farmers are going to hang in. The ones that are milking around three or four hundred cows, they might be looking for a farm to lease to grow their heifers on. Otherwise I don't know what I'll do.

It looks like a nice place to live.

It's a great place to live. Beautiful place. We've got permanent water here all the time. For the kids, you can't beat the lifestyle. It's hard work, but a lot of fun. You've got to love it to do it.

Does it snow around here?

Only forty minutes away, on the top of the hill just there. That's Barrington Tops. I got up to milk here about six weeks ago, looked at the frosts and just rolled back over. It was minus 9 when I finally left the house! You could have skied down the hills. Everything was frozen. It was one of the mornings when you could have just sat there with a cup of coffee with a splash of rum to warm up. The cows were walking around on their tiptoes.

Do you enjoy dairy farming?

I love dairy farming. It's just the satisfaction of seeing the cows drop the milk in the morning and afternoon, watching the vat fill up. I show my cattle; dad showed cattle; his dad showed cattle. We've been going to the Sydney show for fifty-four years. This year was the first year I haven't taken any down. Dad wasn't real happy, but I couldn't afford it.

What about your neighbours, how are they going?

Steve my next-door neighbour's been milking for thirty or thirty-five years. He just finished up. He'd had enough. There's been a dozen go out here in the last twelve months. Back in the 1950s and 1960s there were around 260 to 300 dairy farms around here. And now I think there might be thirty and I reckon in another twelve months there might only be four or five.

Stick at it, mate. Nice to talk to you out here.

Ernie, Kindred, Tasmania

This is Ernie from Kindred, Tasmania

Macca, are you looking for a pea grower?

Well, I saw some peas the other day and they looked really nice. Peas are lovely. I think they're the forgotten vegetable.

We grow peas under contract. We've got about eighteen acres in at the moment. They're about four or five inches high and are a beautiful green blanket.

How long have you been growing peas?

For years and years.

Where are you?

North-west coast of Tassie, about five miles from Bass Strait, in a triangle between Ulverstone, Devonport and us.

What's the place you're at?

Kindred. Three houses. That's Kindred.

'It's a lonesome away from your kindred and all. By the campfire at night . . .'

The peas we grow are harvested in the paddock. They're shelled and the only things that leave the paddock are the peas themselves. All the residue and all the pods are left in the paddock. Off the peas go for processing and within about four hours of harvest they're in the packet ready to buy.

They shell them in the paddock?

Yes. The machines they use cost about $600,000 each.

How long have you been in Kindred growing peas?

I've been in Kindred about six years and growing peas for that period. Prior to that I was in the fruit and vegetable business in Newcastle for twenty-five years, and before that I was an agricultural pilot for fourteen years.

You've led an interesting life. Do you grow other things besides peas?

Onions and poppies, cauliflowers, potatoes.

What's it like being a farmer these days?

Absolutely magnificent. Beautiful red soil, very mild climate. It's a great place to be.

Do you ever go out and pick up a shell and taste a few peas?

You can bet on it.

There are lots of varieties of peas?

Yes. There's only a few that are grown for processing. Mainly because they mature virtually all at once.

Why did you leave Newcastle and go to Kindred?

I've always wanted to be on a farm. This is it. A wonderful place. Really good people and good country. Just a good lifestyle.

And you can throw a stone into Bass Strait? Just a figure of speech!

Well, I can't throw stones for five miles and we don't want to make too many waves.

Good on you. I'll play a song about beans, but it could be peas!

We lived for a couple of years on a beautiful property just west of Murwillumbah. Our house was between two creeks and was not far from the Border Ranges. As a consequence there was an abundance of birdlife, crickets and frogs. The early morning stillness would be broken by the beautiful, pure call of the pied butcherbird, or

Helen Malseed,
Terrigal,
New South Wales

the chuckling and raucous laughter of a clutch of kookaburras and soft warbling of magpies. Sometimes noisy friar birds were the first to greet the morning. Then the rest of the day was filled with a myriad of different birdsongs. Evenings began with crickets and then, if it had rained, the frogs chorused their pleasure. Green tree frogs lived in all the roof gutters and barked to each other at the first hint of rain.

We had to move back south for family reasons and I am now in an area with few birds and no frogs. I miss them very much, so every time I hear bird calls or frogs and crickets on your program I just stop whatever I am doing and let the sounds wash over me. You are my link with lovely memories and I am very grateful.

We listen to you whenever we can and I just had to write after you said you love wrens and that it would be good to live some time in the city and some time in the country. Well, I have that life and it is the best. The country part is far better of course. So relaxing away from the buzz!

My husband and I bought five acres in Gippsland with a view to die for. On one acre there is a house surrounded by a beautiful garden, lots of fruit trees, two hundred roses, different types of native trees and flowers, and a vegie patch. We have parrots, wrens, swallows, yellow-breasted honeyeaters, silver eyes and the most beautiful grey shrike thrushes who love to sing in the big tin shed. We also see black cockatoos and kookaburras. We try to get to the country at least every second weekend. Come Sunday night we hate leaving to come back to Melbourne. My husband was born and bred in the country so he always dreamt about returning. Marrying a city girl he wasn't sure, but we both just love the country life. Some weekends we come back to Melbourne with fourteen different types of produce. We joke that one day we will be like The Good Life television show.

Lorraine,
Melbourne and
Gippsland,
Victoria

Helen, Weipa, Queensland

Hello, Helen. Are you a local?

I've been here eighteen months.

Well, you're a local! What do you do?

I think so! I'm a mother. My husband works with Comalco. He's at work today and not – what's the word – very happy he can't be here!

So it's a shift operation?

Yes. He works two days, two nights and then has four days off.

I'm always interested in what people do and why they're up here. I've never shifted in my whole life. I grew up in Sydney and while I've travelled around a fair bit that's where my home is. Where was home for you?

We're actually West Australian. We came from Tom Price before here. We were ten years there and then down in Narrrogin south of Perth. Nobody knows where that is!

Do you like it?

Yes. We love it. We love the water. We had ten years at Tom Price with just the rock, the dust and no trees! We like the trees here.

What does your husband do?

He's in despatch. He controls the section of the mine where they deliver the trucks to the load out.

So you've got some little kids around the place?

I've got two and they're in year one and year two. I spend my time chasing after them. It's great here for the activities. The kids love the sport. We have things on every day.

They had a fun run this morning, didn't they? Did you go in it?

No, it was a bit early for me on the weekend!

How they can describe running as fun I don't know. But that's what they call it!

Jason, Jabiru, Northern Territory

Good morning, Macca. It's a nice morning here after we had a bit of a storm last night, the first rain of the wet season.

I was just talking to a guy in Broome and they'd had a light sprinkle. He said they expect some cyclones around there this year. Don't know if that's true.

Yes, that's what they're saying. We had a storm through here at about seven last night and had an hour of rain. Good decent rain. So we won't have to sprinkle for a couple of days.

What are you doing in Jabiru?

I work out at the Ranger Mine, which is what most of the people at Jabiru do. I look after all the computers out there.

How long have you been there?

I've only been here two months. My partner and I moved up from Brisbane. We're enjoying it so far.

I bet you are. You're there for the wet season. It should be spectacular. More lightning strikes up there than just about anywhere in the world.

That's right. We had a storm come through last week and the lightning was unbelievable. There was a strike or two every second. It was quite spectacular.

Tell us about Jabiru.

There's about 1,200 in the town, of which about 400 work at the mine. The town's shared between the mine, parks and wildlife and a few other organisations. About eighty to eighty-five percent of the people in the town actually work for the mine. It's one of the smallest mines in Australia but it's one of the closely watched because of where we're mining. Being in the middle of Kakadu National Park it could have quite an impact if something went wrong.

Computers are your speciality?

They are at the moment. I've decided to do some environmental science study next year with an IT stream to it.

It must be really good experience to work in a mine based in such an environmentally wonderful place like Kakadu.

Yes, because you're talking two ends of the extreme. The mine has got certain certifications that have proven it can sustain itself and also keep its influence out of the national park. Studying environmental science will be good. There are a lot of environmental people here who can help me.

Tell people what it's like living out there. It must be quite awesome when you go outside, specially now when it's starting to rain.

People call it remote, but we're only two-and-a-half hours from Darwin. We go there every month and do a big shop. We've got a little food store here, a post office, newsagent, bank and service station. So that's enough to keep you going. A lot of people go to Darwin to get away for a weekend. It does get a little hot. We had forty-two and forty-three last weekend. We'll stay for a couple of years, but who knows. Some people have been here for ten or twelve years.

Have you got Jabirus in Jabiru? Are you a bird watcher?

Yes, definitely. I like doing a bit of photography and there's lots of billabongs around where you can build hides and watch. We went for a cruise down at Yellow Water, which is about fifty kilometres south and saw a couple of jabirus, and some pretty big crocs. They reckon there's two in the lake here so they've set some traps. All they got the other day was a big barramundi!

Hello, over here!

Which they kissed and released!

Molly Sinclair,
Murrindindi,
Victoria

We have lived in this lovely place called Murrindindi for the past ten months. It is approximately twelve acres with a river frontage where trout are plentiful.

The house faces the river with the hills and mountains beyond. The abundance of wildlife is absolutely incredible: wallabies, kangaroos, wombats, rabbits, echidnas, foxes, birds such as cockatoos, galahs, many parrots of all colours, rosellas, bluebirds, cuckoos, kookaburras, swallows, bellbirds, magpies, blackbirds, flocks of budgies and canaries. On the dam between the house and the river you'll find several varieties of ducks, brolgas and ibis. Completing the picture are the cows, sheep and horses contentedly grazing.

Being only an hour-and-a-half from Melbourne we realise how very lucky we are to live in Murrindindi, which means 'Mist of the Mountains', and to live where we live.

Carmen, Mossman, Queensland

Carmen, how are you?

Good thank you, Macca. How are you?

Carmen, where's that accent from?

Germany. I have been here for seven and a half years.

How come you're driving a truck?

I worked on a farm in Western Australia. I was cutting cane. I came out on a holiday, went home and came back again. I live just north of Mossman. Been here three years now and happily married.

You're in the middle of the cane season now. What's this job like?

Just started six weeks ago so it's full-on.

What other jobs have you done in Western Australia?

Working on farms, cotton farms, melon picking.

Germans seem to like Australia. What is it? The wide open spaces?

Yes. Wide and open, free and no stress. Just relax, take it easy.

You're working pretty hard here. What sort of shift do you do?

Usually start at seven in the morning and work till eight at night; whenever we finish. The cane season goes to late November. Depends on the crop. Or if we have trouble with the mills breaking down.

So Carmen do you regard yourself as an Aussie now? Or half and half?

Half and half probably; not a full German any more.

You've got a great Aussie accent. It's lovely, and lovely to meet you.

And you too. A nice surprise.

I'll let you get back to work.

No worries! See yer!

In the early hours of the morning, when the dew is still glistening on the grass, this town I have made my home awakens to the sound of honeyeaters, the smell of freshly baked bread and the drone of the hoop pine mill. A traveller driving from Nanango to Yarraman would be rewarded with a great view. Green flowing hills, with contented cattle grazing and tall bunya and hoop pines mark the horizon.

It's strange how destiny works in one's life. I was born and bred a city girl but I married a country lad and here I am thirty years later still enjoying my country life. The community, although small, are a warm and friendly bunch who pull together in times of strife and rise to meet challenges with enthusiasm. Last year when our police sergeant, Perry Irwin, was slain in bushland at Caboolture our

Julie Sandeman,
Yarraman,
Queensland

town went into mourning. As a tribute to the man and his family the community is raising funds for a permanent memorial in the people's park, a memorial seat will be placed in Yarraman Cemetery where Perry was laid to rest.

Yarraman has a population of 1,500 and is slowly growing. For me the friendships and the knowledge that someone close cares about me is why I live where I live.

Bill Ah Foo, near Kilcoy

Where are we Bill?

About ten kilometres east of Kilcoy

It's a great view. What valley is that?

That's what they call the open ranges to Neurum Hills and looking over is towards Villeneuve, which is a bit scruffy today because we haven't had any rain. When we've had rain it's nice and green and a beautiful view.

How long have you been here?

I've been here fifteen years. I grow strawberries, rock melons and a few other vegies during the year just to make a living. We haven't had much rain. Our main problem is water. Dams are very low. We have three. Two of them are empty and the other one has only got about fifteen per cent in it. We water our vegies underground mostly. That's the only way to conserve water. We seem to be in a dry belt here at the present time. We see the rain come and it goes to the hills. It never comes this way. Goes either side of us. Woodford gets two or three inches and we get two or three points. It's heart breaking sometimes, but every now and then we get something. I wouldn't change it. We're pretty central here and the outlook is pretty good. Not far from Brisbane, not far from the north coast and not far from Toowoomba.

Where were you from, Bill?

I originally came from Longreach out west.

What made you make the move?

Kids going to school. They either had to stay out there and leave school early or come down here and get a job. So it was easier and cheaper for us to come down here and be with the family.

Do you rely on passing trade or send to market mostly?

We send to markets. We're in a co-op. A strawberry co-op where we pick our fruit and send it down there and they pack it for us. We have our own marketing manager. It's a lot easier than when we first started when we could be up ten, eleven or twelve at night packing, and then have to start again at seven in the morning.

And your wife looks like your right-hand man?

Yes. And she makes the jam as the sideline. It's the value-added product for us that does well.

Have you got any theories about the weather?

I think it's a lot to do with the warming of the climate, but it all depends where you are too. Some places get it and others don't. We miss out here a lot because of the ranges. It comes through the gap, if it keeps coming we're right, but most times when it comes through the gap it splits and goes east and west of us. We used to get storms in early September and October, but we haven't had a storm here for about eight years now. We haven't had any decent rain here for four years. We really want it.

Let's hope we get it for Christmas.

Yes and not only for me. There's a lot of people out there going through a tough time. As I said, I come from Longreach in the central west and I've seen seven-year droughts. I just know what people are going through. Some of them have got great hearts to be able to back up again after going through so hardship living in the never-never land.

Tom Milenkovic, Shepparton, Victoria

I met Tom in his coffee shop.

G'day Tom. Running a small business in a big town. How did you get into that?

I worked for the federal government for twenty-eight years. I left ten years ago and bought a seven-day-a-week business. They say I'm now paying for all the slack times I had over the twenty-eight years!

Now that wouldn't be true, Tom, would it!

Not at all! I worked with the Commonwealth Employment Service. We decided to have a life change. A deli-cafe change. We're down here at the Europa Deli and Cafe in Shepparton, but not open seven days any more, unfortunately.

Why not?

Well the industrial award situation is changing and you've only got so much money. Even though people think we have a shed full of it at the back. We just can't afford to pay the penalties on weekends. Three shops in our precinct have closed because the wages are so high. It was a fairly bubbly food corner. I hate seeing one shop open, one shop shut. It makes the area look a bit mish-mashy. Jeff Kennett got rid of the penalty rates in the late 80s. Unfortunately Mr Bracks and whatever have now changed that and reintroduced the penalty rate. I'm not for one minute saying that people don't deserve it, but in our situation it changed the goalposts. We'd financed our business on a seven-day-a-week basis, but we worked out that on a Sunday – one of our busier days – with the new wage rates (we employed about

twelve people) at the end of the day we'd come out with about $100 in our pocket. So, here we are talking instead of making coffee!

What's your family background, Tom?

My mother was born in Austria and father in Yugoslavia. I was born in Seymour so I've come a long way. About eighty kilometres! My parents came here after the war and were farmed out to jobs like the Snowy Mountains. Seymour was a very big railway centre, one of the biggest in Australia. My father was a pilot in his life overseas, but here they sent him to work on the railways. He was a train driver. He studied to do his pilot's licence and learnt English while working night shifts. At the grand old age of forty-four, and a week after he finished his last exam, he dropped dead of a cerebral haemorrhage, which was very sad. Mum raised me and my brother. I did my schooling in Seymour, went down to Melbourne, back up to Shepparton and married a Shepparton girl, and been here since 1981. I love the area.

What's it like running a coffee shop? I've often thought that running a cafe, a motel or a pub is one the hardest gigs. It never seems to stop.

You spend a lot of time after hours, particularly when the seven days were there.

Tom, all around Australia people are in coffee shops and you hear conversations like, 'I'm so over that ... I'm so not into magazines.' Amazing language! What's it like making coffee for people?

Well, I'm not allowed to. My missus bans me from the coffee side! She's a great woman and does a great job.

🐕

Doreen Vance,
Wee Waa,
New South Wales

I am writing to tell you why I live where live. After passing my sixtieth birthday and having lived and worked in Brisbane for the past twenty years, I really wanted a change of lifestyle. I could definitely hear the call of the country and got a position living on a property outside the town of Wee Waa. The town is known as the cotton capital of New South Wales, so of course there's lots of cotton as well as wheat. The place where I live is the famous Cubbaroo Wine Cellars. It has been a steep learning curve for me but I wouldn't change it for quids. Firstly, I got bogged on the black soil road so had to learn how to negotiate the roads in the rain. Secondly, the isolation at first was difficult. Thirdly, sharing the planet with snakes has been a challenge! I needed an attitude adjustment. I am starting to gaze out at the blue skies and comment on the lack of rain. I am enjoying the solitude and time to appreciate the little things. I have a huge garden and have been trying to make friends with the horses by bribing them with thistles. I have been encouraging a feral cat to stay about the house with the idea that it will keep the snakes away. Now that it's spring everything is coming out in bloom and the wildflowers are a constant amazement. Every species of birdlife, especially glorious parrots and galahs, drop down on the lawns to say 'hello' every day.

Life has taken on a different dimension. When I think that if I had stayed in Brisbane I would probably be languishing in a pensioner's bedsit flat. Would I go back? No way! This is why I live where I live.

Charlie Earle, Winchelsea, Victoria

I thought I'd ring up from a free-range egg farm and say good morning.

What are you doing Charlie?

The missus has got me moving the portable sheds. We have to move them around twenty or thirty metres every Sunday morning before daylight so the chooks have a fresh pick. I hope she doesn't catch me sitting here bludging!

So you're really mustering!

Yeah, mustering big time. I've got 5,000 of them to move! We've been doing this for about two or three years. We had seventy acres we didn't know what to do with and thought chooks would be good. Every farm's got to have a chook; we just went a little bit overboard! One of the reasons we move the chooks in the mornings is because early in the piece they put one over me. They get out of the shed in the morning, have a look around, and off they go. We moved the shed at two o'clock in the afternoon and came back at five or six that evening to lock them up, but they were back where the shed was that morning. So we had to move 800 chooks back by hand. I always thought chooks were stupid!

I buy free-range when I can, but are they fair dinkum free-range? Is there free-range and free-range?

There are basically three lots of eggs: the ones you catch in the cage, then the barn-laid in big sheds 300 long – the chooks can move around the shed. Then there's ours, which are totally free-range. We use about thirty-five acres of the farm. We buy our chooks at fifteen weeks old off Lou, who brings them up in a cage to stop them from pecking. We lock them in the sheds for the first day and next day we put a small cage around them so that they can get out on the grass. It takes them about three weeks to learn how to roost. We drive around and collect the eggs on a little Massey Ferguson tractor. When you're feeding them it's nothing for a chook to hop up on the tractor and sit on your knee.

How long have you been at Winchelsea?

I was just about to say all my life, but I haven't finished it yet! I was born and bred here and live in the same house I was born in. I went over to Western Australia – that's where I met my wife – and worked on the road trains and a gas pipeline for a while. Then I went to Gympie in Queensland and worked for my cousin pushing timber.

How do chooks compare with all that?

I'm still an earth-mover, mate. Once you have diesel in your blood you can't get rid of it. That's what I do for five days a week and then I move chook sheds on Sundays!

Where's Winchelsea for everybody?

It's between Geelong and Colac. Winchelsea's pretty famous. I'd guess you've heard of a thing called a rabbit? Well, rabbits were first let out about a kilometre away from here. So, we're famous for something no-one wants!

I'll let you get back to mustering the chooks!

Sue Shepherd, Maralinga, South Australia

Sue Shepherd and her family are the caretakers at Maralinga, the site of Australia's early atomic tests.

Yes, it is very nice here. We meet many interesting people but it's quiet when nobody's around, which is really good. There are beautiful sunsets every night and sunrises each morning. The wildlife around is really good; the birds are beautiful. And we're not really isolated. We have the internet and the people in the store at Ceduna that we deal with are just wonderful. Although they don't know us from a bar of soap, they really go out of their way to make our life more pleasant. We can ring them at any time and say we need some flippers for the swimming pool, Panadol, even wool for the bonbons my daughter wanted to make one Christmas! The Port Augusta post office is wonderful. They accept parcels for us and send them up on the Indian Pacific train.

When it gets boring do you go and watch the train go by?

No! We have been down a couple of times just to see it but missed it as it raced past at 120 km. On Wednesday mornings we pick up our mail bag and the train drivers get off and have breakfast. They're always happy to see us because they're hungry! We've had lots of photos taken of us at the train. We take the kids down and the passengers are pretty impressed to see a seven-year-old running around with a chihuahua in the middle of absolutely nowhere!

Is this the first time you've lived in an isolated area?

Yes. I'm definitely a city girl, definitely a city girl!

So you've adapted.

Yes. It's a little city on its own here. We meet people like you! We've met people from all over the world. French delegates come here, and politicians we would never have had the opportunity to meet elsewhere. We're thoroughly enjoying it.

And how long will you stay here? Could you stay for the rest of your life?

Probably Steve and I could, but for the children, no.

Do you miss the shopping and all the stuff that girls miss?

No, we've got the internet!

Who delivers here?

A truck goes to Oak Valley once a week and so we get any delivery we want then, and as I said, Australia Post delivers via the train. We don't really miss out on anything.

I know kids are on the school of the air, or the internet of the air. Do you talk to mothers on other stations?

Yes, we have what they call a 'supervisors' soup'. We do it on the telephone as well as the internet. Once a week, or fortnightly if things get a bit hectic with schoolwork, all the mums, or supervisors, get together and bash out what we think needs to be done with the school.

Sue, nice to meet you all the way out here.

It's been lovely having you here.

Daria and Pat, Weipa, Queensland

It's twenty degrees, I'm just about to take my shirt off, but Daria's wearing some sort of Canadian Rockies top. She's all rugged up but it's not cold at all.

DARIA: It's freezing here this morning for us locals! We all had our doonas on and the kids were complaining when we pulled them out of bed.

I thought coming from Geelong, you'd have a singlet on, Daria!

DARIA: We've acclimatised now.

Do you like it here, Pat? Tell me about your life here.

PAT: I work at Comalco. It gave us an opportunity to move and we like travelling around. I can't think of too many better places to move to. Weipa is lovely, looking out at the river there in the background, the camping and good friends; we have two boys Michael and Liam, and they are just terrorising the place this morning!

Do you work here until your job finishes or can you live here afterwards?

PAT: You can live here and there are a few long-timers, but on the whole most people move on. It's very much up to you.

It seems like a nice spot. Somebody said to me recently that home is where the heart is. Obviously at the moment this is where your heart is.

DARIA: Yes, few people have family here and that's the hardest thing. Most have families in Brisbane or further afield. You can't have a baby here unless of course it pops out all of a sudden! You have to go to Cairns, so it's quite traumatic.

That reminds me of a lovely eighty-five-year-old bloke in Junee telling me how he went into town with his mum when she was pregnant with him and knew all the bumps in the road. So when she took him home after he was born he recognised every one of them! It's been lovely talking to you.

Graeme and Deidre Brown, Reola Station, New South Wales

I talked to Graham and Deidre during a long, dry spell in early 2005.

Where am I?

GRAHAM: You're at Reola Station, 300 kilometres west of Bourke and about 110 kilometres north of White Cliffs, western NSW.

And it's a sheep station, so you need a drop of rain.

GRAHAM: We certainly do, Macca. We're in our fourth year of exceptional circumstances. We're starting to think it's as bad as the 1902 drought, so it's pretty ordinary.

Deidre, how long have you lived here, and what's it like?

DEIDRE: I've lived here for thirty-five years. I've adapted quite well but I've never got used to the heat. Everything else is good. The isolation isn't really isolation as we have lots of people coming and going all the time, and we're busy with family and jobs. The isolation doesn't worry me and it's a great place to have a family.

GRAHAM: On the health side of it one of the reasons we can stay out here and have a family is the Royal Flying Doctor. It really puts a mantle on safety for people living in isolated areas.

Graham, tell me about living and working out here. How many sheep do you run?

GRAHAM: We normally run between forty and fifty thousand sheep. We're down to ten per cent of that number at the moment and struggling to hang onto those. It looks like we'll probably have to move them off the property if we don't get rain in the next three to four weeks.

How long since you've had rain?

GRAHAM: Our last rain was on the first of November last year, but it was only a passing shower. We've gone the last four months with not a splash of rain over the summer.

People in Sydney and Melbourne can relate to that as they're on water restrictions. So, when's your rain time if you're going to get it?

GRAHAM: It's very unreliable out here. We can get good winter or good summer rains. But if we get most rain in summer we get the grass butts and that takes us right through the year, with just the average bits of rain here and there.

Nice place to live, Deidre?

DEIDRE: Yes, great place to live, Ian, really good.

Do you get to the city? Ladies love to shop don't they – that's what I've heard anyway!

DEIDRE: I've just come back from the big smoke – I had ten days in Sydney. We caught up with a few films, lovely restaurants, and a bit of shopping too. It was great.

How big is Reola Station?

GRAHAM: Reola is six stations together and there's 430,000 acres in the whole lot.

And you've got this really mighty shearing shed. (See the photograph between pages 96 and 97.) What was the impetus to build such a very high tech shed?

GRAHAM: The decision was made back in 1985. We were finding with our expansion and the number of sheep our little shed on the property just wasn't big enough. We just outgrew it. We put together all our good ideas and built one big shed. We get the shearing over and done with in a short space of time.

It's lovely to see you both and thanks.

DEIDRE and GRAHAM: Great to have you here, Macca.

PS On 10 July 2005 Graham phoned to report they'd had excellent rain that week! I'm still waiting for the jar of their delicious apricot jam . . .

3 - My Island Home

I thought I'd met all sorts on my travels, but that's one of the great things about the program, there's always a surprise in store. Pattie Rossie bought forty-acre Puncheon Island between Cape Barren Island and Flinders Island and crowned herself 'Princess Pattie of Puncheon Island'! So, enjoy my first interview with 'royalty'.

Pattie Rossie, Puncheon Island

Here's Pattie Rossie. She's 'Princess Pattie of Puncheon Island'. Hello Pattie, are you a local?

I am, but I'm probably considered a newy by the locals because you have to be here for forty years before you are a local! To make myself a local I bought a forty-acre island between Cape Barren Island and Flinders Island. So I call myself a local out there but a newy here.

What's the name of the island?

Puncheon Island.

I'd love to buy an island. Why did you?

It was my husband who decided he wanted to buy it. We were workaholics in Melbourne. I couldn't understand what we were going to do with an island – we never took three minutes off! He mentioned the word retire in his spiel about why we should buy it. But he's still a workaholic and I have retired.

How do you get between here and there?

I have a boat. I'd never driven one before and only knew the pointy bit was the front! I've got a little nineteen-foot runabout. The first time I had to drive it out there was a bit freaky. Me and my puppy dogs. I'm 'Princess Pattie of Puncheon Island'!

So we've got Princess Mary from Denmark and Princess Pattie from Puncheon Island! You seem a fairly gregarious person. Do you get lonely out there?

I have seven sisters and grew up as part of a large bunch of people. They are in Melbourne though. I have never been lonely out there. I used to project manage trade shows and things, so I called myself a professional exhibitionist before I became an islander!

Why did someone like you, who is obviously involved in the community, want to go out there? You like the solitude?

I don't know. I just feel at home. For people that don't know Flinders Island, this community is the most wonderful group that I have ever come across. They are supportive, warm, and care for each other. So I pop across here to wear their ears off! The bakery is my Flinders Island office. I am known for sitting out there and talking too much. But they understand because I've been on the island by myself and need to do an unload!

Princess Pattie, can I ask you what the going rate for an island is?

It was a bit expensive and there were a few zeros at the end. I thought it was a giggle what we paid for it!

Olga Henwood,
Flinders Island,
Tasmania

The last time I wrote to you I finished up feeling like a hero! I had letters from all over Australia, from people I hadn't heard from for years. I am a permanent resident of a nursing home, and writing and listening to the radio stops me being bored and lonely. I am nearly eighty and our family has had an uninterrupted residency of these islands for eight generations.

My grandson came to see me this week after three years overseas in Europe and the Middle East. He is going to work at Gove. He is adamant that we have the best water for swimming in the world. One of my best friends says his kids are like mutton birds – they always come back!

I heard that you are being invited here and I do hope that you will accept because you have been part of our lives for many years. If I have made any errors in this letter you must excuse me as I am listening to your program at the same time.

We are having glorious weather but really need a lot of rain after the driest November on record. Deliberately lit bushfires are causing much worry and with very little water it is hard to get on top of them.

From my lovely window I can see birds of all shapes and sizes – black cockatoos, Cape Barren geese, black swans, Pacific gulls and black ducks, to name but a few. The honey eaters entertain me for hours as they work so hard getting nectar from the bottlebrush.

A pod of fourteen young male sperm whales beached themselves a couple of kilometres from here this week and only one survived.

I think my daughter could be right when she says that, 'Until we learn their language we may never know what causes this'. Apparently they have been doing this here for hundreds of years.

I was asked by the local newspaper to write a piece on what I want for Christmas and my mind immediately flashed back to my childhood Christmases, when everything was made by hand. Streamers were made out of crepe paper and it took days to put them up.

I could go on and on, but my grandchildren are carrying on!

I came to live at Redcliffe fifty-six years ago when I was two years old. I've lived here for most of that time. Redcliffe is a peninsula. The northern end looks over the Glasshouse Mountains and Bribie Island, the eastern side over Moreton Bay and Moreton Island, and the southern end over Brisbane Airport and the Port of Brisbane.

I recently went over to Moreton Island on the car ferry. It left at 6.00 a.m. and I had my first cuppa for the morning watching the sun come up over the bay. I just love that silvery sparkle on the water. It was high tide when I arrived and I walked fifty paces down the beach to a rusted shipwreck. The sand was white and the water crystal clear blue. During the day the water changed to a light green colour. I spent a lot of the day sitting in the water wearing my hat and sunglasses. There were a lot of tiny little fish swimming around. When they jumped out of the water and the sun shone on them they looked like rows of pearls. During the hottest part of the day I sat in the trees and watched the ships which passed in the shipping channel very close to the island.

If you'd like a nice quiet day away I'll take you over there. But don't tell anyone else about this lovely place!

Carolyn Barclay,
Margate Beach,
Queensland

Esther, Deal Island, Bass Strait

G'day Macca, This is Esther from Deal Island in Bass Strait.

How are you, Esther?

Really well thanks. Are you nice and warm up in Weipa? It's pretty freezing here.

It is nice and warm here. Where about in Bass Strait is Deal Island?

It's half way between the mainland Wilsons Promentory and Flinders Island.

And what are you doing there?

We're just caretaking for three months for parks and wildlife. It's a national park here.

What do you have to do to as caretaker there? Is there a lighthouse there?

Yes, there's the lighthouse that was built in 1848, and there's a lot of old heritage buildings around the island that need someone to keep an eye on so they don't get vandalised or fall to bits.

Does the lighthouse still work? It's unmanned obviously.

It still functions. But there are two little islands just off Deal Island that have automated lights, so the light doesn't work in the lighthouse any more.

Esther, where are you from?

I'm from Tasmania.

You do this caretaking business from time to time?

As much as I can. This island is the most beautiful island I have ever been to. It's a paradise. Everywhere you look is the most beautiful painting you could ever imagine. So we've been doing a fair bit of painting.

You mean the pictures from your eyes that you like to paint?

Yes. I'm looking across to another little island called Erith with a long, white sandy beach. It's just pristine wilderness here. Up at the lighthouse on a clear day you can see thirty islands scattered around the horizon. It's just so beautiful.

How many people on Deal Island?

Just two. My partner and I.

How long will you be there?

We've got three months and we've been here for two. So only one to go.

What sort of animals are on there?

Albatross and millions and millions of wallabies. We've got our mountain bikes here and there are a few tracks we can ride around on. We have to shout out really loud when riding, to scare the wallabies away. I actually ran over the tail of one the other day because it didn't get out of the way in time. There's also lots of Cape Barren geese. Their babies have just hatched. Sometimes they peck at the window in the mornings when we're having a lie-in.

Gee, it's a different lifestyle. I bet it's cold there this morning.

Yes. My toes are like ice. It's a very windy island. Today it's actually really sunny, but it's blowing from the south so lots of Antarctic winds are on the way.

Don Prothroe,
Russell Island,
Queensland

About nine years ago my wife Penny, daughter Bonnie and I escaped from suburban Brisbane to the rural bayside area of Redland Bay. At that time we built a six-metre catamaran called *One and Only*. The name was suggested by old George who lived opposite. George was a survivor of the Burma Railway and used to lend me tools and frequent advice as the boat took shape in the garage. I tried in vain to get him to tell stories of the war but the memories were just too painful. Seeing us labour George decided this boat was the only one we would ever build, hence the name *One and Only*.

We used to sail Moreton Bay at weekends and holidays, fishing and exploring the various anchorages and islands. Often we would anchor overnight in Krummel Passage off Russell Island, set the crab pot and watch the sunset over Mount Cotton on the mainland. The bay never lived up to its promise as far as fishing was concerned. It has so much suspended mud and is badly overfished as well. My grandfather loved the bay and would wax lyrical about the birds and fish but I doubt he would even recognise them now.

One day Penny went ashore on Russell Island to get some fuel. An hour later she returned with stories of helpful people, rich red soil, forest, high country and panoramic views of the bay. In what seemed like no time she decided we were moving there; the house on the mainland was sold and we were soon clearing an old avocado orchard to grow and sell flowers. That was five years ago. There's no money in growing anything, the politicians see to that, but the locals have supported the farm, and the flower trade is improving. Dad moved next door and settled into island time without missing a beat. I suspect he always had island time in him. I suspect we all have.

We are a real community on Russell Island. Dad says if you wait for a bus on the mainland the passengers sit around as if they don't speak the same language. On Russell we yarn while waiting for the water bus, we catch up with friends on the fifteen minute trip to the mainland and on the way home we use the trip to get the craziness of the mainland out of our systems. People ask if we will ever move back to 'Australia'. Perhaps, but only when our councils manage to work out why we shifted to Russell Island and why most of us choose to live where we live.

Cat'omaran

Don, Elcho Island, Northern Territory

Good morning, Macca, this is Don from Elcho Island. You don't need a pilot's licence; you've just got to have a job where you can fly! We're on Elcho Island which is east of Milingimbi, between Milingimbi and Gove in Arnhem Land. My wife and I work with Marthakal, which is a homeland resource centre. We service twenty-one Aboriginal communities from Galiwin'ku. Last Wednesday I flew down to Mapuru, about thirty kilometres south of here. It's twelve minutes flying time. There are about sixty-five Aboriginal people there. They have three washing machines and two of them weren't working so I had to repair them. A vehicle met us at the airstrip. I threw my swag and tools into the back of it, walked into town and greeted two of the old leaders. One of them broke off a piece his damper and gave it to me with half a cup of tea. Later that evening a lady came up and gave me some more damper. It's great to work among these people here.

Tell me your story, Don.

Back in 1970 I was working as a refrigeration mechanic at Woomera and I answered a call to work on a mission field here at Elcho Island. I met my wife Rhonda the day after I arrived. She was a nurse. Four kids later, in 1982 we went to Birdwood in the Adelaide Hills. Lots of people would know me – from Elmore, Henty and Orange, up as far as Darwin and Kununurra. I was selling mousetraps, chook feeders, cattle and sheep yards. Mr 'Easy Feed' they used to call me. I designed a mousetrap in 1984 when the big plague was on. Sold heaps.

You do a bit of flying up there?

I don't fly the planes. I just hop in. We have three Cessna 206 planes here. Missionary Aviation Fellowship supplies us with the pilots and we visit little communities with from twenty up to sixty or seventy people. They all have solar bores, which need to be maintained. Rhonda looks after the older folk, who really need a fair amount of help. She has two Aboriginal girls working with her.

Don this is February and it's wet season. What's it like up there this time of year?

It's raining right now and twenty-eight degrees. If you put on a shirt and go outside and do some work you're wet straight away with perspiration.

How long will you stay there? It sounds like a lovely place to be.

Indefinitely.

In my next life when I get my pilot's licence I'll fly up and see you!

Last night some folk from thirty-four kilometres up the road drove in with a whole lot of shellfish for our tea. That's Aboriginal people for you. There are some fantastic people around. And you're one of them – I've always wanted to thank you for visiting the kids at Walpeup/Underbool school. It meant so much to them.

4 - The Smell of Rain

Most Aussies living or working overseas get homesick. They buy vegemite to tide them over but the pull remains. For singer Enda Kenny it was the smell of rain:

I miss the smell of rain

And the magpies here don't sing

No use trying to explain

I just miss the smell of rain.

Katie Rossie from Paris

This is Katie calling from Paris. I'm only in Paris for a short time. I live in Oman. I'm Princess Pattie from Puncheon Island's daughter.

Yes, I met her on Flinders Island. What are you doing in Oman?

I'm working on the oilfields as an engineer in the middle of the desert. Muscat is the capital of Oman. I get there every now and then, but effectively I live in the desert. I love it.

Are you the reason oil prices are going up?

My wages are pretty expensive, so clearly the price of oil has to go up! I don't know why the price is going up, but I know China's using a lot of natural resources at the moment and maybe that's one reason. But I'm no expert.

What training did you do to become an engineer?

I didn't finish high school. I played around for about eight years then decided to go to uni. They rolled on their backs laughing when I applied because I hadn't finished high school. I did a four-year course in civil engineering and then went into petroleum.

What's it like living in the desert apart from lots of sand?

Lots of sand, and I get to walk past a few camels on the way home from work to my shed in the desert. The people are actually the best bit. The expats can be a bit cynical but the Omanis are fabulous. I work in a settlement – not a town – which services the oil industry. There are about 1,000 people there. Living in the desert is pretty good. We have a bit of a kite flying fraternity and have some stunt kites. But that aside I spend lots of time driving out to rigs. I go from absolutely nowhere in the desert to absolutely nowhere else in the desert. I went on a two-day drive and drove past one tree. I got out and took a photo!

What are the Omanis like?

I haven't been too impressed in the city, but out in the desert where I'm one of seven girls, in a Muslim country, I find the locals the most welcoming. The kitchen at the settlement is pretty crap, and the Omanis take great offence to that and have a little campfire out the back. Like a barbecue, a seriously huge barbecue! I don't know where they get the wood. About two or three times a week they cook for twenty to thirty people. They have three plates. They put it all on the middle of the table. No individual plates, no cutlery, no nothing. You eat it by the handful. The only problem is the rice burns my fingers like hell, but I'm getting used to it.

How long will you stay in Oman?

Until I get a transfer to another country.

What do you actually do?

There are about 100 rigs in Oman and they drill twenty-four hours a day. You end up with a steel-lined hole which goes anywhere from between eighty metres to five to six kilometres deep. After that someone has to supervise the installation of all

Nice day at the office?

the bits that get the oil from the bottom of the hole to the top and into a pipe. That's my job.

Are you missing Puncheon Island? Have you ever lived there?

I love Puncheon Island. I head down there any time I can.

Tell people where Oman is. Our geography's not that good here in Australia.

It's at the entrance to the Persian Gulf, and is known as the jewel of Arabia. I don't know what glitters, but the locals are great. That's what glitters for me.

✈

I'm a Yank now living in the States on a little piece of land on the outskirts of a small town in southern Illinois. I came here after living and working in Alice Springs from 1969–1989. I left the Alice to return to the States and work at NASA on the Gamma Ray Observatory. I retired in 1992 and returned to the family home. I continue to get back to Australia about every two or three years.

Joe Dalrymple, United States of America

I truly love AAO. I still have mobs of in-laws living in Perth, Singleton, Sydney and Wauchope, NSW. I feel very close to them and we exchange email almost every day. Most of them listen to your show and knowing we are all doing the same thing at the same moment makes me feel close.

✈

Rick McAndrew, Whitsunday Islands

This is Rick McAndrew from the Whitsunday Islands

How are you Rick?

Pretty good thanks. I'm just enjoying the beautiful weather here after coming back recently from living in China for five years.

That'd be a bit of a contrast. Where are you from originally, the Whitsunday area?

No. Originally from Sydney. We went to China for five years and then decided to retire and come back to Australia. We are spending most of our time up here in Hamilton Island. We're at a beautiful place called Macona Inlet. It's just glorious.

What was it like living in China?

It was a fantastic experience. It's something you wouldn't miss if you had the opportunity. The impact of the people there and the culture is quite remarkable. Shanghai is such an enchanting city and it really gets under your skin. It was very hard for us to make the decision to leave. You see some fascinating things. The life of the people is so dominated by the culture and history; almost everything they do has some explanation in history. We had the opportunity to see some fascinating things that normal visitors may not be able to do. For example, we went to a place called Thai Phou Town. It's on the side of a lake that is about 100 kilometres wide. You access it by going down a small canal. When you go down the canal it's like going back a thousand years. The people living in fishing boats, hundreds of them, are stacked side by side down the canal. They are really old fishing boats. They've got sails as well. Everyone lives on these boats. At the end of the canal it opens up into a lagoon and there's a huge floating restaurant about four storeys high.

It's interesting to think about the way other people live. I've always been fascinated by China, by the number of people and the way they live. When you say they live in boats, side by side, I wonder how we'd be if we had to suddenly change the way we live? I suppose we'd adapt because life's something that everyone grabs with both hands, whether you're living in a mansion or a humpy.

That's right. The thing that strikes you there is how resourceful the people are. As you know, in Shanghai riding a bicycle is the main form of transport. The things you see people do with their bikes is amazing. For example, I've seen a piano on the back of a three-wheeled bicycle.

You'll tell me he was playing it next!

Well, there could have been someone sitting up there playing it. I didn't see them. And I've seen a guy with three fridges on the back of a two-wheeled bike. We'd complain about having to put them in a ute!

I suppose where there's a will there's a way. So, what were you doing over there and why did you come home?

I was working for a telecommunications company. I'd been working for that company for forty years and I just decided it was time to retire. It seemed about the right time.

So you've decided to live in the Whitsundays?

Yes, we've got a place at Hamilton Island. We are out on the boat now.

That's from the sublime to the ridiculous isn't it? Quite a contrast.

It is a contrast. But you also see contrasts in China. I mentioned before that most people travel by bike and there are nine million bikes in Shanghai. Yet I was able to travel on the new magnetic levitation train at 430 kilometres per hour. It's a real mixture of old and new.

What are you going to do with yourself now you've retired?

Boating, and I also design websites. I've got a couple of good jobs there at the moment. Then we'll do some travelling around of course.

I've always wanted to go to China. There'd be a lot of Australians in China, I'd suspect. Is that right?

Yes. There's a good Australian community in Shanghai and we got together in the pub every Friday afternoon.

To eat Vegemite and sing Waltzing Matilda?

Yes, and have some noodles as well! I'd like to tell you that everyone really appreciates being able to get Macca on the internet.

I've often thought about travelling the world and doing the program just for something different. I don't know where I'd get the money from, but it would certainly be nice to go to France and China and New York and catch up with the Australian communities and do what we're doing here in the park at Grafton. I wonder what the reaction would be?

I think you'd get a fantastic roll-up if you were to do it in Shanghai.

What would the locals do?

They wouldn't understand you!

We could get a translator. Did you pick up a lot of Chinese while you were there?

Yes, I picked up some. I had a teacher for a while. You can get by without learning it, but I think it's a shame to go to a foreign country, especially for five years, and not learn the language.

It is over seven months since we left Australia to begin a new way of life. And I have to say that the Galapagos Islands are all that I thought they would be.

Firstly, I have never lived near the sea before. I didn't realise how dynamic the sea is and how each day it is different. Just like the land, the changes from the morning to the midday light are beautiful, as are changes to its moods brought on by cloudy days. But it's also alive with the rolling swells and the changing tides. Although we are 1,000 kilometres from the coast of Ecuador and also on the equator, the weather is incredibly peaceful, with only gentle breezes and no thunderstorms. I was expecting the usual afternoon thunderstorms of other tropical areas I have visited. And the Pacific Ocean seems to live up to its name in this area. The sea here doesn't seem to have any fury.

Our first months here were supposed to be in the wet season, but it has been exceptionally dry. I am sure that you can identify with that. Here, there are many plants that are semi-dormant during the cool season and they were supposed to spring into life during the hot months with the rain, but many islands are looking very stressed.

I knew that the Galapagos were made mostly of lava rock and so I'm surprised by the amount of plants that grow here. The most recent lava flows don't have any vegetation but those islands that are composed of broken lava are amazing. Very little soil seems to exist between the rocks yet plants thrive. All of these have obviously adapted to the area well. The cactuses are the most spectacular. There are three main forms. One is the opuntia which has large round 'leaves' like the prickly pear. The second is called the candelabra cactus, a name that is very descriptive. It's like those that you see in the old American western movies. And finally, the amazing lava cactus, which is a smaller plant, one of the first to become established on a lava flow. And of course some of Darwin's finches have adapted to be able to feed on the cactus fruit and seeds – their beak shape is easily recognised.

Another thing that I should have been prepared for, but wasn't and feel surprised about, is the lack of land mammals. We were out the other night in the bush and there were no animals to be seen. No eyes glowing in the light of a torch. When you think about this it would have been difficult for land mammals to get here. Of course, on the coast there are the sea lions. And there are two species of bats here.

Pam Cooke,
Galapagos Islands

I have seen them around the streetlights in town hawking for insects. There are, of course, the introduced animals.

The most famous inhabitants of the islands are truly amazing. The wonderfully ugly marine iguanas are everywhere along the shore. Just cycling to and from the shops takes me past the bay where at the moment there are a lot of newly hatched youngsters. These little guys are about ten centimetres long and have a very wise look on their faces. The older ones tend to seem a bit blasé about life. They are irresistible reptiles, full of character, very tame, and I have had to put a ban on taking any more iguana photos. I'm too scared to count the number that I've already taken!

You might have noticed that I said cycling. Private cars are not on the agenda here. There are taxis if you have a lot of things to carry, but everyone has a bicycle and I have to smile at myself sometimes. I would never have imagined a year ago that within twelve months I would become totally dependent on a bike. I just couldn't manage the shopping without it.

Shopping here is interesting. There's not a lot of arable land on the islands and the National Parks Authority has wisely restricted the amount of agriculture to a limited area. The other famous residents, the giant tortoises, live in the areas with soil. So some things are grown here but a lot of food is imported. Vegetables are seasonal which makes each week at the market a big adventure. We are just into the citrus and passionfruit season so you can buy these very cheaply. Until a few weeks ago, I had not seen an orange. Limes are always available. I have only once seen a lemon. So the fruit and vegetables in season are really appreciated and they are always full of flavour. You would kill for the tomatoes here. They are just delicious. Not like the plastic ones in the supermarkets in Australia. I'm having fun leaning to cook with new things. Most common here is the plantain, the large green cooking banana. You can make patacones with them which are really like potato chips but made with green cooking bananas. They are really delicious and are always served with fish.

You would love the birdlife here. It took me a while to get used to the brown pelicans. They don't look as clean and crisp as the black and white ones in Australia. They plunge-dive into the sea for fish, very un-pelican-like behaviour I used to think. In the sky there are magnificent frigate birds with a wingspan of over two metres. The males have a red throat pouch which they inflate to the size of a soccer ball at mating time. They look like pterodactyls gliding in the sky. The blue-footed boobies are quite comical on land but are expert plunge-divers and their feet are truly the most amazing blue. They have a relative on one of the northern islands that has red feet. At the fishermen's wharf, there is always a great blue heron, about a metre tall with a very mean-looking beak. There are wonderful gulls including the swallowtail gull with an impressive eye ring. And, of course, there are Darwin's finches. After a while you become quite obsessed with the shape and size of their beaks. They are quite ordinary birds to look at, the females of many species resembling the house sparrow. The males are varied, but the main characteristic that each species has developed is its specialised beak.

Since we have been here we have become acquainted with the world below the sea and have been amazed by the variety of fishes and other creatures. I have seen sea turtles and marine iguanas feeding underwater. I even saw the flightless cormorant feeding. But on Wednesday when we were swimming, first one and finally five young sea lions came to play with us. They loved Brian's flippers which are a bright yellow. If we dived under they would fly past us. If we floated quietly on the top they came to look in our masks and blow bubbles in our faces. It was fabulous to be able to swim with these wild sea mammals and know that they have no fear of us.

I miss your Sunday morning programs but have to confess that we routinely get up early on Sundays and head along the three-kilometre track to the sandy beach of Bahia Tortuga, or Turtle Bay, where Brian catches a few waves. So if we can't listen to you then I suppose the beach is a not too bad consolation!

Wendy Janini, Italy (formerly from Tamworth)

I'm originally from Nyngan in outback NSW. I left about thirty years ago to go overseas and finished up in Italy. I married an Italian doctor and we're established about 100 kilometres south of Florence.

You grew up around Nyngan. I love listening to people's accent and you've got an Australian accent but you sound Italian.

That's right. I speak fluent Italian, although I'm not absolutely perfect because I never went to school to learn the language. I work for the Ministry of Justice.

It's a lovely accent. Tell me about living in Italy. Are you Italian or Australian?

I feel very Italian over there. I try to get many Australians to come and see me in Aristo, our beautiful medieval city, just to remind myself of the accent. I listen and hear them say 'G'day' and 'Ta-ta' and all those different things.

How often do you come back to Australia?

Two years ago I came. This time I have come back to see my old mum in Newcastle who's not doing so well. There are five sisters and brothers so I have to give them big help right now.

There's something else about her: she's got red hair!

And freckles! I really stand out over there. Even if I wear black, I always stand out. I find Italy very beautiful, and it's all free and hundreds of years old. That's the thing I really love, the history side to it. It's just so inspiring.

Do you still feel ties to Australia when you come back?

Yes, I would like to mingle both Italy and Australia. Take the best of each and put them together.

Ricky, Australia Federal Police in Jordan

Hello Ricky in Jordan. Tell us all about it. What are you doing there?

I'm part of the Australian Federal Police's contingent to Jordan. I'm working at the international police training centre for Iraqi police. It's bloody cold over here!

Sniff sniff

How long have you been there?

I've been here three months. I'll be back in Australia in a month's time and I'm looking forward to the warmer weather. When I heard I was coming over here I imagined desert, sun and sand but we've got snow coming soon.

Gee, you wouldn't think it snows in Jordan. I know there're lots of mountains there.

Yes, there are. Where the camp's situated it's mainly all desert so the wind just howls straight through. We're right next door to a chicken farm so there's a nice smell in the mornings as well.

Where are you from in Australia?

I'm from Sydney. I've been in the Federal Police for about fifteen years now, mainly in Sydney and Canberra. I rang you four or five years ago from Cyprus, where I was serving with the UN for six months.

Nothing can prepare you for what you're experiencing in Jordan?

Nothing at all. It doesn't matter how many briefings you get you never know what you're going to face. The most I knew about Iraqis was what I'd seen on TV. I guess that's the same with everyone in Australia. You see all the trouble and violence and so you kind of stereotype Iraqi people. I got over here expecting to have trouble being a female teaching Iraqi police. I really didn't know how they were going to treat me. But they are amazing people. They have such fire in them and a desire to help their country. It's really quite inspiring to stand up in class and train them.

You've got another month to go. What's a typical day for you?

We split the training in two parts. There's general policing, that's what I teach and it's mainly classroom-based, and the law and theoretical side of patrolling and community policing. They do that for four weeks and then head off to do practical training, the physical hands-on side of things. You get to know them over the weeks and they are really wonderful people. They draw us pictures and leave notes on the classroom whiteboards.

They appreciate the training?

They do. Most of them have never left their home towns. They've just been recruited and shipped here and have never met people from another country before. They're quite open and honest about what they expect when they head back. Often they say that they're fully prepared to die for their country. It's quite moving for us instructors because we really get to know them over the four weeks. You never know how many'll survive. You've done your best by them but how can you guard against a car bomb or an attack on a police station?

Do you train them for that sort of thing, to look out for bombs?

That's a big part of it. We spend a week on terrorism. We teach them what to look out for; try to give skills that will keep them alive. But a lot of the time it's just luck.

Are they positive about the future for their country?

I guess they are a little bit negative. There's a lot of work to be done to rebuild the police force since the fall of the old regime. The people going back to Iraq from here will try to change the system, but it's difficult for them because they're coming in at the bottom. It will take a while before they make a difference.

When you say it's cold over there, how cold do you mean?

We have a temperature gauge in the car and I checked it this afternoon. It was minus three! And as it's now late evening it'll be even less.

Ricky, Keep in touch.

I'll talk to you another time. I've just started two years of missions and when I finish here I'll have a bit of a break before heading to the Solomon Islands for four months. After that, who knows? Two years travel around the world working on these missions is a fantastic job.

Eight years ago my husband, Warren, and I fulfilled a dream by building a yacht and going cruising. We live on a sailing catamaran and our lifestyle is adventurous, exciting and sometimes challenging. We cruise for part of each year and work the rest. And whoever said jobs are hard to get? We are in our fifties and so far have not had a problem. We top up the cruising kitty and off we go again.

Warren and
Rae Mitchell,
SV *Spanish Dancer*

In the seven years since we left Tweed Heads we have thoroughly explored the east coast of Queensland a few times, have sailed in the Torres Strait and the Gulf of Carpentaria. We have just finished working for a few months in Gove and recently sailed to the Wessel Islands, across the top to the Coburg Peninsula and down to Darwin.

We can change our 'backyard' any time we choose. Sometimes we can safely swim in our backyard and other times we cannot as there are things in the water that either sting you, bite you or eat you. But we are in their domain and we respect that. Other times we are able to dive from the stern of the yacht to have a swim or go snorkelling. From our duckboard we can fish or, when we are sailing, tow a mackerel line. We have witnessed some beautiful sights of nature in the sea. I mention a few that spring to mind: a dolphin thrusting her baby above the surface of the water as if to say, breathe baby breathe; a piece of seaweed floating by and a small turtle taking refuge amongst it; a baby crocodile sitting on a riverbank with its chest out and head held high with aplomb; a turtle labouring as she lays her eggs in the sand; small reef sharks right at the shoreline on the incoming tide looking for their next meal. We have lost count of the numbers of stunning sunrises and sunsets we have observed. We have walked and swum on deserted islands with not another boat or person in sight.

At times we have been asked questions like: where's home or what do you do all day on the yacht? Our reply to the first question is home is where the yacht is anchored. And the second, sometimes there are not enough hours in the day to do everything we wish to do. We catch our own bait to go fishing. Other times we gather oysters. Sometimes we get crayfish or mud crabs. One of our favourite things to do is beachcombing. It is not uncommon to walk miles along a beach searching through the flotsam and jetsam. And of course, we have domestic duties like in any home. We also have hobbies and one of mine is writing. One of Warren's is to jump in the dinghy and fish over a bombie, targeting coral trout. Most times he brings one back for the pan.

We always say one day we will build a little shack somewhere. At this stage we do not have a clue when or where that will be. In the meantime we will continue to live our current lifestyle; maybe in our travels we will find a location to build that 'little shack'.

Don Eichhorn, Kangaroo Valley, New South Wales

This was Don from China in 2003.

G'day Macca, I'm in China. You are my link back to Australia. I wouldn't miss you.

Thanks, Don. Where are you in China and what are you doing?

I'm in Tsen Geng, in from Hong Kong, about forty minutes by train. I have designed a factory over here, a joint venture, and we're now building it. We are doing the whole thing from start to finish. I'm missing home dreadfully. With SARS over here it's not helping. People with masks are increasing. Tsen Geng is a fairly new and modern city. It's only twenty years old and the size of Sydney. The population is around six million. It's fairly safe and they screen people. I guess you could get hit by a bus but at least you can be careful and see the bus coming. With SARS you just don't know.

• • •

I often think about the people I've talked to and where they are now. Here's Don again.

I'm back in Australia in the Kangaroo Valley, NSW. Been back a couple of months. I was in Tsen Geng for two-and-a-half years.

Are you a changed man after the experience?

Genuine fake

It was one hell of an experience. Apart from building the factory and getting it up and running, I also started the Tsen Geng Australia Businessmen's Association which then became the chamber of commerce. It's an exciting time over there. I think one day China'll certainly be the economic capital of the world. All the major companies are going there. And it's just like one giant $2 shop. The Chinese have control of the labour so things are always going to be cheap. Women love it there. They can get Louis Vuitton, Christian Dior or Gucci for $20! It's fake but you'd never ever pick it. You buy the genuine stuff and you could pay up to $1,000.

There's a line in a Tex Morton song that goes, 'Roam like a gypsy the rest of your life'. Have you got the travel bug now or have you had enough?

It is enough for me. It's made me realise how good Australia is. Particularly here in Kangaroo Valley. There are other parts of the world that I certainly want to see. I did the whole of China, I guess. I went to all the capital cities and saw all the major sights. It is a fascinating country.

Cheryl from Saudi Arabia

This is Cheryl and I'm ringing you from Saudi Arabia. You sent me an email and said catch me some time. So I'm catching you!

Cheryl, tell me your life story in a couple of minutes.

Well, it was very boring in Melbourne so I decided to pack my bags and see the world. I came as far as Saudi Arabia and have been here for eight years.

How did you pick up an American accent in Saudi Arabia?

Get out of it, this is a Melbourne accent! I do work for an American company here and people do say, 'Gee, you have a funny accent.' When I come home my kids say I talk funny as well.

What do you do there Cheryl?

I'm working in a hospital. The oil company I'm with is the biggest in the world and has its own hospital. It's huge and the sort of hospital any of our state governments would give their eye teeth for.

And you've been there for eight years. Did you really have an Australian accent before you left?

True blue, Macca, true blue. A cultured Melbourne accent, of course! You were broadcasting from Fitzroy Crossing when I last tried to contact you. I wanted to send a big cheerio to my son who's a helicopter pilot on a station up there.

How's the feeling in Saudi Arabia, with New York and all?

Let's put it this way. We're all being very vigilant. The consulate's warned us to be extremely careful and the company takes every precaution. Security in the compound I live on is heavy. People can't just come and go. It's a huge compound of about sixty square miles. It's relatively safe.

Are you there for good?

I'll be going back to the sunny Gold Coast. After living in Saudi I wouldn't be able to go back to Melbourne's weather. Melbourne's a great city but the weather is so unpredictable.

Home base is a suburban house on the outskirts of Perth, but I also have a little farm on the banks of the Serpentine River about an hour's drive south of the city. My daughter lives on the property with her horses, chooks and dogs and enjoys the rural life. The farm was part of a grant of land in 1830 to Alan Armstrong, who worked for Thomas Peel, one of the original settler developers of Western Australia.

    The place I really want to write about is Australia, or more specifically the mining communities of outback Australia. Working in the mining and processing industry over the past thirty years or so I have had the good fortune to visit many of the mining operations in outback Australia. Some of these have been short 'troubleshooting' visits while others have been much longer-term assignments. Most of the mining sites have a history that stretches back one hundred years or more, and

Mark Wanshaw,
Leeming,
Western Australia

the ingenuity of those early mining and engineering pioneers never fails to surprise me. While the work assignment always takes priority, you can usually snatch a few hours or a day to enjoy the isolation, look at the local geographic features, investigate the geology or seek out the wildlife. Look for fossils or fossick for gold. Or just go into the local pub and listen to the yarns of the locals. As engineering is my passion, I usually check out the discarded machinery and discover the history of the place.

I have enjoyed listening to your program over many years and on occasions have managed to pick it up on the shortwave while on overseas assignments. Engineering work has taken me to many interesting places around the world including North and South America, Europe, Africa, Asia, and places like Iran and Kazakhstan. But what I enjoy most is coming back to Australia and that's why I live where I live.

Gemma Jones,
Japan

I could endeavour to give you a 'why I live where I live' explanation, but at the moment I don't quite know where that is! I am originally from Glen Innes, NSW, and finished school last year. I have got a scholarship to study in Japan for a year. So consequently I am not quite sure where home is.

I have never had a decent excuse to drop a 'hi there' to Australia All Over, but I think that Japan probably categorises as interesting enough, don't you?

I am living on the north west coast of Japan's mainland, Honshu. It is quite picturesque, there is the most beautiful sea (almost comparable to the seas of northern Australia) and the pointiest mountains.

I tell you, I really miss the skies in Australia! They are so clean and broad. There is a delicate mist that often obscures the sky here, and the humidity steals the sunrises from me. Although I live in a less populated area there is always a feeling of enclosement because the mountains loom in every direction.

When I first started studying Japanese, one of the first adjectives I learnt was 'wide'. Once here I started to realise the relevance of the word: you never notice how wide Australia is, I took it totally for granted.

At this time of the year, now early spring, the paddy fields have been ploughed and filled with water, and little green rows of 'kome' or rice have been planted. Coming from a farm, I can't help but wince at the amount of water that is used to keep the paddy fields water-bound. You find them in the most amazing places: in between houses, next to the railway tracks, anywhere there is room to cram them in. Come to think of it, my host family has a small crop in a bucket outside the front door!

It is beautiful here. I love the language and the culture. And there is so much history. There is a small town not far from where I live that dates back to the 1600s, the houses and temples still remain and function as they did many hundreds of years ago.

Every year there are festivals and traditions that have existed longer than anyone can recall. And you can often see people in full traditional dress, the yukata or kimono, strolling the street, and no-one bats an eyelid. Imagine how people would react to seeing someone in Elizabethan dress walking the streets in Australia!

But there are no gum trees here. And you can't strike up a conversation with

some random person about the weather, the stock prices, the drought or somebody's grandchildren. And there are no meat pies! Anyway, I will try my luck on the infamously congested phone lines of *Australia All Over* and give you a call one Sunday!

Geoff Williams, Nigeria

We've got an interesting weather phenomenon I thought I'd ring you about this morning, Macca. It's called a harmattan and it's effectively a fog made up of sand from the Sahara Desert that reduces visibility and shuts down not only Nigeria but quite a lot of west and central Africa. It has grounded us for the last three days because visibility is down to less than a kilometre. We fly out to the oil rigs with crew changeovers. Everybody is sitting around twirling their thumbs.

I remember your last call. You're a helicopter pilot, is that right?

Yes, that's right. There's quite a lot of oil activity in this part of Nigeria and so with the reduced visibility it's just unsafe to fly. It's difficult offshore to find the rigs. We can see them on the radar, but we've only got a minimum distance of three quarters of a mile to actually see a rig or we have to turn around and come home. We're not even getting to that point at the moment.

Does it affect the rest of commerce around the place or is it something the locals get used to?

I think the locals get used to it. It mainly affects the oil industry with their helicopters moving personnel and equipment offshore. I know when we came in early January we were held over Lagos for nearly fifty minutes waiting for the harmattan to ease. So it has that sort of impact on the country.

How long is your stint there going to be?

It's an ongoing job. We do six-weeks-on and six-weeks-off tours. The oil industry is expanding at an incredible rate in Africa, not only in Nigeria but also in Angola, Chad and Cameroon. The oil reserves are phenomenal. They're going further offshore now to about 200 miles south of the delta area where we are. I believe Nigeria is the sixth largest oil supplier in the world. I think most of it probably goes to the States.

We're always seeing the price of oil going up, but from what you're saying there's lots of it around the place.

I'm not sure what the reserves are. A lot of multinational companies are still putting money into this country. I think we spoke about this before – unfortunately the people who live in the towns and country areas of countries like this and the rest of Africa probably don't get to share the spoils that unfortunately go to a few.

I'd love to see Nigeria. It must be a great place to live and work.

I don't know whether I'd use the word great. The people that live in the country away from the frontier towns, the oil towns, are genuine and honest, friendly and smiley. But when you come into an oil town like Port Harcourt the people haven't got smiles on their faces. They're just eking out an existence and poverty is everywhere. It isn't the typical African lifestyle you see on TV – grass huts, rivers, people walking around picking bananas off trees and cultivating their crops. It's far from that here. You'd have to classify the towns in the more commercial areas of the country as squalid.

John Pattison, missing Australia like hell, but alive and well in Los Angeles

A fair dinkum g'day all the way from LA. My name's John Pattison and until three years ago I lived in Traralgon about one hundred miles east of Melbourne. About five years ago I met a beautiful lady on the Internet and when I visited her in LA a year later we got on like a house on fire. She came back to Victoria with me and met my family. I followed her back to LA and we were married, on Anzac Day by coincidence. We now have a little fella living with us and this September he will travel with us back Down Under to meet his Australian grandparents, uncles and aunties.

Thank heavens for *Australia All Over* and Macca on a Sunday morning, only here it is Macca on a Saturday afternoon when I listen online. It brings a tear to my eye every weekend when I tune in and remember those Sunday mornings back home. Keep up the great work Macca.

Jeff Shaw, Des Moines, Iowa, USA, ringing from a truck stop

It's Jeff Shaw here. I'm ringing from a truck stop in Des Moines, Iowa. I'm over here driving trucks for a living. On a working holiday I suppose you'd call it.

What's that like. They're eighteen-wheelers are they?

Yes. Life over here driving trucks, I don't think you'd get it easier anywhere. The driver does nothing really. You drop a loaded trailer, you pull out from underneath it, back onto another loaded trailer, and off down the road you go.

How did you get the job? Does it pay well?

I came over here with the Customs Harvest group and worked for a bloke out in Colorado. At the end of the harvest I met people and got talking and got myself a job driving trucks. The bloke I'm working for now has just gone and bought me a brand new Kenworth T600 and I still haven't managed to get 10,000 miles on it.

Where are you now, and where are you from?

I'm on my way over to New Jersey. I've got time to kill so jumped online and started listening to you. I'm sitting here in my truck now. At home I'm from Muswellbrook in NSW, the Hunter Valley.

Sounds like you'll stay there if the truck driving caper's pretty easy.

I've got to be home by March 28 next year. It's my eldest niece's eighteenth birthday and I promised her I'd be home for it.

Just send her an email!

I'll do that when I get the chance, but I'm looking forward to the birthday party. It'll be a good one.

The life of a truckie in America has been celebrated in country and western songs. How do you find the truck stops and the trucking life?

The size of some of the trucks stops is phenomenal, and you can take the menu from one stop and use it at just about every one around the nation! You go in and sit down and there's always somebody to talk to – stories of driving through the snow and how to get out of difficult situations like that. It can be fairly interesting at times.

Is it easy to get a job over there?

They love Australians, New Zealanders and Europeans to drive their trucks. I can't say on the air what I think about their truck driving abilities! It's the Australian laid-back, easy going, 'she'll be right, mate' attitude they like us for.

Are you missing Australia?

Yes. I miss being able to go down the pub and have a decent beer.

The last two letters in this chapter were broadcast way back in 1990 and 1991, from an Australian living in California and a Californian who had adopted Australia as her home. I wonder if they still listen in?

I am probably one of your most remote listeners and you may be wondering how I tune in. My parents who live on Phillip Island, Victoria, tape the program and send them on. I also have some tapes with the songs 'Gumboots', 'The Shed' and 'G'day, G'day', which the kids love to sing. One of our most favourite personalities on the show is Mary Adams.

Heather Hendrickson,
California,
USA

    I live about seventy-five miles north of San Francisco in the rural area of Sonoma County. We tend to have wet winters and dry summers along with the coastal fog that keeps the giant redwoods flourishing. Grapes and apples also thrive along with gum trees and acacias. The Russian River winds through the river valley out to the Pacific. We have raccoons, squirrels and possums in the yard along with noisy blue jays, robins, humming birds, crows and thrushes. Deer are quite common but luckily don't venture into our place to devour the vegies!

    I was born and raised in Australia and many of the names on your program bring back floods of memories, like train trips from Brisbane to Melbourne on overnight sleepers. What a glorious way to travel! I left Australia in the early seventies for an overland trip to England and met my Californian husband in Kathmandu. The US of A was not on my agenda when I set out but life seems to unfold as it will. I do enjoy the program. The true blue essence of Australia comes rolling through each time without fail.

I enclose a poem I wrote for your Why I Live Where I Live segment. I am from southern California and came to Australia in 1965 to see if I could form a better life. I feel Australia is the land of opportunity, and the people I have met have been

Bettie Wessell,
Carnarvon,
Western Australia

generous and kind. I was lucky to meet a gentle Australian with a love for his country, the best possible way to introduce me to it.

We currently live on site at an aquaculture project in WA, rearing oyster larvae from microscopic stage to market size. Western Australia is a true frontier: dry, unpopulated and fragile. Like California before I was born. When I walk in the desert near Carnarvon it takes me hours to get a few hundred yards. I'm always stopping to peer into a bush for the locally known 'did ya get drunk' bird. That's how the locals mimic its call! If you ever make it to Carnarvon just ask for us at the oyster farm.

THE GASCOYNE

It's gone green now,
This dusty, dry, red desert where I live.

We've had eight days straight
of rain.
Red sand is fertile with a drop of rain.

And, oh my, the river,
our wide, red-sand river.
Dry, soft like sand hills to walk on,

Water flowed from inland rain weeks ago.
We've had eight years of drought.

This week we had eight days of rain.
The river swelled and swirled
all over the dusty, dry red dirt.

where bananas grow with irrigated,
gated water.
Now bananas are underwater in places,
and houses, too, some places.

It's gone all green now.
It's time to see the desert bloom, and hear it
make its noise,
after the quiet, dry, red drought.

5 - I Must Go Down to the Sea

Living on or by the water, sailing round Australia or the world, aboard an aircraft carrier or making a living fishing, listeners contact me from the water almost as much as from the land. Peter and Diana Utber sailed round Australia for many years and these verses from Peter's poem summarise its effect on their lives. (The complete poem's in this chapter.)

If but that I with an artist's eye
Could draw a steady line,
I would make a sketch of a little ketch
Her sails all standing fine.

My painting done would be proudly hung
For all the world to see,
So they may know the reason why
A sailor's life for me.

Ron Jones, on the Endeavour River

I'm with Ron Jones, the First Mate on Endeavour River, a bauxite carrier.

I started fairly young on sailing ships in Bass Strait many years ago. It's very unusual to have somebody with sail experience on cargo ships nowadays.

What made you go to sea?

I really don't know. It's somewhere I ended up. I've done a few things. I've worked underground and started off as a boilermaker/welder. For some reason I gravitated this way and never looked back.

I've only been on board for a few days but it reminds me of a team. Everybody does their job whether they're a rating or the captain.

That's right. We have to be fairly self-disciplined. There's not always someone checking up to make sure you're turning up on time or you're doing the right thing.

What are seamen like? I suppose they're like any other people?

No, they're actually a totally different breed. I've worked with overseas crews as well as Australian seamen, and the Australians are probably the best-trained seafarers in the world. They're the sort of people you can trust.

They've changed over the years, I'll bet.

They have changed a lot. It reminds me of an incident at the Melbourne docks a few years ago. It was a really cold, foggy winter's night and I overhead two big, tattoo-covered boys discussing the advantages of disposable nappies!

I suppose it's not for everybody, a life at sea.

No, it doesn't suit a lot of people. It's very hard on those we leave behind of course. They've got to be very strong and organised. And it's difficult to get young people to sea nowadays. Gone are the days where we used to spend several days in a port and had a chance to go ashore and meet new people. Nowadays we're in and out in thirty hours. I wouldn't say the fun's gone out of it, but it's a lot different.

This run from Weipa to Gladstone still seems like a great lifestyle. The beautiful Australian coastline's just slipping by.

Yes, you wouldn't swap this for quids. The Barrier Reef is one of the most beautiful areas in the world and we're extremely lucky to travel up and down here every day.

Reg and Angela Atkins, Hobart, Tasmania

You meet all sorts of lovely people after the program, including Reg and Angela Atkins. They'd been fishing and they had their new arrival Freya with them.

ANGELA: This is Freya. She's our fortieth birthday present! Reg and I own a thirty-six-foot cray fishing boat and I was the deckhand until this little gift arrived!

What sort of fortieth birthday present is that!

REG: A busy one!

Tell me about your lifestyle.

REG: I've fished the west coast for twenty-five years. I did work bigger boats as a younger fisherman.

I've heard working the west coast can be pretty hairy.

REG: It can be hairy, but I'm lucky to have been taught by older fishermen. We used to watch the barometer and as soon as it dropped a bit we'd be off to Port Davey and hide there.

There's not many ports on the west coast, are there? You can't pull in anywhere.

REG: No. There are a few islands you can hide behind and you're quite safe until the sea builds up to five or six metres, but then you really need to be in Port Davey or up the coast in Macquarie Harbour.

Tell me about yourselves.

ANGELA: I'm from Hobart. I grew up on a farm in a country town called Richmond. I've been fishing since I met Reg and we've been around the west coast together. We once did a trip there when it was snowing here and we were catching striped trumpeter in tank tops and shorts! It was just beautiful. It's just the most amazing place.
REG: We're so very lucky to live and work where we do.
ANGELA: We are privileged. This little one Freya is our fourth daughter and she's five-and-half months. We've one just about to turn nineteen as well as a sixteen- and a ten-year-old.

Gee, so life's changed again for you!

REG: Another circle, yes. But isn't that what's life is all about?

Well I suppose so. I'm sure it is. Keep me posted! How's the season been?

REG: It's been very good. Our prices were low earlier but fish stocks have improved immensely because of quotas, and are looking in very good health.

Are you always going to fish, Reg?

REG: I think so. I don't think I could ever really do much else. I did have a five-year spell away, but I'm very pleased to be back.
ANGELA: you get addicted to it.

What do you see from your deck, Reg?

REG: The other morning I was pulling in the gear. It was lovely and calm and on the shore only fifty metres away was a very big sea eagle sitting on a mound. I suspected it was a nest. About ten feet away was a wedge-tailed eagle just watching. Suddenly along came another sea eagle, the mate that had been out hunting, and rolled the wedge-tail down the bank to keep it away. I'm not sure if they had eggs or young, but it was a brilliant thing to see.

They're such majestic bird. I love them. They always seem to fly in pairs.

REG: Yes. I saw a couple the other day that would have had to step sideways to take off because they were sitting so close together on the perch. With whales and seals and sea eagles and dolphins we are very blessed.

Lovely to talk to you both.

Joy Ellis

This is Joy Ellis. She's a yachty and has travelled around the world with her husband. I met her in Toowoomba.

My husband and I travelled around the Pacific. We flew to Alaska and then sailed from there through to Canada, right around the Pacific across from Mexico. It was a wonderful voyage. It was an exceptional wildlife experience. We could actually hear grizzly bears eating the grass, and I went to see the polar bears in Churchill. My love of the sea and respect for it comes from being a lighthouse-keeper's daughter. I started off on Low Isles, a coral atoll outside Port Douglas, which has about 250-plus visitors every day. Then I lived on a lighthouse outside Townsville called Cape Cleveland, and then on Moreton Island when they were still whaling 600 humpbacks every year.

What was it like growing up there?

We had a forty-mile beach to ourselves, my sister and I and the kids next door. It was very isolated and we used to play on 600-foot cliffs as our entertainment, or dare each other to go out on a rock where five fishermen had been swept to their deaths. We grew up wearing very little clothing and no shoes. I was sent off to boarding school at a young age and that was pretty awful, being what I called 'sent to jail'.

What did your dad do?

My father was the head lighthouse-keeper. He was a Kokoda Track veteran and he'd been in signals in the army. He went back to teach at the university in Brisbane and then got a job with the lighthouse department. He used to actually signal the ships with his little lamp. We lived in houses, not in the lighthouse.

That upbringing has probably made you a person of the environment. Do you like the sea and the open spaces and things like that?

Absolutely. I'm a real environmentalist. I'm not involved in radical stuff, but it made me a greenie and water conservationist, something we really have to get to grips with in this country, as well as the disposal of our waste. On the lighthouse

Wanna make an issue of my eating loud?

and the coral atoll you just can't pollute. You've got what you've got there and you can't mess it up.

And you can't have three showers a day.

No, you can't have three showers a day! As a yachty you learn how to wash yourself clean in very little water. We can all do it. We also need to recycle water, and councils have to come to the party on this.

Where do you live now?

I'm still a bit of a gypsy. I'm in Toowoomba with my daughter as I've had a serious health problem. I'm going to live in Proserpine and I'm hoping to build a little refuge there that's environmentally friendly. I'll keep all the wallabies, kangaroos and wildlife on my block and then people will hopefully come and visit me. I'll have a little bit of peace and quiet away from the madding crowd.

You survived the polar bears?

Yes. There was an occasion when one was right outside my motel window. I could hear it in the rubbish tins. I got out of my room and told two guys who were working in the kitchen, but they said they hadn't seen it. Half an hour later I heard a gun. It had been tranquillised and was taken out of town next day. They are just the most beautiful animals. Like our animals and wildlife we need to preserve them. We really do.

Lt Fraser Vergelius

A few months ago I spoke to Fraser Vergelius.

I'm on board the American aircraft carrier USS *John Stennis*. We're doing a big naval exercise and are a couple of hundred miles south of the Hawaiian Islands with about seven submarines, forty ships and 18,000 sailors from eight countries.

How long does this go on for?

We've been at sea for about ten days and basically completed the structured training to bring everyone up to the same level. We're now in a tactical phase where we split into two teams in a 'competition' that simulates engagement between two fictional countries that will go for another couple of days.

Fraser's now my guest this morning. Good morning, Fraser.

Good morning, Macca. I got back to Australia about a week ago. It was a very successful exercise. We got a lot out of it.

You mentioned you were on board the USS *John Stennis* and that it was the biggest ship you'd been on.

For a submariner it was! I'm a submariner by trade and I'm currently working with submarine operation at Sydney's maritime headquarters.

I remember when we were in Townsville some time ago – I think the Coral Sea celebrations were on – an American aircraft carrier inched down the little channel there. It was so huge, I think they had to put it into reverse and back it out!

I think that ship was the *Independence*. It's what you might call one of their baby carriers and is smaller than the *John Stennis*.

I suppose a lot of the boats on the exercise had been over to the Gulf?

The *John Stennis* had done a deployment. The ship is actually based in San Diego.

You don't hear a lot about submarines now. Certainly you did during the Cold War when the Soviets were reputed to have nuclear submarines, the Americans as well. Maybe they don't want us to hear much about them. A bit like our spies.

We've always been the silent service! We do keep to ourselves a lot. We just get on and do the job.

I've been below decks on a normal navy ship, and when we were on the *Endeavour River* in Gladstone the other day we went below decks – it's very confined and claustrophobic. Subs are obviously very claustrophobic and close.

It's interesting how people often ask the question: 'How do you live in a submarine?' The first time I went on board one when I was a midshipman I thought the same thing. You just get used to it. An Oberon Class submarine was a bit like living in a caravan. It really is just a state of mind.

Think of those Japanese midget submarines. Nowhere to go if you were trapped in one of those. So, you're back in Australia. What's your next move?

Submarine operations in Sydney has a staff of fifteen and we plan all of the exercises. My next overseas commitment is in Japan to work with the Americans on an exercise.

It seems that because of things like Afghanistan and the war in Iraq defence forces have a higher profile. There certainly appears to be a heightened state of awareness around the world, and in Australia.

Yes, of course world events require a higher state of readiness. We have a destroyer in the Gulf and we're doing regular rounds of training exercises.

I would have loved to have seen the *John Stennis*. How big was she?

She was 100,000 tonnes full load. The flight deck was about 1,000 feet long (330 metres) and the surface area of the flight deck was four-and-a-half acres. She's basically an eighteen-storey building afloat.

It was obviously a great experience.

Yes. To serve on a ship that size and with the Americans. They love Australia.

Gary, Gove, Northern Territory

G'day Gary, how's things in Gove?

We're having really unseasonal weather up here. It's been raining half the night and it's mid-June. That's about a month late. It should be dry now.

What do you do up there? Where are you from?

I drive taxis and that's why I'm up this early. I've only just got home from work. I left Perth on my yacht *Risky Business* about seven years ago. I sailed up here and this is as far as I got. I fell in love with the place, living on my boat. I don't drive taxis all the time. I've had a few jobs, but you can't always be working.

It's a nice part of the world. How's the crocodile situation? Are there many crocs around the place.

Every now and then you see one, but you don't hear of too many people coming in dangerous contact with them. Everyone's aware that they're here and you treat the situation accordingly.

I know some people get in a yacht and go sailing around Australia. It's a nice thing to do isn't it.

It's a beautiful lifestyle. I'm just sitting on the back of my boat now surrounded by the other boats at their moorings. This part of Australia is on the world trade route, so we're always getting boats through from around the world. You meet a lot of interesting people. It's great.

Well, while you're relaxing up there we're working! I hope the rain stops up there. We need it more down here.

Yvonne Bradley, Borroloola, Northern Territory

This is Yvonne Bradley who writes songs when she's not on the water.

I thought I'd let you know we're still on the river bank about 160 kilometres south-east of Borroloola on the Wearyan River. I'm heading to Bing Bong Port in a barge, which takes nineteen to twenty hours. On a recent trip we came across a little island that had lots of pilot whales washed up on the beach. Looks like they were attacked by tiger sharks. It's riddled with tiger sharks out there. We counted fifty-six dead whales. The whole family'd been attacked, mostly on their tails. The mothers had pushed all the young ones onto the beach first. It was quite a sad sight. Tiger sharks are pretty vicious.

When I grew up we were always told that grey nurse sharks, especially in Sydney's Georges River, were supposed to be deadly. Of course, now they find out it's not a deadly shark. Some sharks are aggressive and some aren't. They all get labelled. A bit like snakes.

What's it like living where you are?

Paradise. We have been here ten years now.

Do you do a lot of travelling on the barge?

We probably spend ninety percent of the time on or near the water. Neil goes away for two weeks dredging and then comes home.

What's it like living so far away from everybody else? You make music, don't you?

The freedom for the kids and a clean environment. We think we have the best of both worlds really. In between teaching the four kids I do bookwork and recording. I have just finished my second album.

And you've got things you can write music about that most people don't see. Good luck with the album

Jim and Linda Collier, on board the *Liberator*

G'day Macca. It's Jim Collier on board the small sailing boat *Liberator*. How do you read me?

I'm all right, Jim, is it? Over.

Yes. We're just coming to the end of a nine-and-a-half-year voyage around the globe. We left Darwin in 1992 and are now seventy-five miles east of Brisbane. We can smell the place. We can't see it yet but the bird life is increasing as we get closer. You may remember on your first program this year we emailed you from Panama.

I do, yes.

Since then we've travelled some distance. We set off from Panama in February then went to the Galapagos Islands. Boy, if you like wildlife you've got to visit the Galapagos. It's absolutely incredible. From there we went on down to the South Pacific. We thought we'd seen the highlights in Egypt, London, New York and Washington, but the South Pacific just about beats them all. If you saw the film *South Pacific*, believe it, it's real. Absolutely incredible.

Jim, you've been doing this for nine years is that right? You haven't worked? You're obviously a man of independent means, or have a woman of independent means!

I'm an ex-public servant from Launceston made redundant to technology. They said we can transfer you to Sydney or Melbourne, or we'll give you a small pension and you can be on your bike. As you can imagine it was a difficult decision, but we had this little boat and thought, let's see the world before somebody blows it up. And we've just about done it.

How big's your boat, Jim?

About thirty-two feet. *Liberator* was built in Tasmania. She's quite solid but small compared with the many boats sailing around the world, and hasn't got much technology in the way of navigation. It's all very basic but we plod along, take our time and get there.

Any close shaves?

Just after we left Australia we got caught on the periphery of an out-of-season cyclone in the Indian Ocean and had to batten down for two days. Boats ahead of us got caught as well. One was laid flat on its side for fifteen minutes and the couple on board were on their hands and knees praying! Then we got wrapped up in a tuna fishing net for a whole night. We couldn't move. We were completely trapped until a fishing boat came to retrieve the net and discovered the biggest catch they'd ever had! There've been a few more things, but you can't make this sort of trip without having some problems.

Nine years is a long time.

It is a long time. In actual fact, by the time we get back to Tassie it'll be just about ten years to the day. We did actually work, Macca. When we got to England we got into a small creek thirty miles south-east of London and got jobs packing apples. Would you believe it, going all the way from Tasmania to the United Kingdom to pack apples!

Jim, there's a book in you I'm sure.

There's a book in all of us, Macca. It's been a wonderful time but there've been ups and downs. We were devastated to hear about New York on September 11. We visited New York and went to the site like lots of others. The people in New York were so friendly. They really went out of their way to help us. From there we went up the Hudson River and into the Great Lakes, went down the Lakes to Chicago and into the Mississippi River, and into the Gulf of Mexico.

You're modern-day explorers, Jim. You'll find it hard to settle down.

Well, there's still a big world out there. But we've got to give *Liberator* a good renovation. She's a bit tired and weary now like us. By the way, before I forget we were listening to you in the Mediterranean – you're heard all over the world!

A hot, humid breeze is trying to find its way down the windscoop on this second day of November 2000. We are currently anchored in beautiful Florence Bay on the south-east corner of Magnetic Island. The weather has been coming from the north for a week now as a large low pressure system passes through the Cape Byron area.

Peter and Diana Utber, Cannonvale, Queensland

We have just enjoyed the annual Townsville Wooden Boat Show. A wide variety of fine old and new vessels was on display, along with the *Duyfken* which just had sailed in from Western Australia. It would seem that Townsville is to become the home port for the rich sailing history of the Queensland coast. A museum has been built which houses an amazing display of artifacts recovered from the *Pandora* shipwreck. Graphic film and audio detail takes one back in time.

Last year we were at Onslow, Western Australia, where we battened down and rode out Cyclone Vance. *Leah*, our thirty-two foot ketch was safely out of the water and escaped unharmed. Not so lucky was our mate's fishing vessel, *Zora Dawn*, which was blown four kilometres inland by the one-hundred-and-fifty-knot winds. Cyclones are a fact of life on the north-west coast and good anchorages few and far between.

My wife and I have been on board for thirteen years now, and have sailed across the top of Australia three times. We have usually managed to find work even in the remote places like Groote Eylandt and Onslow. Favourite cruising areas we have enjoyed are Yampi Sound in the Kimberley, the Clarence River of New South Wales, the Cape York area and the spectacular King George River located right at the top of Western Australia. It was in this river in 1996 that our friend Gypsy wrote his song 'The King George River' that we have heard you play on your show occasionally.

During the more quiet moments I have attempted to write a little poetry. I draw upon a love for my country that began in the tiny townlet of Murrabit West on the Murray River. I also draw upon a sense of wonder and fascination of all that is around me and the lifestyle we have chosen.

CANVAS

If but that I with an artist's eye
Could draw a steady line,
I would make a sketch of a little ketch
Her sails all standing fine.

With artistic flair I would daub with care
And paint the living sea,
And place upon its living back
My little ketch and me.

With my artist's quill I would draw until
My canvas told a tale
Of a wind-filled sky, a sea bird's cry
And a lifetime under sail

My painting done would be proudly hung
For all the world to see,
So they may know the reason why
A sailor's life for me.

Sue Prider,
Goolwa,
South Australia

I live permanently on a houseboat in a marina, which is not as expensive as living in the suburbs. I consider myself very fortunate and privileged to live in such an idyllic situation. I have spectacular water and sunset views and much wildlife and natural beauty which keeps me gazing out of my windows whiling away many hours. It's a fantastically quiet, peaceful environment which completely enraptures anyone who visits my corner of paradise. The spirit of the community here is so very heart-warming. If I, as a pensioner, can do it, so can others.

I DREAM OF BONNY HILLS

While I am living inland
The thing that I miss most
Is to see those distant freighters
Plying up and down the coast

While I listen to those breakers
I forget about my ills
I think about the ocean
From the cliffs at Bonny Hills

The nostalgia of that scenery
Is with me for e'er, it seems
I may forget in waking hours
But never in my dreams

And so I'll go to bed tonight
With some potions and some pills
But I know I'll wake refreshed, because
I dream of Bonny Hills

➥

Syd Easton,
Wauchope,
New South Wales

Finally in this chapter, read about a couple who live surrounded by water, have a seven-mile-wide swimming pool, and the largest flushing toilet in the world!

I would like to tell you why we live in our very unique water situation. We live on a 350 x 250 metre coral island that's located approximately 100 kilometres from Gladstone, Queensland, and twenty kilometres from Heron Island. One Tree is a scientific research island run by Sydney University. My husband Mark and I are the only permanent residents as caretakers.

We had intended to escape our jobs in Sydney by travelling round Australia, but instead were lucky to get this job. One Tree got its name when HMS *Fly* surveyed the Capricorn Bunker group of islands in 1843. The large clumps of pandanus palms in the centre of the tiny island were said to look like one tree! It's certainly not your typical tropical island. There is no sand, only coral rubble, but somehow vegetation manages to grow through.

During the summer months many thousands of nesting terns visit. You can't imagine how many thousands of birds squeeze onto a ten-acre island. They are all beautiful, although rather noisy. Some are ground nesters (bridle terns) so we are limited to only a few hundred metres of 'beach' during summer. The buff-banded land rails are my favourite bird. They have so much character. We have named a few – there's Beer Beer and Laurie, who somehow lost a leg and has been christened our Minister for Mono Rails.

One Tree is surrounded by seven miles of reef, which at low tide prevents us leaving the reef. This presents us with a seven-mile-wide swimming pool that provides great research opportunities for the scientists who come here. It also gives a

➥

Maryanne Sewell,
One Tree Island,
Near Heron Island,
Queensland

degree of isolation. We have radio communication with Heron Island and Gladstone and the Royal Flying Doctor Service transmits our telegrams and telex messages via Charleville.

Recently One Tree had a facelift in the form of new accommodation. The original buildings were a bit like glorified tents. The floors consisted of coral rubble, which prevented us going barefoot. Now we have a house that is like something out of *Vogue Living*! We still have coral rubble on our verandas, which helps retain some of the old character. And the shower is a bush shower, which is probably the best shower I've had. I'm not sure if I should go into too many details about our toilet. It's the largest flushing toilet in the world and it does allow us to get a wonderful view of the stars at night!

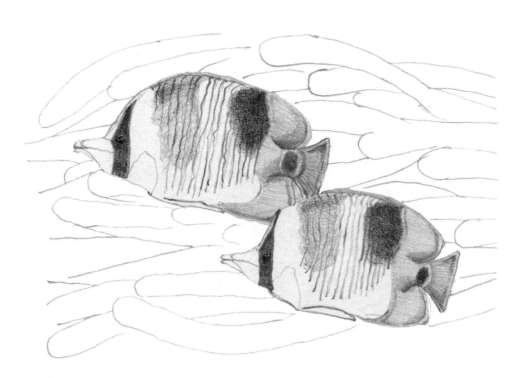

6 – Follow the Bed

It never ceases to amaze me how many people are travelling round Australia all the time. Letters and phone calls pour in from grey nomads, as they sometimes describe themselves, making contact from all parts of the continent. I met two of them, Eileen and Kevin, during an outside broadcast at Grafton, NSW. Eileen was quite pragmatic when I suggested it was an exciting life. 'I just follow the bed!' she said. By the way, these nomads are Ron and Gladys Bone.

Eileen and Kevin Kennedy

This is Eileen and Kevin who were at the outside broadcast in Grafton, New South Wales in 2004.

Where are you from Eileen?

EILEEN: Broken Hill. I came here today because my friend Blondie said I had to take a picture of you Macca.

How's the Hill. Has it changed a lot from a mining town to one of artists?

EILEEN: Yes, thirty-eight of them. Menindee Lakes has dried up; you can walk there. I'm originally from Taree and I've only lived in Broken Hill for three years.

What did you go to the Hill for?

Eileen. Because in the middle of the night my husband Kevin decided he wanted to go somewhere. He turned left and went somewhere else.

That's the sort of husband most girls want!

KEVIN. We liked it a lot out at the Hill and bought a place there.
EILEEN. Now he's sold the house and bought a caravan. He said if I didn't come he was going without me, so I had to sign the paper and go.

So you're on the road?

KEVIN. Yes, just want to see the country.

Are you going back to Broken Hill?

KEVIN. Probably later on.
EILEEN. We left in February and we've only got this far. He changes his mind in the middle of the night and says, 'I think we'll go to Nambucca Heads tomorrow. I never know where he's going.'

That's probably exciting, is it Eileen?

Eileen. Doesn't worry me. I just follow the bed!

Dave and Jocelyn, on the road

We live out of a self-storage unit. Let me qualify that. Our work takes us all over the outback and the unit is used to store our gear between and sometimes during jobs. My job as a remote-area nurse takes us all over the outback. Although we keep trying to escape the desert regions, we find ourselves continually drawn back through the courtesy and politeness of the people who live there. My wife (and hence family) is Aboriginal, from the Gulf of Carpentaria, and she enjoys talking about her culture.

Travelling the outback allowed our children to see much of Australia. They have met a swagman, albeit pushing a wheelbarrow! We knew he was authentic because his yarns were only briefly interrupted when he asked for a cigarette, tea or sugar. There's so much to see in the bush – orchids growing up the trunk of a gum tree, old wells used by Aborigines, wildflowers, rock formations, old structures.

Like a recent caller to your show we are concerned about litter along the roads. 'Green Can Dreaming' is a worry, as well as the streams of toilet paper left in road-side parking areas. Another unpleasant trait we've noticed is the indiscriminate emptying of caravan portaloos.

On the happier side, as we travel my wife is able to look at the slightest rocky outcrop and point out indigenous dreaming sites. Living the way we do, we found that our children developed a better understanding of not only Australia but the world in general. You spoke to our son Stefan back in 1997. He's now sixteen and studying broadcasting under BRACS and is an ambassador for Aboriginal culture. Our eldest son Allister is eighteen and studying Aboriginal mental health as a result of the problems he's seen first-hand in the bush.

We do visit cities regularly to see family and regale them with stories we have about how mail comes once a week on a small plane, how the weather means that Christmas needs to be planned from August in case the wet season isolates us, how we stop for a dip in a creek or waterhole if we get too hot, the food we enjoy such as honey ants, and the pets we have like a poddy calf Norma who thought she was a dog and swam in the river with us!

So, we live throughout the outback because it offers so much enjoyment, learning and a chance to be of service. And now you see why I suggested we live out of a self-storage unit!

I was recently on a trip from Perth to Port Hedland to help out a mate who need-ed some plumbing work done. I flew up there for three days and as I had a window seat I was able to observe our wonderful country. As I was looking at the remote roads below I penned this poem (see below).

Warren Murray,
Bridgetown,
Western Australia

I trust you'll find it as inspirational as I did as I looked out on the vastness of the Australian outback; roads going in all directions; tracks of wilderness com-pletely devoid of roads; roads that seemed to form impractical shapes as if drawn simply to please me; roads that seemed to go nowhere for there were no towns or settlements for two hours; spectacular remote ranges and gorges.

I listen to your show whenever I can and have been doing so for twelve years. I think I have some gypsy blood in me for I have never been able to quite settle down and have travelled the country I call home for most of my life. Perhaps when an Aussie says he has gypsy blood what he really means is: we are so blessed to live in Australia with all its diversity, how can anyone call any one particular spot 'home'.

Your show is so unique because it shows us all the beauty of being Australian, and it doesn't matter where we live – be it in Sydney, Melbourne, Bourke, Wilcannia or even Canberra!

I ponder the lonely roads below
As I look down from a mile high
Where do they go
From whence have they come?

Some go straight and never deviate
Still others they twist and turn
They meander ever forward
Indelibly imprinted upon the earth below

Others criss-cross as if lost
Seeking their way through this vast land
An obstacle here and there
A reflection of me perhaps

Perfect symmetrical shapes some be
As if to signal an artist has been at work
I am gob-smacked at its sheer beauty
I ought be ashamed – but I am not

Where do these highways and byways lead to?
A lonely prospector perhaps
A fella looking for his pot of gold
Will he find what he seeks?

The roads to riches is plain to see
Nickel, iron ore and precious metals galore
A newfound wealth waits below
Fly-in fly-out, go to blazes

Long forgotten roads I see
Paths our pioneers dared to blaze
Their bones scattered – bleached and dry
A past forsaken but still remembered

Roads to progress – right or wrong
National park or two below
A reminder of what once was
Symbols of the terrible deeds done

A road to a quiet billabong
Scraggly trees clinging to the desert sand
Clutching to life itself
Roaring, take me if you can

Roads to nowhere and everywhere
Like ants as we busy ourselves with enterprise
We leave our tracks on the earth below
'Tis a mystery to me

Reba Candy Avery,
'Pedals', the cycling
swaggie lady

Thanks for your card to remind me to ring some Sunday morn. It also reminds me to get back where I belong – on the road again. As I rode into Coraki, I knew I couldn't go any further. Four long months off the road and it's discovered I have a hernia so now I am on a waiting list to get repaired. Now I know what a truck feels like with a flat tyre.

My bike tent has extensions, with a forty dollar TV, thirty dollar fridge.

My tent is on the banks of the Richmond River. Fish jump calling one to come and get them – and I do.

After twenty years on the road I am starting a new book. Sure I will tell you when I quit being a swaggie but I am not old enough to quit. Thanks for the card, it made my day.

It's hard to believe thousands of old Australians are looking at four walls, when with a bike and a tent they can go everywhere and visit relations all over Australia. There's no hurry, it's like a second life, a new learning adventure. I will be seventy-six years old in May. I hope to have moved on by that time.

Ross Kennedy

G'day, I'm on a couple of shire horses and a gypsy wagon. I rang you in March last year.

Had you just crossed the Murray?

Yes. I was just near Yarrawonga. One of your listeners wanted to know the size of the shire horses and I gave you a call.

Where are you now?

We're about sixteen kilometres east of Camooweal, heading there from Mount Isa.

How long have you been doing this now?

We started in September 2002. We had a bit of a break earlier this year. But we got going again in May, just crossing the rivers and channel country and watering our horses in famous creeks we'd read of in books about the pioneers.

Where are you from, Ross?

I'm originally from Wollongong. We've got one more river to go, the Georgina.

One more river and that's the river to Jordan …! One more river and then you'll have done them all.

Not all of them, but a lot of them. We'll give the horses a good break and decide where to go from there.

How many horses have you got with you?

We've got two, Mother and son. Holly and Morgan. She's fifteen, he's ten.

How are they holding up?

Fabulous. Fat as mutton they are. We've been feeding them all the way of course. The big horse race is on Tuesday, when everybody in Australia is thinking about horses. Well, I *think* they think about horses. We'll probably be in the pub at Camooweal and watch from there.

We always talk about why I live where I live on the program. You've been doing this for nearly two years. When do you plan to go home to Wollongong?

Over here!

We don't have a home now. Our home is our wagon.

Where are you heading for after Camooweal?

I don't know. We might hang back, get a bit of work and wait for the wet to be over.

When you say 'we', who's 'we'?

My wife Denise and I, two dogs, two birds and two horses.

What's it like living in a wagon?

It's fabulous. We haven't got any lawns to mow!

Do you stay in caravan parks?

Sometimes in caravan parks. Mostly showgrounds or on the side of the road.

Has it changed your lives?

We really appreciate the pioneers and what they went through. It's something we've been wanting to do for the past twenty years. We waited for the children to grow up and get their lives in order.

I can hear the horses clip-clopping in the background. Wouldn't it be nice to do a program from your cart one day. I guess you see the world in a different perspective from a horse and cart. My friends live in the city, and they're doctors and accountants and lawyers and Indian chiefs, and they'd be listening to you now and thinking 'If only'.

We love doing what we're doing, so we're very lucky and fortunate. For many years we were stuck in jobs that we didn't like and now it's a chance to have a bit of fun.

Ross, it's been a long time between phone calls. Keep in touch. Don't make it two years. Say g'day to Denise, Holly and Morgan, the two dogs and birds.

Roy Fursman,
Everton Hills,
Queensland

We are regular listeners to your program and have tuned in when caravanning all around Australia. So long as there is a faint crackling signal, then that is where the glowing red bar on the dial stops. We were present some years ago at your concert in the old Rialto Theatre in Brisbane and recently were part of the large crowd of 'around a hundred' to join you under the Story Bridge in Brisbane.

Last Sunday we heard you talking to a woman from Sydney and she made reference to friends she had in Hervey Bay (Qld). Unfortunately you 'corrected' her pronunciation when she said the name as it is spelt, that is Hervey with emphasis on the 'Her' as opposed to 'Har' in Harvey. Now, I suppose you could argue this point all day long, in the same way you would with 'Mackay' and 'MacCay' and many others. However there is one important difference. Hervey Bay was named after Lieutenant Hervey aboard Captain Cook's ship the *Endeavour*. He pronounced his own name as it is spelt, i.e. Hervey and not Harvey.

My wife and I both grew up in 'The Bay' as it is known locally, and in the 1940s and '50s it was widely referred to as I have said. The population of the whole Burrum shire, which embraced Hervey Bay, was then around 8,000 people, and it was not until the 1960s and '70s when development started with an influx of people from southern states that the pronunciation altered.

I recall that sometime in the early 1950s it was debated at some length in the *Maryborough Chronicle*, a newspaper which was widely circulated in the area, and to coin a modern phrase, one we both draw breath on, 'the bottom line' was that the correct pronunciation was Hervey, for the reasons I have mentioned.

I suppose my letter has the potential to open up new debate. We have long since left the bay area and now reside in Brisbane, or should that be 'Brisbin' or 'Brisbun'?

This week we are living in a 'ghost town', Gwalia near Leonora in Western Australia. Last week we were living at Niagara Dam near Kookynie, which is north of Kalgoorlie, next week next month somewhere else!

Sometimes we wonder what it would be like to live in one place and one house all our lives, but we enjoy seeing new and interesting places and wonderful people. The people of Leonora, with the help of the Sons of Gwalia Mine, have restored the abandoned town and it is so interesting to glimpse into the past.

We join in and help where we can and have more friends Australia-wide than we ever had in the suburbs. It has taken us seven years of travelling to get west of Port Augusta. It is a very big country – so much to see and do. There is no need to go overseas.

When I hear you say, 'I'll go there some day,' I feel sorry for you stuck in Sydney, but you are only a kid yet. When you get more wrinkles and greyer you can do what you want to. Hopefully!

That is why we live where we live, 'Australia all over'.

Anne and Ray Corbin,
Clontarf Beach,
Queensland

On your show one phrase caught my interest and that was when you said, 'Nobody lives in a shack anymore.' Our residence for the last three years ought to come close! It is a World War II Nissen hut cum unused service station. We have been renting these premises while converting an old forty-foot bus into a motorhome, which has been a long time dream of ours.

'The Birth of a Dream' was hastened along almost four years ago by a serious car accident. My wife Ellen and I were travelling south on the Hume Highway near Sutton Forest with an 87-year-old friend. I was driving and had just passed a fully loaded petrol tanker when all hell broke loose. One of the brake calipers on the car dropped out against the left front wheel, jamming it solid. My brain was too busy trying to keep the car on the road to worry about where the petrol tanker was, though his presence was definitely in my thoughts whilst we were spinning on the bitumen surface. The driver tried valiantly to miss us but the tanker hit our little Corolla, instantaneously spinning us in the opposite direction and almost demolishing the car from the windscreen forward.

The tanker then went onto the centre median strip, rolled one and a half times, burst the tank and spilt 30,000 litres of petrol onto the Hume Highway, closing it for two days.

Erik and Ellen Dempsey,
Dapto,
New South Wales

The three of us were able to get out unhurt, if only quite a bit shaken up. The truckie was in hospital for a couple of months. He is thankfully okay now.

Over the next couple of days Ellen and I individually came to the same conclusion: you are a long time dead, and it can happen so quickly, when you least expect it. Six weeks later we shut the doors of our thirty-year-old business, renovated the house over twelve months, sold it, and moved into the Nissen hut to start the building of our mobile home.

'Chez O'Dempsey' as it is fondly named is as large as King Solomon's Temple and situated on four blocks secured with six-foot-high chain wire fence. Having lived in a small bush community it took us a while to acclimatise to the ten thousand cars a day passing on the highway. One great thing is that I have a shed, which is 100 feet long and eighty feet wide plus.

The rusting roof is like looking through a colander, especially after rain when more holes appear. During summer the temperature soars and in winter it plummets (one reading was three degrees inside). We converted the old office into a lounge room, dining room and kitchen and installed a hot water service, sink, stove and furniture. The bathroom is corrugated iron and partially open to the elements. There is no need to queue for toilet facilities as there are both male and female outside amenities!

Basically, that is Why I Live Where I Live and we shall phone you from 'somewhere' when we are on the wallaby as grey nomads.

Russell Hartley, travelling Australia on a motorbike

For ten or twelve years I've been doing seasonal work, sugar cane, mangoes and driving trucks. I get away from home and take a look around the countryside just to do something different for a few months. This year I intended going on a motorcycle trip around Australia but the weather was too hot to keep travelling. The last few years I've been going down to a little town in northern Victoria called Robinvale and working in a winery, so I rang the boss and asked if he'd have me back for a few weeks. We've just finished so I'll rest up for a week then get the bike, hit the road and finish my trip.

Is this the motorbike?

Yes, an 1,100 Kawasaki. Been a faithful old girl. I've had it for about ten years or so now. You get little problems but I know every nut and bolt and connector so there's nothing that I can't fix.

So you're a bit of a gypsy. Do you like that lifestyle?

Not a gypsy as such. Ayr's my home base and I've got family there, but it's nice to get away and do something different for a while. I'll never be content staying in one place. I've been travelling for nine years or so in between seasons and I've only seen half of Australia. While I'm single and able to do it, why not?

So, where are you heading next?

I'll just head across the Nullarbor to Perth and go around the Top End. I have to be back home the day after Queen's Birthday to start work so I've got ten weeks up my sleeve.

It seems like a nice lifestyle.

Yes. It's not too bad. I enjoy meeting people and having a look at new things. I like your show because you go to a lot of places I can relate to. Somebody'll ring you from somewhere I've been. Then I hear about places on your show that sound pretty good and go and see them.

I'm sure many people envy that, but then again a lot of people do it as well, don't they.

Yes. It's amazing who you meet on your travels. I've come across people that either know folk from my town or used to live there. About four years ago I saw a friend who lives across the road from me hitchhiking in central NSW!

Good to talk to you and good luck to you.

Travelling Australia by caravan 'on the wallaby' has given us a different perspective on life. Prior to setting off life revolved around our lovely home and the possessions that adorned it. In other words we were caught up in materialism.

Carole and John McGuffog,
Foster,
New South Wales

Away from all that, living a less complicated and very simple life in a caravan, our pride and delight now comes from viewing pristine beaches, rainforests, mangroves, unusually shaped rocks, cassowaries in the wild and delicate geckoes; hearing new bird calls, tasting hitherto unheard of exotic fruits, communicating with interesting people from all over Australia, learning something new almost every day; from listening to the silence and feeling the tranquillity.

Then, as if to really seal our changed perspective for good, we received news that our newly renovated home, once our pride and joy, had suffered a serious fire. Everything was a terrible mess, what the fire didn't destroy the smoke ruined.

Apart from the initial shock our reaction was amazing because we now considered the caravan our home and the other didn't seem quite as important anymore. We were just so thankful that it was saved before it burnt completely to the ground and that no lives were lost.

At home our lives revolved around modern technology, phones and computers, but on the road we have fallen in love with the silence. I have returned to the lost art of letter writing and in four months have sent off more than a hundred missives.

After five months we have returned home, but as soon as the repairs are complete we are off again. We can't wait! I can now understand why some people sell up and stay permanently 'on the wallaby'.

We live wherever people need help. In our pop-top campervan we move around west Queensland enjoying and experiencing the good and the bad of outback travel and living. We are full-time volunteers with the VISE which is connected to the school of distant education. We travel all year to properties as tutors and 'angels'. Our placements on properties are six to eight week blocks and then we move onto

Bev and Alan Kennedy,
en route

the next one. Tutoring is full-on whether there are two or three children. Angel's work is required in places where drought has become too much of a burden. Mums, who have to do everything, plus teachers welcome us with open arms. We've even been out helping the men muster!

The birds, abundant wildlife, clear night skies where you could touch the stars, the clean fresh air, the peace and quiet, small country towns, the friendly and helpful locals, the mailman's smiling face, and ABC radio are all things we remember when we come across negatives like dusty and rough roads, drought, the bad telephone service and snakes!

Michael and Annabelle Chambers

We're on the road to Grenfell, NSW, with Michael, two dogs and a mob of sheep and his wife's somewhere up there ahead. This is what they call the long paddock?

MICHAEL: Yes, that's right. We've got the sheep on the road trying to steal a little bit of feed and keep them alive. It's been very tough for too long. The rain's been good. I hope this is the end of it, otherwise I might look for a new career. I thought today we'd have trouble because it's a long weekend with lots of tourists on the roads driving too fast. But it's been pretty good. Have to watch for the dogs though. Bundi's the old one and a bit of a sheepdog. Max is a golden retriever who thinks he's a sheep dog! As long as he's tied on the bike or ute he's great.

Here's Michael's other half. Annabelle, you're from England?

ANNABELLE: Yes, and I've been here for about four and a half years. I met Michael while backpacking around Australia. Some mutual friends took me to Cowra for a couple of days and I went to help him in the shearing shed. I couldn't leave him so have been here ever since. I love life in the outback but it's taken a bit of getting used to. I moved from London where I worked for a travel magazine publisher. Sheep and wide paddocks – I couldn't have changed my life more if I'd tried!

There's something about the wide open spaces.

ANNABELLE: There is. As I said, it took me a while to get used to it, but I wouldn't change it now. I've just spent a month in England. I couldn't wait to get back here. I thought I should go home just to see if it bought some rain. Which it did! Everyone keeps telling me that there's feed up to your knees in a normal season. But I'm waiting to see it.

Jan and Ian Oakhill,
Yulara,
Northern Territory

You might remember me as the lady you interviewed at Molly Clarke's first ever bash on Old Andado. She was the lady who said she'd never leave the Territory except in a pine box, but who subsequently wrote to you from the tiny town of Mole Creek in northern Tasmania where she had moved to!

I just wanted to tell you that my partner (also named Ian) and I have returned to our beloved Territory after an absence of eight years. We are living in the resort village of Yulara here at Ayers Rock. To say that this part of Australia exerts an almost magical pull to the heartstrings is a complete understatement. We had great plans to travel Australia as itinerant workers after we sold our cafe in Mole Creek. We actually started to travel until the need for more money than we had to build our dream house on wheels became all too obvious.

Things have changed a bit from when we left, but the Territorian camaraderie remains and we feel complete again, right down to silly things like having Territory plates on the car! We both want to see the rest of the country though, and during the course of my day I see many photos of other people's travels – they serve to whet my appetite for travel even more. I come home from work and drive poor Ian crazy with my tales of what I saw and where I travelled to each day. He reckons he will never live long enough to go to all the places he wants to in Australia. He says he wants to be in each place for a long time to really enjoy the experience.

Hope to catch up with you somewhere out on the track.

John Boode, Barooga, New South Wales

John's an employment consultant. He told me about the people he meets and why he changed his life.

I meet some wonderful people, average Joe Blows like Justin Case and B. Quick and James Boag who come in and have something to hide. I just send them out to be fruit pickers.

They use those names?

They use them on the orchards. I see their driving licences in the office when they identify themselves. I get some fantastic stories from grey nomads as they travel around Australia, and from the guys who make a living as gun pickers and are earning $400 a day.

What did you do before this?

I used to be general manager of a local fruit juice company but had enough of management and stress and opted out.

What was the impetus for that?

There were too many long hours. Life's not all about that. A couple of close friends of mine died of pancreatic cancer. Tested today, get it tomorrow and dead in six weeks. Not for me. So my wife and I took three months off to decide what we wanted to do for the next decade. Had to be near water, and the Murray sounded a great place to live and we did it. My wife's Lady Citrus and I'm Lord Navel! She looks after the 400 orange trees on our five-acre block and life's idyllic.

Lady Citrus and Lord Navel, that's very good! How long are you going to do this do you reckon?

I'm a grandfather twice over and may sell up in four or five years' time, but then again I might make the farm a hand-me-down for the kids. We're going to be grey nomads and wander Australia for a year or two. I want to show my wife. I've been all around – Alice Springs, Darwin, Melbourne and Tassie – for BHP as an engineer. I started as a fitter and turner, did an engineering diploma and then moved into management.

Do you find the employment agency rewarding?

Absolutely rewarding. No day's the same. A lot of people look for a life change and I can help them with that. There's a harvest trail from Darwin right down the east coast to South Australia and back. You can work in the industry the year round; it's a good lifestyle, you don't have to work too hard and can make good money.

Carol Smith,
Port MacDonnell,
South Australia
(camping at Mary
Pools, Western
Australia)

My husband Dennis and I are exploring parts of WA, dragging our 'wobbly' over roads I'm sure it wasn't built for! We have enjoyed listening to your show and there have been coincidences of us travelling through a place when, lo and behold, someone will ring in. One instance which springs to mind is a lady who had bought a caravan park at Peaceful Bay. She described the tranquillity and beauty of the area and we knew exactly what she was talking about.

We are relatively young to be grey nomads but this hasn't stopped us meeting several wonderful people, and many don't hesitate to ask you to visit if you're ever their way in the future. And of course we have offered the same – just hope we remember their names if they knock on the door!

You have often mentioned Fitzroy Crossing on air and I had no concept of what it would be like. Indeed, I didn't even know where it was. We spent the night there and I will now have an instant picture when it's mentioned in future.

Life has been wonderful travelling from place to place. Even though home is in a place described as 'the fourth worst to visit in Australia' I will enjoy returning to see huge white waves crashing on our rugged coastline.

7 – Macca's Top Twenty

I have to thank the bloke who helps put the books together for this 'mission impossible'. He'd just become a happy 'Pa' for the second time so maybe he reckoned all things are possible! 'Select the twenty best letters or phone calls to Why I Live you've received,' he suggested. Well, it'd be easier to hunt for the needle in the proverbial haystack – I've received literally thousands of letters and phone calls over the last twenty years. Anyway, a book editor must be obeyed, so here goes . . . but I could have selected hundreds of top twenties.

✏️
Sue Robinson,
Trentham,
Victoria

Nocturnal Grunt Choir

In a time when all we hear about is elections, war, trauma, hard luck stories and greed, Sunday mornings are like an oasis in the desert. Why is it that the media focuses on the negative when we could be hearing from people like: Peter guiding ships into Gladstone, Dick Smith's adventures, the Fergie tractor trip, Ted the farmer from the West and Gilbert, remarkable and funny at 106. What a rich tapestry of guests you have from all walks of life, all corners of the country. True inspirations all – it lifts the spirit, revitalises the soul and ignites my passion to explore this magnificent country of ours!

I live where I live because it reminds me of what life is all about – away from the urgency of the city, the traffic snarls and road rage where you can still leave your keys in the car and the house unlocked. The locals have time to talk and show genuine concern for each other without invading your privacy. There is a true sense of community, a community that mobilised to stop destruction of our local native forest, a community which twice in recent times threw a benefit for someone's uninsured house that burnt down, providing clothing, furniture, funds and promises of assistance with rebuilding. True community!

And my modest patch? I look out onto the towering gums in the forest, kookaburras on the fence posts, over one hundred species of birds in the garden, flocks of cockatoos and galahs overhead. There's a paddock full of kangaroos opposite, koalas and possums grunting at night, the occasional visit from an echidna or wombat. The air is so fresh, mornings crisp, nights cool and starry, and snow at times to delight. Seasons are distinct – winter refreshingly cold, spring full of brilliant bulbs and blossoms, summers mild and dry and autumn trees spectacular.

To me, this is heaven on earth – and only one hour from Melbourne.

✏️
Sue Parker,
Brunswick Heads,
New South Wales

You recently spoke about your visit to the Gold Coast and how it reminded you of some of the big coastal cities of the United States. I know what you mean. There are people who like the big cities on the beach, but I find this type of thing too ritzy and always feel I need a fashion pass and lots of money to be a part of it. My favourite beach is south of the Gold Coast, over the border in northern New South Wales at Brunswick Heads. In place of towering high-rises grows bush and scrub, the beach goes further than the eye can see, or sometimes not very far at all when shrouded in a mist of sea spray.

I haven't been there for a long time now but have fond memories of holidays with my parents when I was a teenager. There was always plenty of room on the beach, room enough to be yourself. You could walk for what seemed liked miles and the Byron Bay lighthouse never seemed to get any closer. This beach, to me, is a spiritual place. Its wildness reminds me of what vulnerable and contrived creatures we humans are. If stranded on this beach, could you survive as well as the sea eagle whose ghostly shadow on the sand haunts you as you walk along? The breaking waves, green and foaming, wash up meek as a child to your feet, enticing you to come play in the cool green water (never mind the tidal rip). The relentless heat of the sun makes you sweat off the much-needed sunscreen and still the beach stretches on. The sea wind tilts at your hat and shouts its song in your ears reminding you that for a moment you are alone in an environment that has no need for money.

Money won't buy you a cool drink and somewhere shady to sit. Calvin Klein, Georgio Armani and even Versace have no relevance there. You might as well be naked (as some there choose to be).

Considering the relative historical short time of white habitation in this country, it was not that long ago that the Gold Coast was like this. Industrious aren't we!

'Good Morning from Goodnight.' It really was quite a while ago that I rang you. I have tried to ring you recently but then again so does everyone else which is great. I thought I would drop you a line when I heard you talking about your twentieth anniversary. I really can't believe it has been that long, but then again I can't remember you not being on the radio on Sundays. Yes, it's Jenny from Goodnight who is now Jenny from Doncaster in Melbourne. Peter and I left the farm twelve years ago and moved to Melbourne, a big decision at the time but when we look at some of our friends still struggling with drought and markets and governments, it was the best for us.

Jenny Cecil,
Doncaster,
Victoria

When we left many people said, 'It won't be the same in town, people are different in the big smoke.' Let me tell you we have found people wonderful. When we were moving into our new house the neighbour next door (we had never had a next-door neighbour) came up the steps with a big pot of soup. She was seventy and noticed that we had New South Wales number plates on our car and thought we must have had a long drive. (Guess she was checking us out too but what a lovely thing to do!) We became great friends. All our neighbours are wonderful people. We are a bit like the United Nations here. At the back are our Malaysian friends, Raj and Indra, also our other eighty-year-old friends Peg and Jack who were born in Australia and their little dog PJ. Down the side its Brian and Mary from England, then Mano and Melissa from Greece. Across the road are Helen and her four daughters from China, and the others next-door are Helen and Tony. Helen is from Malaysia also.

When we came to town we gave ourselves long service leave for a while, then Pete got a job with a boss (he had always been the boss.) He was the best employee in the company but soon found out that the only way to get ahead was to work for himself. What can a farmer do? The answer is anything he wants to. He can fix anything, find anything, talk to anybody, get things done. He is working at schools doing repairs and fixing things. He started at one school, now he has five and two others have approached him. If you are honest, reliable, affable and game to have a go there is plenty of work.

I work part-time in a ladies 'frock shop'. I think it must be the last frock shop in the country but on our Bankcard dockets that's what we are classed as. We cater for 'mother of the bride' and the more mature lady and thus I get to meet a lovely lot of older ladies. I love it.

There are things we miss about the farm. Pete needs a shed, he still owns the 1951 Morris truck his father bought new the year he was born that he is going to restore. At the moment we have only one dog and we always had two or three, and also a couple of cats.

We always have people coming to stay and dropping in, so that hasn't changed at all. Did I say that when we look out the front door we can see Myers. That is really amazing when you think where Goodnight was and what was there. I remember when we first moved in here I woke up to the sound of a lawnmower. It was strange because on the farm if the mower was going I was pushing it! We are very happy here but I think we will probably finish up somewhere with a couple of acres and a big shed. We just haven't found the right spot yet. A famous man once said (it may have been Lincoln) 'You are as happy as you choose to be.' I think that is exactly right.

Helen Rose,
Thangool,
Queensland

Well, it is truly amazing how you can have so many changes in your life in such a short time. When I last wrote to you we were chasing wedge-tailed eagles and living in the wild wild west of Australia in Newman, WA. We left there in November last year, packed up our children and drove back across the Nullarbor for the second time in twelve months, this time with me thirty-six weeks pregnant and with very few toilets between Norseman and Ceduna. What a trip! Whilst we were glad to be returning to civilisation in Brisbane, we were sorry to say goodbye to a place of such rugged beauty and isolation. Surely it will be a chapter in our lives we will never forget.

The pages have turned and we now find ourselves living outside a small central Queensland town called Thangool which is approximately twelve kilometres from Biloela. The area we live in is surrounded by hills and we are fenced by fields which at the moment are growing sorghum. As it ripens it turns from green to a burnished red with all the colours of autumn in between. This place we call home is one of peace and gentle, green beauty. But only when it has rained. The farmers have done it hard for the last seven years or so. The quiet determination of these people is truly inspiring and with their welcoming ways and sometimes brutal honesty we have felt at home.

We have an acre fenced off in the middle of a farm, an old-style house with much land for the boys. Every day is an adventure for them. The very large vegetable patch provides us and the birds with food. Various birds of prey impress us with their aerial acrobatics and in the evening, when the shadows grow long and the hills in the distance take on a misty charm, the sulphur-crested cockatoos screech and squawk as they find a perch for the night in the gum trees by the creek – which they share with the koalas. We will never be in the same league as the Packers or Murdochs but we are richer, so much richer.

Robyn and Matt,
no fixed address,
from the banks of the
Dawson River,
Theodore,
Queensland

Presently we are huddled up in the tent while the rain taps menacingly at its shell. The tent is old and it's hard work keeping dry. But luckily it's Sunday morning and as not all our batteries are flat the radio is keeping us company. You've just been talking to a fella who owned a trotter. It got me thinking I'd tell you about Matt's two horses. They are trotters bound for the doggers before his timely intervention. I often think of what a different life they are living to the one they had. From the flat track to boulder-laden gullies; from the hand feeding to foraging; from bottomless troughs to hours without even a sip; from pulling a gig to lumping one of

Santa takes a breather the morning after a hard day's night doing the rounds in Newstead, Tasmania. Or, as Heather Hastings suggested when she sent in the photograph, perhaps he's just forgotten where he left his sleigh!

Casey's camp in the Northern Territory. In a lovely Why I Live letter Casey described it as, 'A simple place in a valley at the bottom of a dirt road. I wake to the sound of blue-wing kookaburras and bowerbirds dancing in their nest.'

Lance and Marlene Fairlie sent in this photograph of their peaceful bush humpy surrounded by wattle near Narooma, NSW.

This is *Norfolk*, the replica of Flinders' boat, off the NSW coast. Bern Cuthbertson wrote to say that three gales in the Bass Strait resulted in the worst experience at sea he'd had in sixty years.

Margaret McKeachie and her husband lived at Pittwater, NSW, on *Fancy Free*, the thirty-foot wooden boat they built. A long-time listener to the program, Margaret wrote to say she's listened to *Australia All Over* all over Australia.

Robin Tiffen's photographs are always great. This one shows stormy weather approaching Tasmania's idyllic Binalong Bay.

Ross and Denise Kennedy travelled Australia in their wagon with two horses, Holly and Morgan, two birds and two dogs, and phoned in along the way. When I asked Ross what it was like he said, 'It's fabulous, we haven't any lawns to mow!' Here they get camping instructions from Reg, a local at Julia Creek, Queensland.

Here's Ivan Gellie ringing the program from Bright, Victoria (photographed by Bev his wife), from his 'self-built, telephone red, genuine Ivan phone box'. When I asked him if Ziggy knew about it he said he didn't know, but that Telstra had hooked it up!

Greetings from

The Big Shed "Reola"

This is the mighty 'Big Shed' on Graeme and Deidre Brown's Reola Station in western New South Wales. I visited them during a very long, dry spell, but a week or so before this book went to press Graeme phoned to say they'd had their first excellent rain in months.

Pears ready to go to market from Andrew Prentice's place at Shepparton, Victoria. His grandfather planted the original orchard. Andrew sponsored Guri and his wife Luma from Albania, and when I asked Guri how he liked it he said, 'I'm lucky, I'm second time born here.'

'Fore!' Mary from South Yarra, Victoria, was playing golf at Wagga Wagga, NSW, when she came across this football-size bunya nut.

When Shirley Mealey from Mount Warrigal, NSW, mows the lawn her husband insists she protect herself like a gladiator! The enormous bunya nuts from their forty-foot tree (at rear of picture) crash down on the unsuspecting.

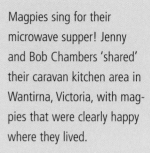

Magpies sing for their microwave supper! Jenny and Bob Chambers 'shared' their caravan kitchen area in Wantirna, Victoria, with magpies that were clearly happy where they lived.

Every day many white cockatoos drop in for a feed here. And they are just one of almost thirty species of birds that live in this area.

Penny Murphy from Meandarra, Queensland, shares her drinking water with these frogs! And there's an upmarket room with a view for sixty frogs that have taken up residence in her Hotel Plant Pot. The frog might have taken on more than it can chew!

I know what you're thinking: 'Who's the pretty boy?' Gabriella Hudson's poodles certainly caught the eye at the 2004 Australia Day outside broadcast in Sydney's Hyde Park.

To the manor born! Bill Scott came across this sign somewhere between Noosa and Pomona, Queensland.

Ubobo! What wonderful country town names we have. We did a great outside broadcast from here, and Paul Neville wrote this 'Ubobo Lament':

His honour, Mister Justice Gobbo,
Said to a dog named Hobo,
'For not chasing foxes
And messing with phone-boxes
You're banished for life from Ubobo.'

The Amiens Branch Line exhibit of railway station signs of First World War battle sites in France and Belgium is just one of many highlights at the Stanthorpe Historical Museum, Queensland.

Well, the mail's obviously delivered to this place in Lighting Ridge, NSW, by pigeon. The local postie would find it a bit of a challenge!

Jenny Weyman started building this 350-straw-bale, 'thermally excellent' house south of Nowra, NSW, in 2000. When I first spoke to her the straw had just been delivered, and here it is placed in the walls ready for earth/clay rendering. Jenny looks as though she's rendering herself as well!

Sue Shepherd and her husband Steve (here with Lee and me) are the caretakers at Maralinga, SA, the site of early atomic tests. As you can see from the WARNING, it's still a pretty forbidding place. Passengers on the passing Indian Pacific are amazed to see Sue, Steve, their children and a chihuahua in the middle of nowhere!

A land of contrasts. The view from Margaret McKeachie's place near Kendall, NSW, looking across the flooded river to a dairy farm; a dry country view at Werris Creek, NSW, from Yvonne Shirley.

A stunning sunset over the Plenty River, the life blood and source of Melbourne's water supply, sent in by Brian 'Rowdy' McDowell, who lives nearby.

Irene Shanks, Mareeba, Queensland, went seriously bush to take this stunning picture of Barron Falls, or Din Din, in flood. It was ninety-four years ago, way back in 1911, since they'd flowed so dramatically.

us or our packs full of gear; from a stable to a different camp every night in all sorts of places. They were definitely city horses when they came to us. Totally bomb-proof as far as traffic went, but the sight of a white cow sent Willy into reverse the first time he spotted one. And Not Willy shook with fear as we tackled an infamous section of the National Trail. The trail was narrow, the sides were steep and at one stage he even sat down! But now they are both bona fide trail horses who think nothing much of anything any more. Except the odd log monster (snake) which if I look hard enough I can see too! I also thought I'd give you our 'why we live where we live'. And it's simple. We live in Australia because we have the freedom to live the lifestyle we do travelling with our animals. There is space, grass, water, work and very little political unrest, except at the public bar or in Parliament House of course! We can live a simple lifestyle because we want to, not because we have to. Personal freedom is Australia's greatest gift. Hope you're enjoying yours.

I'd like to tell you why I live where I live.

I doubt if many people would relate to why I live here. Statistics tell us that as a nation we are gradually becoming coastal, especially city dwellers. But not me. I've moved the other way.

I moved to Wagga Wagga a bit over twelve months ago from Taree on the mid north coast of NSW. Taree is close to miles of beautiful coastline, is situated on the Manning River and it's close to mountains too. But I didn't like the coast. I grew up on a wheat and sheep farm near a little town called Eugowra in the central west of NSW. When I was thirteen we moved to residential Taree. But I yearned to go home. I missed my friends a bit and I missed the lifestyle a lot. But most of all I missed the land and the open space. It was a loss that never quite went away.

I lived near Taree from then on, with a few breaks away in Sydney (yuk!) and a little place near Mudgee (nice!), but mostly I lived at Taree. But I felt a bit like a lilac bush. The lilac bush will grow but not flower on the coast. It lives, it exists, but it doesn't thrive. It doesn't pulsate, explode colour, or celebrate life. It doesn't flourish because it's not a 'coastal' warm-climate plant. It really belongs in a colder, drier place. It doesn't belong on the coast . . . and neither did I.

Then my husband left me. I'd spent too many painful years in Taree and I'd had enough. I resigned from my job, gathered my courage and three adolescent children and moved to Wagga Wagga. I'd never been there and I didn't know a soul.

I didn't realise how the shroud of dark years and painful experiences hung around me until I moved away. My friends thought I was crazy to leave the green of the coast for the dusty brown interior, but I came here because I wanted to be close to the wheat and sheep country. To many people the brown landscape looks uninviting, drab and unproductive, but to me it's comforting and familiar. I love the wide, brown paddocks and hills, the fertile granite soil and the river red gums. I love the smell of the earth at night. I love the distinct seasons; the dry heat of summer and the crisp frost of winter. The dry furnace heat in summer is preferable to the insipid, greasy humidity of the coast. And how do you know if you're alive without the bite of a frosty morning?

I had to be practical though. I had to choose a place big enough for the prospect

Susan Howard,
Wagga Wagga,
New South Wales

of employment to be good. Wagga is the biggest inland city in NSW yet it seems to retain its big country town atmosphere.

Wagga is lovely. It has wide, tree-lined streets. Many of the trees are deciduous. The Murrumbidgee ambles it's muddy course through the city as though there's nothing new under the sun. It tells its serene and calming tale to me and I could sit and listen for hours. The bird life is beautiful too, from the superb parrots and the cheeky willy-wagtails, to the tame ducks that wander about like pets. They all tolerate frail humanity on their patch.

One of the highlights of moving here has been my involvement with the local choral group. The people have been warm, welcoming and friendly and we've been on a few really fun singing excursions. I enjoyed our participation in the Mangoplah Christmas service. Mangoplah is a little one-pub town about thirty kilometres away. At 7.30 pm the air was still oven-like and it was stifling inside the simple hall. We were in good humour though; it's fun to sing with a group. People dribbed and drabbed inside to take their seats; there was much talking, hand-shaking and nods of greeting. We sweated and smiled and sang (they loved our 'Hallelujah chorus'). The kids waited, hot and fidgety on the stage to do their nativity play. There were no fancy costumes; it was towels and tinsel for the wise men, stripey dressing-gowns for the shepherds. The Christmas story was narrated by a gracious lady with the bearing and presence that a lifetime on the land brings. Mrs Claus arrived to bestow gifts wearing a simple navy skirt, white blouse and smart shoes, but with bright red necktie and blinking Santa hat! At the end the Christmas pudding was brought in, flaming, while we all sang 'We Wish You a Merry Christmas'. Then we crushed into the supper room for a delicious repast, plied with hot cups of tea and Christmas pud – home made of course! Outside in the starry, still night there was the smell of sheep and earth and gum trees too. It was an enjoyable experience; it was simple, it was sincere. It was the result of local denominations cooperating and it overflowed with the essence of country people. I felt blessed.

The yearning to live west of the Great Divide is something that has stayed with me since I moved away as an adolescent. It defies logic. But it wouldn't go away until I answered it and moved back. I'm feeling pretty optimistic about life these days. In fact, I think the lilac bush is beginning to flower.

I suppose my reason for writing fits into the area why I live where I live. I moved up here to Beagle Bay just over two years ago to become the assistant principal at Sacred Heart School. Many of your listeners would know Beagle Bay for its famous church, which is decorated with pearl shells. The history of this form of Catholic mission goes back to 1890 when a French order of trappist monks came to the Dampier Peninsula. They came with the then common view of many Christian missionaries at that time, to convert the Aboriginal people to Christianity. These Frenchmen suffered great hardships but were able to develop a close relationship with the local people, learning their Nyul Nyul language. One of the monks put together a dictionary of the language and the book is still in existence.

In 1900 the monks returned to France and in 1901 the Palatine order of priests

☞

Frank Birrell,
Broome,
Western Australia

and brothers arrived from Europe and worked with the Sisters of St John of God to develop a self-contained community. During the period of World War I the German priests and brothers were confined to the Beagle Bay mission. To keep themselves occupied the present church was built with the help of many of the local Aboriginal people. It was completed in 1918. Many of the Aboriginal families of Beagle Bay have very close ties with this historic building. Today there are plans in the pipeline to completely restore the church to its former glory.

I said earlier that I teach at the Beagle Bay School. We have about 110 students from kindergarten to year ten and these students are the future of Beagle Bay. I'm continually amazed at their optimism. They are always keen to learn and do very well in their work. This enthusiasm is what keeps me here and encourages me to keep going into the classroom. I see great potential here for not only the Aboriginal people, but also for the whole of Australia.

Every Sunday we put the billy on and sometimes we even call you from our bush haven, 'Swamplands'. We don't have electricity here. We connect our Walkman to speakers attached to a car battery to listen to your fabulous show and have a woodchip heater to fill the cast-iron tub with hot water. It's luxurious living. Although the bush is dry we have an endless supply of spring water gushing down from the Great Divide. Apart from a trace of lyrebird poop the water is pure, a delicious gift from below. Neighbours tell me it takes fifteen years for our water to percolate up through the coal seam or, as the American Indians say, 'the liver of the earth'. Some even say it's got an extra oxygen molecule, and I don't doubt it. It tastes that special.

Over one hundred springs dot the mountain and during the past century and a half or so a healthy farming community has established itself here. But we are now under threat of losing our spring. A coal company wants to gouge out our water filter and sell it for a song overseas. A mine like that would more than likely crack the rock strata causing our water to burst through like a fire hydrant. Needless to say, lack of water would kill the land and all the creatures that live on it, including ourselves.

Anyway, we've rallied our community to form the Running Stream Water Users Association Inc. Some critics tell us to go freeze in the dark but there are other alternatives. It's not an easy path we've chosen so how about cheering us up with Anne Kirkpatrick's 'Train Wreck of Emotion'?

Nell Schofield,
Clandulla,
New South Wales

This is the year that Australia celebrates one hundred years of Federation. Most of the celebrations focus on the many human accomplishments of the nation, and rightfully so. But for me there is little to celebrate.

On the 1 April you will be at Belair Recreation Park celebrating the Centenary of Federation. Look around this park, a park for wildlife and people. The large gums have been there as long as Federation. What stories they could tell. But the understorey has changed — weeds, olives and other introduced plants now abound: a symbol of progress and Australian endeavour?

David C. Paton,
The University of
Adelaide,
South Australia

What other changes have taken place? Listen to the birds that are calling: do you hear the scarlet robin, black-chinned honeyeater, restless flycatcher, diamond fire-tail or brown treecreeper? They should be in your audience for they were once common in the park. But now they and other species have disappeared, many in the last ten to twenty years.

In fact the last brown treecreeper disappeared only a few weeks ago. For this last bird, a bachelor male, it was a sad and lonely life. Born with a sibling in spring 1996 he survived but sibling did not. Mother died at her next breeding attempt, leaving father and son to guard the family block – both waiting for another female to arrive. With brown treecreepers, as for many other birds, it is the young females that leave the natal territory in search of a vacancy and mate. But now the next nearest colony of brown treecreepers was more than twenty kilometres away, across freeways and urban sprawl, too far away and isolated. So no female ever arrived and when his father died in 1999 Belair's last brown treecreeper was truly alone against the world – a bachelor all his life. A sad life for a highly sociable bird, but symbolic of the irreparable changes we have made to this great country, changes that are still ongoing. Consider that last treecreeper – none of us would enjoy being dealt such solitude.

What birds do you hear? Perhaps the raucous cries of the ubiquitous rainbow lorikeets – harsh requiem for the others.

So what should we celebrate and learn from the Centenary of Federation?

As we start the second hundred years as a nation, will we learn from past mistakes? Or will we just celebrate a hundred years and not reflect? What do the words biodiversity and sustainability mean to us? Do we only judge performance by the bottom line, by the size of annual profit and how much larger it is from previous years? Is this really sustainable? Is profit-taking good for the environment?

If what we do as a nation was truly sustainable then the common birds of our parks would not be continually disappearing. But do we truly care as a nation that this is happening?

So what will make this country stand out from all others in the next one hundred years? It won't be our wines or multiculturalism or belated reconciliation. With global communications and markets and international travel the peoples of the world will be less diverse in culture and ideas. What makes this country unique is our environment, the flora, fauna and indigenous peoples. Will we continue to let these treasures deteriorate or will this nation finally mature and develop its own identity and sense of stewardship for the landscape that we should all love and cherish and protect – the landscape on which we all depend.

No signs yet of any maturity. Just look at how the various states overexploit and bicker over access to water in the Murray-Darling Basin. I am humbled by our past and daunted by the tasks ahead – celebration seems premature.

John King,
Musgrave Hill,
Queensland

We have travelled a lot throughout the country by car, caravan and motorbike since retiring some nine years ago and there is no end in sight to those travels. Being city slickers, born and bred, we like to hear the country folk giving their side of life and how much they seem to enjoy it, drought, flood and locusts notwithstanding.

However, we do bridle occasionally when the odd letter or comment slips through from someone terrified of progress, who invariably states rather emphatically that they do not want their town, suburb, locale to become 'another Gold Coast'.

Obviously we live on the much maligned stretch of coastline but we'd just like to tell you why we live where we live.

Nowhere else can become 'another Gold Coast'. The Gold Coast is unique. It is brash, tacky, beautiful and ever-changing. It has everything from golden beaches to a wonderful sub-tropical hinterland bristling with diverse wildlife. Fair enough, there are the 'dreaded' high-rise buildings, but they themselves have a strange beauty and once you get used to them they don't seem any impediment to life. They do, in fact, serve their purpose – which is to allow a maximum number of people (both local and tourist) to enjoy living virtually on the beachfront. Some are a bit shabby, but most are pristine with immaculate, well-tended landscaped gardens which complement the naturalness of the beach itself. I defy anyone to come up with a better photograph than Surfers Paradise at night during the height of the tourist season, taken from the Grand Hotel wharf across the Broadwater. Or from the Chevron Island Bridge looking south up the Nerang River. Magic.

The Gold Coast is the sixth largest city in Australia and it is probably the most successful, multiculturally. We have a mix of all nationalities which leads to a greater cultural understanding. Oh, we have crime here, as does every other place in Australia. But we like to think we have a better class of crim!

Tourists, of course, are both our bread and butter and also the source of our frustrations. Try getting a parking space in the main street during the Christmas period. Buy a lottery ticket if you succeed because your luck's in! Having said that, we love them. Because of them and the income they generate employment is plentiful. Every industry, no matter how, benefits in some way from the tourist dollar. Whilst we suffer the crush during tourist season we enjoy the added benefits of more and better medical facilities.

Competition for the tourist – and local – dollar also benefit us Gold Coasters through cheaper meals and heavily discounted visits to the local attractions. Having travelled all over Australia we know our prices and defy anyone to match the evening roast at the Southport Workers Club for only $3.00! Or you could splash out on a steak dinner for $6.50 if you're really flush.

Do you wonder why we love the Gold Coast and shake our heads in disbelief when people bag us?

I was cheered this wet and stormy morning listening to the letter from the couple that lasted almost ninety years at their place in the country before calling it quits and going into nursing care.

This couple spent most of the night awake fearing the roof panels might blow off, or that one of the two large gumtrees ringbarked decades ago – but unwittingly 'case-hardened' by fire against slow demolition by termites – might drop in.

That letter has given me hope that there might still be some mileage in me. I'm not even halfway through building a big shed intended to warehouse all the things Bianca, my wife of thirty-six years, blithely terms 'junk': furniture, computers, an

Luis M. Huesch,
Pacific Palms,
New South Wales

endless array of tools and builder's equipment now stacking up in the purported living quarters.

You see, Bianca and I were sitting up in the kitchen at around 3 am discussing our 'options' after eight years of roughing it on the bush block we've owned since the early 1970s in one of the most pleasant parts of the eastern seaboard. I know because when we first arrived in Australia thirty years ago we travelled along the coast in our Kombi right up to Cairns with four bairns in tow!

Bianca wants out, particularly at times like this after three days and nights of winter gales and incessant rain. I, on the other hand, am rather content with my current place in life, particularly when the sun breaks through as I'm writing this. I'm looking out from my 'office' through large sliding doors onto the bush. A gaggle of geese are cleaning their plumage a few metres away on a patch of lawn; half-a-dozen hens are preening themselves.

Bianca strides purposefully past in gumboots and a hard-hat (thin branches are still falling down like spears). She's armed with secateurs ready to redress some of the rampage of the few days and nights.

When the wind dies down I will be able to hear the noisy nibbling of the red-tailed black cockatoos again in the dense dark she-oaks twenty metres from the house, and their harsh shrieks as they fly about, batlike, as mating-season minstrels.

Why would I trade this for, say, a neat little unit in Brissie, when we both know, deep down, that we'd never thrive in such a setting, never mind the convenience, the culture, the crowds! Give me our 'Clod Nine' any day! (The unofficial name alludes not only to the original Lot 9 number and our early delight in this piece of paradise, but also to the deep clay soil of the place.)

The other thing I found most interesting in today's program was some in-depth information about 1080 poison baiting from both the parks and wildlife bloke in Jindabyne and the Top End grazier.

We've been putting out 1080-baited liver for many years on our fifty-acre block and it was hard at first convincing the neighbours that it was reasonably safe as long as they kept their dogs in check. But in recent years more people have asked us about the program.

Dealing out death is not an easy way of life, to coin a phrase, even when directed at supposedly harmful animals. (I must also plead guilty to having beheaded a goose and six roosters in my brief time on the land, each with increasing reluctance, and the last few only after stiffening my resolve with a big glass of red!)

After last year's baiting we heard strange whimpering noises nearby at night. I dragged myself out at about midnight to investigate and found a lone fox cub cowering next to the carcass of his kin thirty metres from our kitchen door. He was a beautiful greyish animal, already almost fully grown, and for a moment I thought of taming him and putting him on a leash for trips to town. We fed him nightly on scraps of meat and homemade bread and called him Freddie. But we also called the ranger who brought around another serving of liver bait. The soft nightly howling then ceased. Instead, the crows made their raucous rounds once more.

We rationalised our guilt by identifying this fox – and his parents and siblings – as the beasts that had ravished hens and sent our geese flying at night. Come to think of it, Freddie might well have been the one who grabbed our leading gander

Jochen one night and tried to pull him through the electric fence. Bianca, alerted by the racket both had made, dashed out and pulled Jochen back, with Freddie definitely determined not to let go. (Bianca prevailed in the tug-of-war.). Or the one who attacked some hens in broad daylight and carried their fearless defender, Ruby, off into the bush and only relinquished his prey when yours truly ran after them shouting and throwing sticks? Whatever, he must have had it coming to him.

This is not so much about where I live, but more why and where I've worked.

Roger Oxley,
Deniliquin,
New South Wales

As a small boy I found great joy and pleasure in collecting and cataloguing things natural. Insects, especially cicadas in the summer, feathers from all sorts of birds, and flowers and leaves of native plants. I had a particular fascination for the seemingly endless numbers of different trees, shrubs and small flowering plants that grew in the bush behind the house where I lived. The passion has never deserted me.

Of course, plants are only one component of any landscape. There's also the terrain, the rocks, the water, the animals and the colours. Landscapes are also comprised of other attributes that are not physical or tangible. They often have a particular historical or sensual element about them. If they have all these things then in my book they rate the highest score.

My work has involved attempting to understand the life and times of plants, and has taken me from the alpine grasslands to the dry deserts of the interior and everywhere in between.

In springtime, the high country above the tree-line is the domain of the snow daisies and other spectacular small flowering plants. They cover the hillsides and valley in a riotous cloak of colour. The valley is long and narrow; one side is steep and is strewn with steely-grey gigantic boulders, weathered and worn smooth by glaciation. This is the realm of the alpine shrubs and heaths. Here the mountain plum-pine sprawls over and between the rocks, enveloping them with a dense cover of branches and foliage. Hidden beneath this canopy is the favoured habitat of the rare and elusive mountain pygmy possum, a tiny little creature that feeds on the female cones of this very long-lived shrub. Other shrubs, too, can be seen growing in little clumps of their own. Grevilleas are resplendent in their cream or red spidery flowers. Just along the way, where the soil is always damp and squishy, lovely aromatic baechias and eparis are dressed in their mantle of white flowers. Here, too, the kunseas are blooming in all their glory. Their pure golden petals surround scores of long yellow stamens that burst forth like a spray of gleaming sunbeams.

On the other side of the pretty little valley, where the slope is gentle, spring has been exceptionally generous. Here is a patchwork of the most intricate design. Laid on a carpet of the dark green leaves of the snow grasses is a mosaic of flowers in full bloom. Extensive patches of pure white snow daisies dance and sway to the most gentle of breezes. A little further off, a great splash of the golden yellow flower heads of billy-buttons nods in time to the breezes. Still there is more: a patch of pretty pink trigger plants adds another hue. A frenzy of other flowers intermingles and sprinkles the ground in springtime all across this lovely valley.

Just below where I'm sitting, where the sun's ray shortly shine, the last patch of winter's snow remains. As it slowly thaws it creates its own little icy streams that playfully splash over the rocks on their rush to the valley floor. The rays of the sun capture the droplets of the splash and hold them motionless for a moment, like diamonds suspended in mid-air. Onward the little stream rushes.

In a good spring the grasslands of the Riverina rival the floristic displays of just about anywhere else. But what about the vast sandy stretches of the interior where the wildflowers stretch for countless miles across a seemingly endless desert? One of the most spectacular sights I have ever had the joy of seeing was the massed flowering of daisies on the edge of the Sturts Stony Desert. The yellow and white flowers, each one resembling a poached egg, clothed the red dunes in a wondrous mantle of gleaming, glowing, gold and white.

A grassland, resplendent in its spring finery, is more than just the pretty flowers. If you get down on your hands and knees and have a look, there is another little world. In the tussocks and between them, amongst the leaves and flowers of other plants and on the soil surface, there is a thriving metropolis. Tiny little animals are busily going about their business. If you wait and watch, dainty little yellow butterflies flutter to and fro, a native bee silently hovers over the golden flower head of a daisy, sips its sweet nectar, and suddenly darts off to another. Strange-looking beetles and bugs trudge along, their burnished backs of black, blue or brown gleaming like precious stones. A grasshopper, dressed in a drab gown of brown and green, camouflages itself on a dead leaf. And there's the constant scurrying of ants – red, black and brown. Within this domain spiders find it a good place to live. In the early morning their diamond-dewed webs, slung among the slender stems of the plants, sparkle in the sunshine.

Landscapes are not monotonous, boring and flat; even the flat saltbush plains, the vast expanses of Mitchell-grass, the desert spinifex country, the sombre mulga and the mallee will eagerly reveal their secrets to those who wish to indulge them.

Having the opportunity to study the plants and the range of landscapes in which they occur has given me, and will continue to give me, great pleasure. To have seen the colours, to have smelt the sweet scents, to have experienced the awe of sunrise over the desert, or to have been humbled by the majestic fury of a summer storm on a saltbush plain, I'm glad I work where I work.

Sharon, Norm,
Stephanie and
Heidi Allan,
Tjirrkarli Community,
Northern Territory

We live now in the Gibson Desert in a remote Aboriginal community. Originally we came from Gippsland in Victoria, a place called Mallacoota. We, that is my husband and three daughters, decided to see a bit more of Australia before we got too old.

Our first stop was Kalgoorlie for three years, involved in tourism there, which is our background. The opportunity arose to run an Aboriginal community so here we are, and after six months have decided this is what we will do for a long time. The people are wonderful, very simple in their needs and still adjusting to amalgamation with our society.

The community we are in is called Tjirrkarli and is part of the Ngaanyatjarraku Shire, 1,250 kilometres west of Alice and 1,000 kilometres north east of Kalgoorlie near the Tropic of Capricorn. There are eleven communities and we're the smallest with fifty to sixty people. This area is also known as the 'lands'. It is very interesting learning their culture and beliefs, but also sad to see it dying, as the younger generation's more interested in the outside influences our own teenagers come under. The shire is 'dry' and no petrol is sold between Laverton, 600 kilometres west of here and Giles on the NT border to lessen the opportunity to 'sniff'.

We have two mail planes a week and a doctor visits once a fortnight. There is a school here, a store and office. Police are based in Laverton and visit Warburton, 140 kilometres from here, fortnightly. Our two daughters, living with us, do their schooling via Schools of Isolated and Distance Education, based in Perth. They do very well at this but next year may be going to boarding school for their senior years. They miss the social side of life and friends their own age so we think it best if they go to a mainstream school.

It gets very hot here, but is bearable because it is dry most of the time. There has been a bit of rain from the cyclones up north which fills the swimming holes and provides activities for the kids. There is even a waterfall. Sounds wonderful, the water thundering in the middle of the desert. It is very green at present, good for the wildlife. The camels have moved further out now, as feed and water are more plentiful away from the community.

We had a gentleman here last year measuring our water usage. He commented that the people are very quiet. After dark they do not wander by foot without a light, or they light a trail of fires to light the way as they believe the 'wati' or feather foot will get them in the dark. Unlike us, if you want to have no-one around your house you have no outside lights on! Keep it all dark. This is true in our community, but in the larger ones there are the more streetwise who have lost the fear of the feather foot.

Dress has to be modest for men and women when in the community. In our own yards we can, within reason, dress as we please. Certain colours and patterns are not worn by the people, mainly the men, as it has cultural significance. We are still trying to learn the language which creates much amusement at times amongst people, or 'yanarngu' as they are called. Each area refer to themselves differently, like 'koori', 'noongar', 'anarngu' etc. Even the craft is different here; they make tapping sticks, lizards, snakes, baskets, boomerangs and paint. Up north they do bark paintings and make didgeridoos and depict different animals and happenings.

So from the coast to the desert we are enjoying it all. We may try the Kimberley at some stage, but for now the desert is fine. Watching distant fires, the magnificent thunderstorms roll in and the huge willie willies is fascinating.

A town with no pub (yes, its true), that's where I live. After a number of previous short visits, early this year I made my home at Yowah, which is a tiny opal-mining town approximately 100 kilometres west of Brisbane. The climate is arid and the homes are clustered around the town's lifeline: a hot artesian bore.

Why do I live there? You well may ask. I often do, especially when I shake the dust from my freshly laundered clothes or watch the mercury climb to 40 degrees for yet another scorching day. But when I wake in the cool first light of a new day, I know why. I feel a special peace, a sense of oneness with my surroundings. The

Jennifer Loh,
Yowah,
Queensland

blushing pink of early sunrise envelops the entire sky, only to be chased away by fiery orange and pale yellow as the sun peeps above the horizon. Kangaroos withdraw to the scrub, birds nestle back into the trees, mother emu takes her chicks for a morning stroll and sleeping lizards stretch as the sun radiates life back into their bodies.

Everything seems to belong here, to share a purpose: the stunted trees, the dust, even the heat, which seems somehow to cleanse and relax a tired body. There is no battle against nature. Instead I learn to understand and work with it. In my house, which is still under construction, I use local rocks and stone and make bricks with clay from the mining area. Time is not measured by the hands on a clock. When there is daylight I work. As the sun begins its final descent in the west I pause and wait for nature's artistry to once again colour the sky. Soon the stars take over and wink down at me in silent laughter. Another day draws to its conclusion and as I lay my head on the pillow I smile, content in the knowledge that I, too, belong here.

Thyra Harland,
Ludmilla,
Northern Territory

My husband and I have lived in Darwin now for the past four-and-a-half years and tune in every Sunday even though it is still quite dark. In the tropics there is no easing into daylight; it is suddenly light within a half-hour. Another interesting facet to living in the Top End is the climate. Most people are familiar with the 'wet' and the 'dry' seasons up here. In fact there are six! They are named and described by the Aborigines and I shall attempt to tell you about them, using the terms of the Kakadu region.

Through July to August it is 'wurrgeng', the cold season when night temperatures can go as low as 19°C and we actually need a blanket! But the days are simply magical. However, the lush grasses and undergrowth become dried out and a lot of bush fires occur, sometimes caused my man, but sometimes by lightning or dry storms. The sky is often dulled by smoke, yet it is this smoke-filled air which is the cause of the spectacular sunsets over the harbour. Darwin's nickname is Sunset City. It is this time of year when the water in the harbour is so clear from the lack of run-off it becomes a glorious ultramarine colour in the evening light, and a stunning turquoise during the day.

August to September sees a very hot, dry season, with bright clear days. By now the creeks and waterholes have dried up and everything settles in to a waiting period. Through October, November, December along comes 'gunumeleng', the 'build-up' or 'silly season' when people blame the weather for their behaviour (or anything else that happens)! It is the pre-monsoon season, very hot, with rising humidity and violent electrical storms. It is the most visually dynamic season with immense storm clouds of intense colours building up usually late in the day. Everyone looks skywards hoping for the relief of rain, only to see the clouds disappear as quickly as they came, with not one drop. Towards the end of December there is usually very intense rain, over and done within minutes, with a bright shiny day following, but cooled by the rain. Such a relief.

From January through February to March we have 'gudjewg', usually very heavy rain for days on end and extreme humidity. But although uncomfortable at times we can usually keep cool with overhead fans in all the rooms, and of course a lot of people resort to air-conditioning these days. This is the true monsoon season and relies on the monsoon trough coming down from the north. It is also the growing season and everything has an enormous burst of growth. Including mould!

The next season takes up most of April and is called 'bang gereng'. This is the season of the 'knock-em-down' storms, in fact high grasses are literally knocked down, flattened from the south east. At the end of April the air is still steamy, but suddenly each day becomes filled with dragon flies. It is an amazing sight and a sure sign the 'dry' is just around the corner.

Early in May the air gradually dries, and the next sign is the arrival of the wood swallows when powerlines become covered with thousands of birds. Now the season 'yegge' heralds the cooler dry winds and takes us into June. The land dries out and gradually the season 'wurrgeng' comes again. And so the cycle continues, very subtly, but very definitely in place.

· · ·

Hearing my name on your program last Sunday was a big surprise, especially as the letter you referred to was written at least fifteen years ago while we were living at Ludmilla in Darwin. We left there in 1989, finally retiring to Deception Bay just north of Brisbane. However, I can truthfully say that nowhere has any part of Australia made such a lasting impression on me as did the Top End.

Thyra, now at Deception Bay, Queensland

The subject of Aboriginal weather observations is still relevant. Their seasonal descriptions are well documented and certainly bring home the fact that the indigenous people were very observant and protective of their environment.

Wendy and Barry Austen, Medowie, New South Wales

This is a salutary lesson for anyone tempted to go on the land at a late age. Wendy and Barry Austen went to grow lettuces, and this is their tale.

BARRY: We have a little hydroponic lettuce farm at Medowie just outside of Raymond Terrace in NSW.

How long have you had it?

BARRY: Seven very, very long months! We came from Umina down on the central coast to Medowie to indulge in this lettuce farm business. It's very time consuming.

Had you had any lettuce experience?

WENDY: Not a thing We know a little bit more than we did seven months ago!

How did you get involved in it?

WENDY: The kids had moved away from home. We were getting ready for a bit of a change. We saw a little ad in our local paper for a lettuce farm and thought, we can do this, what can there be to growing lettuces? Well, the truck got bogged the day we moved in, and it rained for about two months and then for another two months after that. Then we got the dreaded black spot. I've been in the nursing game and I'm sure it is related to the bubonic plague!

Was this your idea, Barry?

BARRY: It was a joint effort. We tossed it around for a while. It sounded like a pretty good idea when we ventured into it.

I thought water was good for lettuces?

WENDY: Not for hydroponic lettuces. No, no, no! They're the most temperamental thing you've ever come across in your life.

They're grown in hothouses?

WENDY: No, outside on PVC tables with little holes. We bought the house and gear and the previous owner stayed with us for about two weeks and told us what to do. After the 'bubonic plague' we got snails. So we found some stuff that you paint on the table legs. We crawled around on our hands and knees painting 1,000 legs.

I thought you meant the snails, but they don't have legs!

WENDY: Then we got a frost. Stiff as pokers they were, all of them. Apparently you have to hose lettuces when they get frostbitten. There's one hose on the property and it weighs a ton – it's like a fireman's hose. So, here we are five in the morning racing around spraying the lettuce! We lost about 2,000.

So you have to pick them and send them to market.

BARRY: Yes, on a Sunday morning while we're listening to you we pick them, usually about ninety boxes. We take them to the markets and they sell them for us.

Are you going to stick at it?

BARRY: Probably for twelve months. I don't think it's a permanent thing.

Wendy, any advice for people thinking about getting into rural pursuits? You're city slickers aren't you?

WENDY: Don't! It just rolls from disaster to disaster. We got a windstorm that went on for a month. The lettuces were like little helicopters pirouetting out of their holes. We had to race around like maniacs picking them up and putting them back!

It's obviously been an educational experience.

BARRY: It's has been a very, very educational experience. We start at daylight and finish at dark. Today we made a special effort to come in here.

You should have brought me a lettuce!

BARRY: Wendy suggested that but then she said she wasn't going to make a goose of herself walking around with a lettuce! We do enjoy your show.

I wish I could say I enjoyed your lettuce.

WENDY: Other than your show we've got the air force that goes over all the time.

Strafing you!

WENDY: We sometimes look at them and say, 'We're here, drop one on us!'

What possessed you to leave the normal . . .

WENDY: Why was it?

BARRY: In 1995 we got the travel bug and did a twelve-month stint around Australia. Spent our children's inheritance! We've got no big supers to fall back on, so we have to work.

WENDY: I think we've been off the property once in seven months. We've been to a wedding. But we have to come home because we have to feed these jolly things at night. They have to be fed and put to bed!

Nice to talk to you both. I want one of those lettuces next time!

Dave Rundle, Yakanarra Community

G'day Macca. I was born at Mount Barker about 230 miles south of Perth. My father owned a big property but unfortunately he got cancer so we sold the farm and moved to Perth in mid-1940s. I came up here first to the Kimberley in 1959. My twin brother and I were stockmen on Nookenbah sheep station. It was one of the biggest stations in Australia in those days and the record shearing was about 112,000 sheep. That was too many sheep for the amount of country of over a million acres. We reduced the numbers to about 65,000. My brother and I left in the mid-1960s and went south. I did have a private pilot's licence and I got a commercial one as well. I was the first pilot to be based in Fitzroy, aerial mustering. I used to work for all the cattle stations around here until I turned fifty and gave it away.

What's your job now?

I own an air charter company. I've got four aircraft and we service all the many Aboriginal communities in the area. We do a lot of emergency flights. I did two yesterday. Young Aboriginal kid with a gastro complaint and another who slipped over and hurt his back. We also do a lot of flying for the government and education department.

What do you like about the Kimberley?

I love it. I've been here thirty years. I like the wide open spaces and I like the people. When I first did aerial mustering up here I had an all-black crew. Ten to fourteen Aboriginal stockmen and they did a really good job. There wasn't the alcohol problem then. I hope it improves for them over the years.

What's the nicest part about flying round the Kimberley?

The beautiful scenery up over the Leopold Ranges, Durack Ranges, Argyle and of course the Bungle Bungles. I just enjoy the Kimberley and the wide open spaces. I had to land on the road once. About eight or ten years ago I took off from here with five or six passengers. I'd just passed over the Kununurra main road on descent to the Bungles and when I eased off the throttle it was just flopping around in my hand. I was losing power so I told the passengers I was going to have to make an emergency landing on the road. It was in the middle of the tourist season and there was a lot of traffic around but I got down okay. The throttle had disconnected from the throttle arm.

Will you stay up here? This is home for you?

I'll probably think about selling up in three or four years. Yes, I'll settle down in the Kimberley but keep a plane for myself. Shoot down to Perth to see my mother and my brother who lives near Geraldton. Just cruise around. I like the desert country. I flew down there three weeks ago over sheets of water which I've never seen before. After flying over the area for thirty years, I was absolutely amazed that the tropical lows that have swung in south of Broome over the last two or three years have dumped all this water on the desert. There was some absolutely magnificent bird life – pelicans, ducks, swans and water hens. That's the country I really like. The wide open spaces.

Malcolm Mitchell, Muloorina Station

We're with Malcolm Mitchell at Muloorina Station, which is just near the dog fence, not far from the Birdsville Track, not far from Lake Eyre, a long way from anywhere! Malcolm, how long have you and the family been here?

My family's been on the station since 1936 and I've been here all my life. Did my schooling here and been working here for thirty-five years.

And it's a cattle or sheep property?

We're got the dog fence ten miles south from here so we've got some country inside the dog fence. We run sheep inside and cattle outside.

Does the dog fence work?

It's not one hundred per cent. We tried to run sheep outside it but the dogs got too good for us.

Are there a lot of dingoes?

They come and go in waves. Sometimes you see five or six a day for two or three months, then it gets quiet and you might only see one or two.

Now this station's famous because it's where Donald Campbell and his entourage came to break the world land speed record. You were a little feller then.

Yes, in 1963 and 1964, I was in short pants. I was only ten or eleven but I remember them clearly. There were five or six hundred people here for about three months. Media, engineers, army and police.

Was it a big deal at the time? I suppose it was going round the world.

Yes, it was huge. The government put in a lot of money to help him out and put Australia on the map. There were ten or eleven kids here at the time and we had a ball. Donald was good to us. He used to take us out to watch some of the attempts. I didn't actually see the one where he broke the world record.

That fence is a disgrace. He, he!

As I said before, you're a long way from anywhere. Lake Eyre has filled a couple of times. What was that like?

The big filling was in 1974. There was fourteen feet of water where Campbell had been. I fly over it lots and never get sick of it. It's always different, depending on the light.

Have you ever been out on it in a boat?

Yes, in 1974 we bought a speedboat and skied on Lake Eyre!

Tell us about your grandfather

My grandfather was Eddie Price. He started this place and built it up and the last two generations have just kept it going. He had no education, couldn't read or write, but was a really good engineer. He built a couple of gyrocopters and in the early 1960s had one flying. He had an electric fence back in the mid-50s and used to make his own welders out of generators. He was a very clever man with his hands.

He was a conservationist as well.

Yes, he set aside 100 square miles out on the edge of the lake for conservation only, purely to see if in 100 or 200 years it's any different to the country being grazed around it. The only people that go up there are doing research.

As humans I think we're good rationalisers about where we live. What do you think about living out here?

In the years I've been working here, thirty of them have been really good, but when it's dry like now you wonder what the hell you are doing here. It's tough and hard work but it's been good to us and I have really, really loved it. I guess I don't know much else. I was born here and this has been it. You have to do everything yourself – all the plumbing, electricity, building, mechanics. There's nobody within hundreds of miles, and it's just part of life for us.

Do you ever think about living in other places?

Only when it gets dry! When you're in a drought you think there must be something else. I do like to see the sea, to smell it and hear it, but I don't really like going in.

What's the best time of the year here when you wake up and think it's great to be alive?

May is a particularly a good time. There's no wind and you wake up to really crisp mornings. The air seems to lift the horizon. You can see the sand hills and think they are eighty feet high. The trees stand right up. It's just beautiful. They might be fourteor fifteen miles away but they are standing like a three-storey building.

It's five-thirty in the morning and I'm sitting here with a mug of tea thinking about why I live where I live.

    I live in a rundown miner's cottage on about an acre of land in the bush with my

Early morning listener,
Daylesford,
Victoria

three dogs. It's cool and damp and the mist is creeping up the hill. The gums are laden with moisture and look as though they've been washed clean of summer's dust. The smell of eucalyptus, moist grass and soil drifting on the cool air is heady. My dam has a little water in it and the sound of croaking frogs is wonderful. The dawn's just breaking and seven or eight 'roos have just wandered lazily past the gate. They've been eating the apple and bread scraps I leave out for both them and the possums. Now the birds are awake and it's very noisy. The kookaburras and magpies started and now the currawongs have joined in. The kookaburras in the fruit trees drop to the ground every now and then for a worm feed, and a blackbird sings away by itself just for the joy of it. Some folk may like the sound of the city waking up, but to me the sound of the bush awakening, the dawn chorus, is perfect.

I think it's time for another cuppa, and a bit of toast would be nice, too. And that's why I live where I live – and I love it.

Hoo roo.

We live in Yorkeys Knob, a northern beach suburb of beautiful tropical Cairns. It's one of a string of beaches about ten minutes north of the CBD and I think it's the best. At first mention of the name you always get a raised eyebrow or a wry chuckle. It's a real place! It's a nob or bluff at the northern end of our three or so kilometres of golden pristine beach. It was named after George 'Yorkey' Lawson who was a one-armed bêche-de-mer (sea slug) fisherman who settled in the area early last century. He was quite a character and there are many stories about him. In fact our local residents' association is putting up a memorial to him in 2007.

Yorkeys, as it is known locally, is a beaut little place full of 'knobbers', colourful people from all walks of life: escapees from harder times down south, retirees, yuppies, dinks, young families, extended families, first-time-out-of-homers and an increasing amount of regular returning holidaymakers. We pass each other with a knowing camaraderie either at the local IGA, boat club, or just walking on the sandy tidal flats at low tide where we take a bag and pick up any rubbish, obviously left by 'non-knobbers'.

Our foreshore has lovely barbecue areas, kiddies' playground, lawns and lots of native trees that hold it all together and avoid the erosion that plagues other beaches. There is no absolute beachfront development, and a three-storey limit for unit blocks, so you can walk along the beach and not see any ugly buildings – hopefully it won't change.

The beach walk finishes at a very beautiful mangrove clustered estuary called Thomatis Creek (the kids call it 'tomatoes'), a tributary of the Barron River, and it's one of those magical spots where you really feel in touch with Mother Nature. My partner and I work at a large local hotel and on our days off we often sit there for hours quietly absorbing the majesty of the area. There's a pair of sea eagles (I call them Manly and Wharinga) getting to know each other and hopefully build a nest, and a hawk (I call him Hawthorne) looking for a mate to do the same. There's a regular 'mob' of pelicans out on the largest sandbank (I call it Pelican Island) and the ubiquitous gulls and terns. A resident egret (Mr Fisher) gets around up the creek,

➡

Ali Harper and
Phil Gibson,
Yorkeys Knob,
Queensland

which abounds with sea life of all sorts, like Hermie a hermit crab that lives in a pretty cowrie-like shell and gets stranded on the very low tides. I fear it will be taken by a tourist one day. I often hide it near old submerged logs and my partner reckons Hermie lives in fear of me picking him up and putting him back just when it's got so far up the beach.

Sometimes we are truly blessed by the presence of Feather and her family. She is a bottlenose dolphin with a white 'splash' on her dorsal fin. I call her hubby Old Salt and they have a little one Little Salt. They just cruise along the beach only about ten to twenty metres from the shore. Feather teaches Little Salt the things that a baby dolphin needs to know and Old Salt circles around them stirring up the fish and keeping an eye on things. They usually end up just off the rocky point of the nob and you can watch them for hours. You really feel a spiritual presence and privileged to be invited into their lives. David Attenborough eat your heart out!

We moved into Yorkeys permanently three years ago, having spent ten years in another part of Cairns and being sick of having to drive here each time we yearned for the sea air. We have a duplex and we live in one side and rent out the other. There was nothing here when we moved in – barren, sandy and lifeless. Since then I have grown lots of native shrubs and trees and some lovely flowering tropical gingers and shrubs, in particular Miss Ritzy, a named variety of hibiscus, and Miss Moira the jasmine bush/tree that was originally a cutting from my friend Moira, are doing very well. I built a med-style raised courtyard for veggies and herbs and potted fruit trees. My two guinea pigs Parsley and Crackers compost the leftovers and keep the small lawn area well trimmed. I planted some banana trees because it is considered good luck and also in memory of the Bali bombing victims, and I think I'll get a crop this year. We put in a pool that catches the winter sun, and on the odd day we can't get to the beach we 'bubble up' (Australian fizz of course!), fire up the barbie, play by the pool and enjoy the cacophony of the birds, insects, lizards and frogs that I have attracted to our place.

Just on sunset we watch the magpie geese return home from feeding on the wetlands and the fruit bats head out for the night. During the day we enjoy the presence of the sunbird family – cute little hummingbird-like nectar and insect feeders, rainbow lorikeets, friar birds (so called because they have a sort of baldy head), rainbow bee-eaters, a regular migratory pair of Torres Strait pigeons (I call them Warraber and Ngrapi – TI names for Thursday Island and Horn Island), kookaburras who warn me to get the washing off the line, cranky little Willis and Wilhemina, the willy-wagtails, and lots and lots of pretty bugs and butterflies. At night when the moon is bright we are blessed by the call of the bush stone curlew I call Luna and her family. Monsieur the white-tipped green treefrog and Flip the green treefrog are regular visitors. Luckily I don't have many toads. My fourteen-year-old son is quite vigilant and over the fence to the main road is a six! There are some very cute native bush rats (the rellies) that occasionally come in from somewhere and feed off the scraps left on the grass.

We are also blessed with a 'codger' who lives over the 'six' side of the main road and sits on his steps finding fault with the world around him. I feel he will smoke himself to death eventually. We are on a corner that leads to the school and directly across from us is an indigenous family from somewhere up the Cape. They are

Friar Bird

lovely people consisting of Mum, Dad and three kids under four (sometimes Nanna comes to visit). They only speak our English when we speak to them. The rest is in their native tongue, which I think is great in this day and age. They play with, nurture, chastise and educate the little ones who are absolutely drop-dead-so-cute and very active. Occasionally rellies come to visit and under the mango street shade they go and out comes the guitar and they sing and play the most wonderful music.

Anyway, that's why I love where I live. I believe that home is what you make it. I love listening to everyone; it shows what a diverse lot we all are and what a wonderful country we have.

8 – The *Sell Fish Man*

I don't know why it is that kids surprise and delight us.

Maybe we don't expect them to be intuitive, clever, insightful

and dry, matter of fact, all the things that adults can be.

But they are, and listeners are always delighted with kids

like Eric who rang in and talked about life on board

The *Sell Fish Man*. Here, Eric is on the lookout for crab pots

while his mate steers. The *Sell Fish Man* is in the background.

Eric Finlay, Gulf of Carpentaria

G'day Macca. I live on a fishing boat in the Gulf of Carpentaria about three of four miles from Karumba. I'm ten years old and listen to your show all the time so I just thought I'd ring up. We've pulled all the nets up but we haven't really caught anything.

What's the name of the boat and how big is it? You'll have to send us a photo.

The name of the boat is the *Sell Fish Man*. We're not selfish, we just sell fish. We've got a couple of good photos of the boat. Me and my mum are going to get a big portrait done of it and give it to my dad at the end of the year for Christmas. The boat is about fifteen metres.

Do you meet other kids?

I do on-air lessons for school and talk to other kids online. But next year I'm going to boarding school in Cairns.

What sort of fish do you catch?

Barramundi, king salmon, all the regular fish. There's not many others. But we target the barra and king salmon. We're on board the boat this morning. I don't really know where we are. I just know about fish.

So, you listen to us on Sunday mornings and thought you'd just give us a call?

Well, mum bullied me into it, but I was going to ring you anyway.

So, who does all the fishing?

My dad does. I go out to help most of the time. My mum does the crab pots and when she's in a bad mood she makes me pull sixty crab pots. Six o'clock in the morning to seven o'clock at night with only an hour's break. She doesn't often get in a bad mood, really.

What are you going to do when you grow up?

I'm going to be a fisherman or else a bank accountant.

No, don't be one of them, mate. Be a fisherman, it's much more interesting. Keep listening.

Tracey, Eric and Greg Finlay, Karumba, Queensland

Well, 'grumpy old Mum' thought she'd better write as now we are currently on land during our four-month fishing closure. Eric has his land legs and I've hardly seen him, he is so busy playing with other kids.

I thought I'd tell you how the name of the boat came about. As my husband, Greg, was building it he thought to himself, 'Man, I'm going to have to sell a lot of fish to pay for this'. So, the name was *Sell Fish Man*.

The boat's ten metres long with a double wheelhouse and four metres wide. It has an enclosed processing area and is fully air-conditioned.

We're all itching to get back fishing. The boat's a flat-bottom barge which is ideal here as the waters are very shallow. When the tide goes out we just sit there on the sand and fish.

Waking up on the water watching the sunrise is great. But going to sleep is even better. It reminds me of a baby being gently rock to sleep.

Eric has started taking the dinghy out by himself but is not allowed out of sight. He puts out about six crab pots which he baits and then checks. He was told five dollars for every crab he caught but he's never caught any. Mind you, he still manages to get money out of me!

This is the first time I dared to write to you. I just felt a bit shy, as I always do. I really like your program and listen to it nearly every Sunday even when we are travelling somewhere. I take my ABC radio cap. I think your program is really good because it helps the tourists. If they listen they understand more of Australia and its customs and traditions.

Now I live in Randwick in Sydney. It is a nice suburb, very quiet and still. Originally I came from St Petersburg in Russia. It is a good place but hard to live in now. You know the situation there, heaps of people out of work and many not paid. We will try and stay here forever but my dad's position is not permanent. I don't really want to live in Russia long, maybe only to visit our friends.

Actually, what I wanted to tell you in this letter was that you are always talking about Australian kids getting to know their country more. Well, the science teacher at my school has organised a tour of country NSW in the holidays. We will be away for seven days and visit many historic country towns, caves and national parks. We will even go to the Lightning Ridge opal mine.

My family and I really like your show and have been to your Christmas concert. Keep up your good work.

PS If you can please write back.

Lera Onbakina (14 years),
Randwick,
New South Wales

IT'S MY HOME

When I wake up in the morning
I look out the window
And see the sun shining down
I can hear the kookaburras calling
In the big old Manna Gums

I can see the kangaroos
Bouncing across the hills in the sunlight
Wallabies and possums
Magpies sing good morning
And a brown snake lying in the sun

(Chorus)
It's my home
Where the farm land meets the forest of the Otways
It's my home
When I see the wedgetail eagle fly I know
I'm coming home

Written and performed
by Deans Marsh Primary
School students and
Tiffany Eckhardt,
Victoria

There's three shops and a school
A skate park where we can all relax and be ourselves
We all go see the music Friday nights
When we go down the hill

Deans Marsh rich in history
Folklore and mystery
Shadows of black panthers creeping in the bush
I see Marjory Lawrence's face in a picture on the wall

(Chorus)

As the sun goes down on Deans Marsh town
The cows are in the dairy standing round
I see the stockman and his kelpie bringing in the sheep
Before the rain

The spirit of this town is in the people gathering round
In the paddocks and the sheds
Laughing and singing no matter where we go
We will know Deans Marsh is our home

(Chorus)

Lorna Ginn from Childers, Queensland, sent in this letter in 1991. It was written by one of her primary school students. Let's hope all these years later his dire warning about his home hasn't eventuated.

Andrew Davey

I am Andrew Davey and I am living in Childers this year.

I am originally from Cooktown where I live on our 500-acre property called Mungumby. The property is seven kilometres from the nearest road or people. Our house which we built is very open and it looks over a lawn and swimming pool to a great mountain covered in rainforest. The mountain has a waterfall running down a valley. I miss the peace and tranquillity of our small paradise. I get to school by driving seven kilometres to the gate and catching a bus about thirty kilometres to town. Some mornings we stop the car to let a herd of wild pigs cross the road. The bush is a great place to live and relax. Enjoy it while you can because in the future there will be no places like Mungumby and the only great forests will be made of steel, glass or concrete.

This is an early kid's poem, sent in 1991 by twelve-year-old Lana Hegarty, Coonamble, NSW. She lived on a farm and her favourite place was the Castlereagh River.

Lana Hegarty,
Coonamble,
New South Wales

THE CASTLEREAGH

Birds sing along the Castlereagh,
Children splash in waterholes.
The tall, white gums sway in the wind.

Early in the morning the old
Kookaburra laughs its jolly laugh.
The day passes,
Hot in summer
Cold in winter.
Then slowly the sun
Sinks behind the gums of Castlereagh.

In flood, in drought the Castlereagh has its beauty.
Let's hope it always will.

I often ponder where kids like Jacinta, who wrote in 1990, now live. She asked me to 'keep doing a great job on the radio' – I wonder if she still listens fifteen years on.

Hello, my name is Jacinta Murphy and I'm fourteen. I live 100 miles west of Cobar, NSW, on a property called Neckarbo. We're also 100 miles from Wilcannia and Ivanhoe so we have to travel a fair way to do the shopping. I often listen to *Australia All Over* and I think it's great. My family listens as well.

Do you have any pets? I have four dogs and a pony. The pony's name is Tony and I often take him to gymkhanas where he's won lots of ribbons and prizes. My favourite dog is a cattle dog. His name is Harry and he does things like sit, heel and shake hands.

I really like the bush life and have been at Neckarbo for about ten years. There's nothing better than wandering out in the scrub, lighting a fire and boiling the old billy. Well, I hope this letter finds you well. Keep doing a great job on the radio.

Jacinta Murphy

Yeah, g'day

Liam on board a ten-metre catamaran, *Cheers*

Hi Macca, this is Liam.

G'day Liam. How you going? Where are you from?

We're from Melbourne and are at Bundaberg on a ten-metre catamaran sailing around Queensland for a year.

That sounds nice.

It's great. Sunny all the time. We just decided to take a year off. My sister Emily and I are doing school work on the boat.

You can do that in the car when you're travelling around Australia and it's called school in the back seat. Yours could be called school of the poop deck!

We've just been up to Lizard Island near Cooktown. It's really great up there. About fifty boats and twenty kids. One day we had the Lizard Games, like the Olympics. We had sea boot throwing, line casting and everything like that. It was really great.

How long have you been at sea, and how old are you?

We started in April this year and have been going about seven months. I'm thirteen. The snorkelling is great. I'm not used to it because it's usually raining in Melbourne. We're still thinking about sailing around the world next.

Do you miss school, or do you like doing school in the poop deck?

I like doing schooling on the boat, but I miss my friends. We got to Bundaberg last Sunday and will stay here for a week. We're planning to head down to the Gold Coast for Christmas and meet some friends there.

That's the beauty of life, Liam: you can change your plans mid-stream. I suppose that's what you can do with a boat

Yes, we just make it up as we go!

What's the name of your boat?

Cheers.

Cheers! Well, we'll keep an eye out for it. You keep in touch. Any questions with your school work just give us a ring!

Jenni Hodgman,
(7 years),
Captains Flat,
New South Wales

I agree with you about gumboots. We wear them all around the property except for in the house. I like to wear them because I don't have to do up laces every time I go outside. They are also a lot safer from snakes and it is easier walking up the creek. We always bang out our gumboots in case something is inside them. The other day we went outside and my little brother Lewin forgot to bang out his gumboots. He put his foot in and he felt something inside. He screamed and ran away saying, 'There is a creature in my gumboot.' We looked in and saw the blue-tongue lizard that lives around our veranda. It must like gumboots too. I listen to you every week but I can't this week because it is Clean Up Australia Day and we are going to Captains Flat to help.

Jessie-anne Butler,
Blackbutt,
Queensland

I live where I live because I was born in the area. My name is Jessie-anne Butler and I am ten years old. I live twenty-five kilometres out of Blackbutt. There is a view that is fantastic. The birds there are great as well! I love animals and all sorts of animals are at my home, like wallabies, bower birds and bandicoots. My dog Boots loves chasing turkeys! My pets are my dog Boots, my bird Lucky and my horse Dinnie. I would never like to move because I have a high house and after school sometimes I go and sit outside on the veranda and look at the view while holding my dog and watching all the different birds that fly around to get a drink out of the bird baths. I like where I live because I have a great house and great neighbours and great friends as well. That is why I live where I live!

9 - Keep Movin' On

Where are they now? Mostly I don't know. They may have died, the kids will most certainly have grown up. Everyone moves on but their letters, and pictures like these, are timeless. Who knows, maybe they'll buy this book, read their letter and get back in touch. But perhaps we'll just use our imagination . . .

Margaret McKeachie,
Kendall,
New South Wales

It is nearly twenty years since I first wrote to you. At that time we were living near Yandina, on Queensland's Sunshine Coast. You were winding down the Great Shopping Trolley debate. Thinking back I must have been one of your original listeners, and still am. I have listened to *Australia All Over* all over Australia.

When I was born at Collaroy, in 1931, Collaroy plateau was still covered with wildflowers and was the home of wallaroos that hopped down past our place on their way to the beach. I married a Manly boy in 1952. His grandfather was master of the SS *Collaroy* when she went aground in a heavy fog on an unnamed beach just north of Long Reef in January 1881. That's how Collaroy got its name. We lived at Fairlight, overlooking Sydney Harbour, for about three years while we built our home at Elanora Heights, travelling back and forth by bus to clear a site and set out the foundations. Across the road was a dairy farm where we took our billy each day to be filled with real milk. Acres of bushland surrounded us, giving our kids an unlimited area to play out all sorts of wonderful adventures.

When traffic lights were installed at the bottom end of our road we knew it was time to move. The kids had all grown up. We sold our home, lived on Pittwater in the thirty-foot wooden boat we'd built. Then, leaving our boat in good hands we took off for all points north in a Hi-Ace with an attachable tent. We gradually worked our way up the east coast looking for a suitable place to put down roots again. We found it at Yandina, a house on ten acres on the northern side of a hill overlooking cane fields, with a wonderful view to Mt Cooroy and the Blackall Range to our west. Kangaroos and colourful birdlife our daily companions. We lived there for eight years and would have stayed longer but care of my aged father brought us south again.

We still live on the side of a hill, on five acres in a beautiful valley in the Camden Haven hinterland, on the mid north coast of New South Wales. The Comboyne Plateau, with its spectacular scenery and waterfalls, is at the end of our valley. It is only a twenty-minute drive to the beach with Port Macquarie our nearest big town. Since dad died in 1992 (two months short of ninety) we travelled north, south and west in our caravan until we decided the roads and caravan parks were getting too crowded. We've been here for seventeen years now. Part of our land backs onto a state forest while the rest adjoins grass paddocks where wallabies from the forest come to graze. Across and up the valley is a dairy farm. The milking cows chomp happily on the lush grass on the hill over the river from us. The birds congregate in our native garden and the air is always filled with birdsong. You couldn't find a more peaceful 'caravan park' if you tried. And that's why we live where we live and don't plan on moving again!

Keith Doyle wrote this in March 1986

Keith Doyle,
Upper Lansdowne,
New South Wales

I have lived in Rose Bay, NSW, as an insurance broker, fourteen years in Vaucluse as the state member, and now, would you believe, on 300 acres twenty miles west of Taree growing kiwifruit and fattening cattle. I have always been happy. It struck me that you might like this little jingle 'I like where I live'.

Bricks and mortar matter not nor do the locale rate
Provided love dwells in the house you can leave the rest to fate.
A kindly thought, a helping hand, where weary limbs do rest
Are more important than the place and are the only test.
So I like to live where 'ere I go because there's sure to be
The warmth and love my wife provides which so refreshes me.

I am now completely converted to 'Taswegianism' and am busily travelling Tasmania All Over so that I can show it to my interstate visitors in all its beauty and variety.

This seems to be a place where good friends can be made in a few minutes of conversation if you are an older person. I think it must be because we 'oldies' have time, an ever decreasing commodity in today's world. The frantic rush is missing here and the rat race is more like a ramble. We find ourselves sitting and chatting in the shopping malls. We wander about in craft shops and amble along at the weekend outdoor markets. Nobody ever need be lonely for long in this friendly place. I haven't met a grumpy person since I came here and the place is so clean. Very little graffiti is to be seen.

Last week in an antique shop there were so many items I recognised as having been part of our household when I was young. Things I had almost forgotten about but which now qualify as antique because they are over fifty years old. Since I am now three-quarters of a century old, I laughingly asked the proprietor what price he was prepared to put on me!

Earlier in my life I learned to look for the ridiculous in any given circumstance and I am seldom disappointed for life has held much more laughter than tears. I love to photograph silly signs and have found a great number all over the rest of Oz, as well as down here. A few weeks ago I found that a park has two large ornate gates all securely chained and locked up, but with no fence at all. Near my house there is an older-style Ford Falcon, bronze coloured, which is usually parked on the roadway. It has become quite a landmark because it has a P-plate hanging in the back window, a big 'ding' just below the latch on the boot, and on the side of the boot there is a picture of a large dog rising from a mud puddle with 'Bugger' written beside it. I have no idea which came first, the 'ding', the dog or the P-plate. But I do know that it puts a smile on the faces of most of the people passing by.

Not far from here there is a handwritten sign, high up on the right-hand side of the road, reading 'MEALS $4.00' and underneath, in smaller letters, 'With Petrol'. I haven't tasted this new delicacy. You see, I am obviously a simple soul and it doesn't take much to keep me happy.

Together with two friends, our ages totalling 222 years, I am having some lovely car trips about this beautiful state. Sometimes, when the weather is kind, we take picnics, at other times we go in somewhere for meals. We never have a set destination in mind when we leave home. Sometimes we get lost. Once we even finished up on a logging road too narrow to turn round on. After driving right up to the top of a mountain in heavy fog and sleet we came to a felled tree across the road. With one of us at the back of the car, one looking out one side and the driver doing what

Heather Hastings,
Newstead,
Tasmania

Will that be premium or regular unleaded?

came naturally, we made a twenty-five point turn and returned the way we'd come. It was so pretty up there in the first snow I'd ever seen falling it was worth the anxiety.

I have begun a computer course for older folk in an effort to master this darned machine or die trying. To my utter surprise I find myself managing to even squeeze some information into this old brain after all.

Nearly had a catastrophe this morning as we'd had a blackout some time during the night and my alarm didn't go off. Thus I missed the first quarter hour of *Australia All Over*. I've been listening since 1987 – even the little budgie listens in and is very appreciative of the birdcalls each time they come on.

Did I hear you say you will be in Narrandera next week? I well remember staying a night there in the motel on the main street. It was our first trip over the Nullarbor en route to Perth in 1969, the road wasn't completely sealed, and we were driving in a little Morris 1100 car towing a fold-down van. We felt like pioneers as everyone waved and beeped the horn at us as we went across!

You have been talking about why I live where I live lately. I am reminded how I wrote to you some years ago to tell you that we often lived part-time at Port Albert on weekends where we had a caravan on-site. We would travel to the beautiful little spot where enormous eucalyptus trees grew, where birds sang in the branches and life was as it should be. But my husband's stroke in 1997 ended all that for us. He is so much better these days but we don't go there any more.

The home we had in Traralgon is sold and we have moved to an easier-to-look-after unit. We have a birdbath to feed the native birds that visit. You should see the mother blackbird and hear the splashing she makes when she washes. She sits on the edge of the birdbath and chortles in the sunshine. She brings smiles to our faces.

Sometimes it's sad to move on from the place that you call home, but at this stage of our lives we are lucky to have each other. After fifty years of marriage we are happy to live where we live . . . together.

PS I enclose a poem I wrote while watching the birds come to bathe. I hope you like it.

Kay Ruane,
Traralgon,
Victoria

THE BIRDBATH

Deep in reverie I sit
I'm distracted
By a thrashing, slashing sound
I turn to watch
As the blackbird splashes water all around
I watch
And as the little brown bird bathes
She ducks and dives and splashes
She's alert, her head moves side to side
She watches
She knows that danger is ever near
While bathing in my birdbath

As I watch, I almost feel her fear
As she watches
She shakes her feathers
And preens a bit
I've spread some crumbs
She feeds on them
Her head moves side to side
While she watches
She's come to share
A little time with me
But I have cat, so I watch for her
While all the while . . . she watches

Nev Richens, Boree Creek, New South Wales

Nev Richens phoned from Boree Creek, NSW, back in December 1995. Ten years on I wonder how he's going.

I left school early and educated myself to get into the Air Force. I did a bit over two or three years in the Air Force, came out and worked for my father at fifteen shillings a week for a year, then went share farming at Boree Creek.

How did the drought that we had . . .

. . . that's what started the problems in the rural industry here. In 1981 and 1982 we had the drought and interest rates took off. Most fellas, particularly the young ones who'd bought land between 1980 and 1990, got into financial difficulties and they never got in front.

And you lost your place.

Yes, we lost our place twelve months ago.

Was that a big blow?

You just can't describe what it's like. It was a shocking blow. I started off with nothing, built it all up, and it's all gone. I can't go out to the farm now without shedding a tear or two.

And all your farming expertise is lost too, isn't it, Nev. It's lost to the nation.

I guess so. I say to my son, 'There's a week to sow and a week to harvest.' They're the most important weeks in the calendar year. Nobody can tell you when to sow; you feel it. It's only after living all your life on a farm that you can experience it. It's something that gets in your blood. You work a plough and you know by the smell of the soil it's the right time. You can't teach young people that. They've got to learn by experience.

And you still enjoy work?

I love work. Let's put it this way, I've got to work. I think it's bred in you on a farm. There's different things every day, you never get sick of it.

You like living in this area of the Riverina?

Well, I was born here, at Ardlethan. Apart from time away in the Air Force I've lived in the area all my life.

What do you like about it?

The freedom and the big outdoors. I did some flying with Frontier Services out in the Centre, and if I didn't have a family I'm sure I'd go and live in Alice Springs because of the open air and freedom. Imagine arriving in Finke one Sunday afternoon and going to a barbecue in the bed of the Finke River with not another white person for 150 to 200 miles. We stopped at Andamooka, and people never shut their doors there.

But you don't lock doors in Boree Creek do you?

Oh, yes you do. Those days are gone.

Peter Mack,
Geraldton,
Western Australia

I once wrote to Why I Live Where I Live when I was holidaying at a place on the tourist trail in north-west Australia called Warrora Station. With my wife Fran I have lived a rather nomadic existence for the past fifteen years since we retired, and have been able to spread our wings a bit. I'm sure that like a lot of the grey nomads I know we have returned to one of the spots we found agreeable in our past life, and it looks like being the end of the road. We are close to the beach where I can catch a fish or two and Fran can walk the dogs, and it's a pleasant, quiet neighbourhood – who can ask for anything more?

Fran penned this poem about our life, though most of your listeners would never have heard of the towns mentioned.

There is a nice old couple who can never settle down,
Through all their life together they've moved from town to town.

From Drummonds Cove to Coral Bay to Jurien and back,
Like gypsies in a caravan this couple have the knack.

They buy a house and fix it up and plant a grape and fig,
Then before any fruit appears they find the house too big.

Back and forth they travel on looking for a new home,
That'll make them really happy so they'll never need to roam.

So if one day you see this pair some advice you'll need to give,
Because it is quite likely that they've forgotten where they live.

Lucy Faithfull,
Moree,
New South Wales

I live in an area that used to be called the 'pig leather' and is now known just as the watercourse, about 70 kilometres west of Moree. I have lived in many areas of NSW but I believe this is the best one. Our place consists of red ridges with wigas, leopardwoods and capparia (nepine), low clay areas with myalls, belahs and coolibahs and occasional sandy areas containing the beautiful carbeens.

I spent the first year of our marriage identifying trees and shrubs. My collection methods were rather unorthodox. We would be out mustering on the motorbike and I would yell out, 'Stop the bike, I haven't seen that flower before.' Tom would come screaming to a halt. I also learnt to identify many of the birds as Tom knows most of them. He would point out a silhouette flying into the sun and say 'blue bonnet' or 'jacky winter'. One day (again out mustering on the bike) he shouted 'Duck' – I looked for the duck and collected a branch instead! We are still married!

Duck!

Some of our place has never been cleared and contains flood country plants and birds. But these areas are now threatened by a proposed dam further upstream. The area used to be renowned for its 'sag' beds, a sort of reed that was very good cattle feed, especially during drought, and for the egret and ibis rookeries. Black swans and brolgas also nested there. I think there is nothing more beautiful that watching seventy to eighty black swans and their cygnets floating on the bull-couch grass that grows up through the water, or the Vs of ibis or brolgas flying at dawn with the sun flashing on their wings. I don't want to lose all this, so Tom and I are doing a lot of praying, writing letters and going to meetings to try to save it.

· · ·

My name is Lucy and a neighbour rang to say that they heard you reading out a letter I wrote to you a few years ago. We now live on the edge of Toowoomba which, if you have to live in a city, is a nice place to live. We still have lots of birds, different varieties of course, brown snakes and wallabies. It is a lot easier to get the children to school, a fifteen-minute ride on their bikes rather than a one-and-a-half-hour trip on the bus, and the shops are far too convenient! We now have a lot more time for community work, especially through church.

Lucy Faithfull, now at Toowoomba, Queensland

I do miss the bush though, and it took a good eighteen months for me to get used to seeing a house whenever I went outside. Teaching the kids about living in town was interesting as well. They were so nervous about sleeping with their windows open that we had to get security screens put on (we had no locks out in the watercourse, let alone security screens). Also, teaching my four-year-old about boundaries – 'That's the neighbour's gravel driveway you're making roads on and they rake it every day; 'Yes, I know there is no fence but it's still out of bounds.' The first time the kids came to me and said, 'We're off for a picnic,' I just said, 'Okay, don't forget your water bottles.' About ten minutes later I remembered we were in town and they couldn't just wander off anywhere and set up a picnic. When I found them they had set up a camp fire under someone's hedge and were wondering if they could camp there. (No, it wasn't alight, they were never allowed matches.) Teaching them to swim was another interesting issue. Having spent years putting the fear of dams into them we now paid to have them jump in voluntarily!'

I live in a lychee orchard next to the rainforest between Tully and Mission Beach. Many birds, including the wompoo fruit dove, eat the black fruits of the rhus trees in the rainforest, and then fly to the orchard to sit high up in the lychee trees while

Dave Kimble, Tully, Queensland

they digest their meals in the sun. Before they fly off again they deposit the seeds with a little dollop of fertiliser, and in the shade of the lychee trees and in the endless heat and humidity, little rhus trees pop up all over the place.

When they are a few inches high they can be transplanted into pots, and when they are two feet high they can be planted out. They can grow nine feet in their first year (mind you, we do get 3,700 mm of rain here in an average year – this last year, the longest time between rains was two and a half weeks).

You can keep your dry, dusty, red heart of Australia, where just staying alive is a major achievement for a tree. Give me the rampant jungles of the wet tropical coast, with the spectacular cassowary, the impossible Ulysses butterfly, the elusive mahogany glider, crocodile-infested swamps, and the view from Mission Beach out to Dunk Island and the Great Barrier Reef. It's the most beautiful place in the world, bar none.

This is Dave Kimble again. He wrote the above letter in 1996.

Where are you now, Dave?

We're at Uchee Creek in the catchment of the Johnson River near Innisfail.

The last time I spoke to you, well actually you wrote me a letter, nearly ten years ago, you were down near Mission Beach living on a lychee farm. You've moved since then?

Yes, I went down south to Mission Beach and stayed on the beach for a while, then I moved to live in the town of Innisfail, I went back into the Tully Valley and lived in a shed on the edge of the valley, and now I've moved up to Uchee Creek. I'll shortly be moving on again.

We talk to people about why they live where they live, but you keep moving. Is it your lifestyle, or what's the story?

Well, I like moving around. I used to live in a caravan for about twenty years, although the caravan didn't move very much. It was always in my mind that it would be ready to go if ever there was a time to go. Now I'm renting houses as I go and it's a bit easier in my old age.

You surf the internet a fair bit. Why's that?

Well, I get to talk to people that have the same view of the world as I do. There's not many of them around. I think my views are somewhat apocalyptic . . .

Doom and gloom . . .

. . . doom and gloom. They're knocking down the rainforests and losing all the habitats for our precious animals up here. Most people don't seem to be bothered about looking after animals in the rainforest; they just want to get on making some money. But to me that seems the most important thing to be doing.

So you're on the net. How do you try to stop what's going on?

Well, I watch the notices that get published when people put in applications to clear vegetation. Then I look them up on my computerised maps and work out what kind of vegetation is involved and look at aerial photos of the area. If the information on the application form is not right, or it turns out to be a really precious block for cassowaries or whatever, then I put in a submission objecting.

Have you been successful any time?

Yes, here and there I've been successful. I once managed to get 172 hectares turned over to national parks.

So you're a bit wrapped up in the net. What did you do before the internet came along?

Well, I used to do computer work, but I can't imagine now . . .

How life existed before the net?

It just seems impossible that the world could function.

Well, it does and people still exist without it, Dave. We're up almost on Queensland's highest mountain Mount Bartle Frere. Why do you like living up here?

Well, just when I look out of the window and see that mountain I think there's not many people have got such a beautiful view. I get a lot of pleasure out of doing things that don't cost any money, like staring at the sky and the clouds, or measuring the rainfall. It manages to fill my live up amazingly.

Dave, it's lovely to talk to you. Thank you.

Nice to meet you too.

It's been a few years since we've written to you but thought we could again add to your segment why we live where we live. You read a letter, written by Tina, on Mother's Day 1996 on that very subject. We had only been here less than a year at that point. After hearing this morning that people are living in larger houses, I thought I should put pen to paper to reassure those concerned that there are still those who love life in a small cabin in the bush. We have settled in well over the last seven years or so. The block is fully fenced and we have a bigger dam. Our fruit trees grown from seed have just started to give us the freshest, sweetest fruit ever eaten! And not forgetting the fresh vegies, eggs, beef, pork and poultry.

Recently we were presented with the opportunity to purchase an adjoining property. We took our little farm from thirty to sixty acres. The cow was rapt! On the block is a professionally built, three-bedroom (with spa off the main) air-conditioned house. Well, we thought. Wow! So, we did the big move from a crowded little cabin to the spacious 'hacienda' with all the mod cons. We lasted about four months! Missing the cabin life was too much. So now we are back in our not-so-crowded cabin and visit the house to do those jobs required to upkeep the yards and fittings. (Although having an automatic washing machine is a definite advantage, and with summer coming we might give the air-con a whirl.)

We attribute our good fortune to keeping a positive nature and working as hard as health allows at home and in the community. Being members of our local rural bushfire brigade gives us the chance to mix with like-minded people. What it comes down to, Macca, is you get back what you put in. So far we are on the right track. Thank you for your part, Macca, in making ours a better place to be.

Kevin, Tina and Farm,
Tara,
Queensland

Alison Morrison,
Royalla,
New South Wales

I last wrote to you in 1990 explaining why I live where I live. I hadn't mentioned to my husband that I had written to you. We were laying back in bed when you started to read my letter. When my husband heard you saying my name and that I was from Royalla, he soon jumped out of bed!

Fifteen years later we still live at Royalla. However, it has changed dramatically. Royalla is twenty kilometres south of Queanbeyan and ten minutes south of Canberra. Our southern neighbour sold to a developer and we now have 206 small-acreage rural subdivisional blocks to our south, sixty-six similar blocks to the north and forty to the west. Fortunately most of our neighbours are nice people seeking a rural-type lifestyle away from the 'rat race' and within commuting distance of their work.

However, farming has been made very difficult. In one year we lost over 300 sheep to domestic dogs. We have now got rid of most of our sheep at Royalla and pray that those dogs don't attack children. There have been reports of cattle being attacked as well as wildlife.

I thought you might enjoy this true story that my late father-in-law once told me. Years ago a chap who had owned the property next door also used to own lots of other property throughout NSW. He had a very long moustache and the locals called him 'Horny' because of it. Horny used to inspect his properties by travelling on trains. One day he dozed off as the train was approaching Molong. So, when the train stopped he put his head out of the window and asked a bloke standing on the platform, 'Excuse me mate, is this Molong?' The chap replied, 'It's the longest one I have ever seen!'

Yes, I am still here living in my cottage in the country. I have been here for ten years now. When my alarm turned on at 6.00 am and I heard you talking about the full moon, I just had to write and tell you I had been woken up about 5.30 am by the full moon beaming in my window.

Jenny Lacey,
Benalla,
Victoria

You see, sometimes during the year the moon shines right in my window early in the morning, and other times it shines in the other window when it is rising. Because I live in an old house my bedroom has two windows, one that faces east and one that faces south. They are small windows that you find in old houses, just big enough for a full moon and the silhouette of a branch. So, I had the full moon right in my face as you were talking about the full moon!

People still ask me, 'Why did you live out here on your own in that old house?' and I never know how to answer them. And then the moon sets in my window and reminds me why I love it here. I don't know where they expect me to go, probably back into town. But I have been there and didn't like it; too many people and too much light. That is why I like to live here.

Lance and Marlene
Fairlie,
Narooma,
New South Wales

Three or four years ago (in 1987) we wrote to you about a humpy we lived in near Morton National Park. Well, we are still in the bush in a humpy at a beautiful spot near Narooma. The fishing is good and the climate mild, the birdlife is prolific and strangely there are red-tailed black cockatoos which are well out of their area. The marsupials move into our camp each night and native mice have made a camp in my haversack. As for wattle day, I enclose a photo of our home among the flowers. (See between pages 96 and 97.)

I wonder where Alice and Val are now. They wrote this in 1990.

Alice and Val Hayes,
Dulwich Hill,
New South Wales

When I was a teenager (pre-war) we lived in Croydon, NSW, and one of my most pleasant memories was walking on Sundays with my sister and our Scotch collie Laddie to Yeo Park on the border of Ashfield and Summer Hill. Boys and girls and families strolled around, listening to the band playing in the rotunda. In 1965 we moved; guess where? Into a house opposite Yeo Park. It is a lovely park, well tended by Ashfield council with lovely flower beds, annuals and roses. There is an air of spaciousness and tranquillity about it that contrasts with the traffic noise. The lily pond forms a moat around the rotunda and during the week, when my husband and I can't manage our stroll there, we can hear children's voices floating over from the infants' school which is set in the park. What a wonderful introduction to the world for those children. No fences or railings, only trees. Certain trees are chosen and then the children are taught to love them and recognise them as their boundary. Other groups of children have exercise days there, and any day of the week cars pull up and people step out to lie in the sun and eat their lunch.

Alas, the snake has invaded Eden. The school is to be sold and presumably a good section of the park. Nothing seems to change for the better, does it? Older people are asked to look after themselves in their own homes but things are taken from them – transport, maybe the park, and the children. How sad it is. I saw an advertisement once and the last sentence said, 'Frank, tell me about obsolescence.' Sometimes I think that applies to us – the older people, the children and the parks.

I wonder, are Sophie and her now grown-up kids still in Guyra? This is what she wrote in 1988.

Sophie Masson,
Guyra,
New South Wales

Sometimes I wonder . . . in winter when the southwesterlies blow a howling gale, all the new plants die of windburn, when the outdoor toilet is like an icebox and we have to tramp through the snow so that the kids can go to the loo, when the garden will only grow cabbages and cabbages and cabbages, and the harvests of summer are a memory you're sure will never return!

Then spring comes round, and you remember . . . as you face platefuls of corn, asparagus, strawberries, raspberries, beans, peas, you name it, when the ridiculously fertile soil springs to life again and every seed you drop bursts out of the earth, the time before the flies when the sun is warm on your back, and even after the flies when the roses, the hops, the grapevines are clambering madly over the fence, when the kids can spend all day outside playing with the other kids on our great country street . . . then you stop and say, 'Well, I'm lucky, we're lucky, how could anyone be so lucky!

Pat Giles,
Hamilton,
Victoria

Even though it is ages since I read my story 'Father's Hat' on your program, I still occasionally receive enquiries, referred on by you, for copies. I thought I had better let you have my new address!

After forty-three years together on a soldier settlement block my husband, Tom, died in 1998. Not wanting to make any big changes in a hurry I remained on the farm on my own. Drought and my advancing years made me realise that at my age there were better things to do than run around after water for sheep and cattle. So I decided to make a change while I was still capable of making a new life, and before the kids felt the need to make decisions for me! None of my sons being interested in taking over the farm, I auctioned it and moved into a brand new house in Hamilton, just two blocks from the shopping centre. I am quite enjoying the change of pace, although I regret none of those years on the farm. But there is a time for everything and this was my time to move on.

Being involved in driving for Meals on Wheels and working in the local Red Cross shop has restored some badly-needed structure to my life, and I have a lot of friends in town. Funny, though. I started off in a city (Sydney) and now I look like finishing off my life in one (admittedly it's much smaller). Life's wheel goes full circle – almost.

Peter and Susan Lendon, Yallourn, Victoria

Years ago when I wrote to you about this town in Gippsland I was a relative newcomer. The locals probably still think that, but twenty years after our arrival we are more entrenched than ever. The herd of donkeys is now reduced to one and the children have moved into their own homes not far away. On a slightly poetical note let me tell you more. This pretty town in the foothills, with four churches and one pub, has a multitude of small businesses flourishing throughout its two thousand or so inhabitants, and skills abound in all sorts of areas. The people in this town seem to turn their hands to anything that is needed. You can have something welded, baked, cut and raked, painted, sewn, mended, grown, built, bred, plumbed, electrified or organised; you can dance, walk, explore or pray, swim at the pool, drink, be a sport, sizzle sausages in the park or look at the stars after dark. Our community op shop dresses us well and the church it supports rings the bell.

We have well-kept parks and home gardens, too. Children ride horses, play tennis, fish, or just be kids doing whatever they wish. There is cricket and football and bowls of course, and reverence for our older, more senior townsfolk. It is also said, 'You can take the boy out of Yallourn North, but you can't take Yallourn North out of the boy'. There is some truth in that because they all seem to come back.

Best of all we have the most valuable commodity, good friends and neighbours. This town is so great – maybe I shouldn't spout about it but keep it a secret. Where else can you have milk and papers delivered daily, a dressed pheasant dropped in by a neighbour, and where next-door's goat who wanders into your backyard is requested politely to leave, and does so!

We love the place.

Pauline Harris, Timbeerwah, Queensland

Last time I wrote about why I live where I live, about six years ago, I thought we had found the perfect spot, a lovely house by the beach where the sound of the pounding surf sent me to sleep each night. But after a while we didn't visit the beach any more, didn't swim in the ocean, didn't walk on the sand and even began resenting the salt spray on the windows and the constant replacing of rusting items.

So we went country, and I think we've really found the perfect spot this time. The back veranda overlooks four acres of bush which is home to regular visitors: a few roos and wallabies and their joeys, black cockatoos nesting in a big hollow tree, goannas climbing that same tree, wood ducks swimming in the dam hiding their young among the waterlilies, occasionally a few deer with their magnificent antlers, white cockies screeching overhead, rainbow lorikeets by the tree load, countless little birds of all sorts flitting about, not to mention the kookaburras waking everyone early each morning. And what about the animals we don't see, like the bandicoots who dig little holes all around the place, and carpet snakes who leave their skin on the veranda railings? And where are all the frogs that croak at night?

What a peaceful spot it is and such a time waster. How often I venture into the garden to trim a branch and don't return for three hours. There's always another bush to trim, fallen branches to pick up, beauty to admire, fruit to pick – citrus, mangoes, macadamias – jumping ants to avoid, birds to watch, fresh air to breathe, a rustling noise to investigate, and so it goes on.

There's lots of uncleared bush all around us and it feels like a world away from anywhere. But in fact it's only one kilometre to the corner store, ten minutes to shopping centres, services and a train station, and fifteen minutes to the lovely Noosa beaches we visit more often now than when we lived there!

Good morning!

Karen Ambrose,
West Cambewarra,
New South Wales

I am responding to your idea of following up on why people move. After nine years in Cairns, my husband was suddenly and unexpectedly made redundant from his job as an aircraft engineer. This happened just before the collapse of Ansett, making his situation worse. He survived on part-time work for two years, after which he realised he would have to seek permanent employment elsewhere, not only for more income but to boost his fading confidence. Reluctantly he applied for jobs outside the state and as suddenly as we went to Cairns, he was on his way to a new challenge in Nowra. I unfortunately had to close my thriving small business and sell our gorgeous house in Cairns to follow him.

We are now happily settled in the lovely NSW town of Nowra on the Shoalhaven River. We have a very comfortable home on an acre of land surrounded by trees and birds and nice neighbours in a quiet area only ten minutes out of town. Most of all, we are closer to our grown sons and other relatives after so many years of missing out on family events and always being the last to hear any news. To top it off, my husband is very happy in his new job. We have many fond memories of our time in the tropics, of snakes and frogs, of geckoes and toads and so much more. I learnt a lot about beautiful plants and trees and how to keep my lipstick from melting and how to prepare for cyclones. We wouldn't swap those years for anything.

Ross (Roscoe) Taylor,
Thirroul,
New South Wales

I have previously written to you outlining why I live where I live. It was some ten years ago. Things have moved on since then and retirement has a certain air of adventure about it. In addition I have managed to catch up with (in part, at least) computer technology which has prompted this current revision of why I live where I live.

WHY I LIVE WHERE I LIVE

Macca , I once wrote to tell you that I'm no fool,
And why I chose to live here in Thirroul.
Some could disagree and argue that I'm wrong,
But Thirroul is the light of Wollongong.

Some forty plus years I've worked eight till half after five,
I'm feeling burnt out and I'm losing my drive.
Well the clock's moved on, it's time for a change,
To say farewell to my home under the 'range'.

The decision's been made, I've lightened the load
Hooked up my caravan to hit the 'frog and toad'.
Another grey nomad out on the bitumen band,
Leaving behind the life of sun, surf and sand.

What about the 'cheese and kisses' I hear you say?
Wouldn't leave her behind, not likely, no bloody way!
You see we get on real well, everything is fine,
Besides if she didn't come, who'd pour me wine?

So where will I live and find a place to relax?
Out there in the bush on some of those tracks!
I don't have a gun and I don't care to shoot,
Maybe I'll travel that famous stock route.

Be assured whatever I do won't be done in a hurry,
I might catch and kiss that cod from the Murray.
If I get bored and there's too many frowns,
I can turn them to smiles when out on the 'Downs'.

To travel across Australia would be terrific,
Trail the car and van behind the Indian Pacific.
Perth to Monkey Mia and then onto Broome,
Such wonderful scenery would prevent any gloom.

Into the 'top end' where the weather is warm,
With my sort of luck I'll be right in a storm.
It doesn't matter if it's wet or fine, there's no need to stew,
Just unhook the van then drive down to Kakadu.

Well Macca you can now see where I call home,
It's anywhere in Australia that I care to roam.
Although with no permanent abode, I assure you it's true,
I still get my mail each day so long as it's addressed DOT COM DOT AU.

10 – An Aussie Tapestry

Dorothy Watt has sent in her wonderful poems for more years than I can recall, and many of them, like this lovely tableau, have appeared in earlier books. This is a little beauty. (You can read the whole poem in this chapter.)

Across a canvas made of air
Each Sunday from the dawn
Our Macca weaves his magic threads
A tapestry is born.

Each varied thread with care combined
In unique artistry
The blend from this great land of ours
A wondrous tapestry.

Barbara Bufi,
Innisfail,
Queensland

WHY DO I LIVE WHERE I LIVE?

My old house sits on a hill,
faced west towards high mountains,
tried by cyclone many times.
I rejoice in its windows,
kept wide open to the world
to bring in the cooling breeze.

Through these oblong openings
wonders enter every day
to enrich my living space
Bartle Frere, head wreathed in cloud,
greets me in the predawn hush
as sunlight gilds its summit.

North windows in December
show bright lights twinkling nightly
on the Tower Christmas tree,
red berries, golden blossom,
decorate green-strapped palm fronds,
Christmas dress for the tropics.

Eastward, morning colours glow,
bathing grass where white ibis
probe for food with billhook beaks:
day's end from my veranda,
sunset's redgold evening kiss
paints the western windows pink.

At night a tropical moon
lends silver incandescence,
gleaming softly off the glass,
as I sleep the Southern Cross,
low in the starspangled sky,
shines blessings through my windows.

That's why I live where I live.

My Shadow, My Dog and Me

Jan Doust,
Balwyn,
Victoria

I long for the open wheat plains
Of outback New South Wales
The yellow-ochre paddocks
Where only heartache prevails.
My thoughts wander back to my childhood
Where sometimes I'd rather be,
Secure in the knowledge of hindsight
My shadow, my dog and me.

I'd visions of freedom and fairness
And love of the great outdoors.
I was sometimes accused of mooning
Instead of attending to chores.
Often I'd sit in the coolness
Of that old kurrajong tree,
For hours on end, just dreaming
My shadow, my dog and me.

As I watched the kelpies scamper
Across the yarded sheeps' backs,
I had plenty of time to ponder
The way we'd treated our blacks.
When their kids won school races
It was always a puzzle. You see,
'Their wins were never counted
'Cept by my shadow, my dog and me.

And when it rained for hours
After two successive droughts,
I watched the water rise
Six inches in the house.
I checked the dams were filling
And dragged the bogged stock free.
Nature spun her endless riddle
For my shadow, my dog and me.

The stupid, senseless slaughter
Of animals and birds.
The 'sportsmen' sought no quarter
Their victims' cries unheard.
Animal life surrounded our dams
And birds filled every tree,
Refusing to shoot and dreaming still
My shadow, my dog and me.

Many a day I spent mooching
As I dawdled behind the sheep.
And many a night exhausted
I dreamed as I fell to sleep.
In a never-ending cycle
In a different economy,
Our banks refused their credit
For my shadow, my dog and me.

Now I drive the streets of a city
In a battered half-ton ute,
There's often a quizzical look, or of pity
And I smile as I commute.

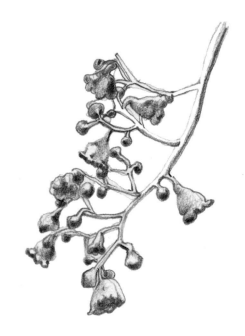

A bewildered, mid-aged eccentric
With a dog in the back, they see
My squint at some distant daydream
My shadow, my dog and me.

Through the distance of years I watch the galahs
Wheat-laden on the ground
And see the farmers harvest their wheat
Stripping it, round by round.
For now that I live in the city
And have my privacy
I spend hours on end, just dreaming
My shadow, my dog and me.

Helen Brumby,
Hobart,
Tasmania

RIVER DERWENT HOBART

Ever-changing as the sea
Is what the river is to me.
Sometimes it's reflection-filled;
Surface gloss all bright and still;
Other times the white-caps rise
Everywhere I turn my eyes.
Boat horns, using too much power
Wake us at the witching hour.
Kayaks, sabots, big yachts too,
Like butterflies, adorn the view.
Sometimes Jerry takes a ride
Across the river, and it hides
The mountain, and the city too,
Just a bit of bridge looms through.
It could never be a bore
To see the view from my front door.
Ever-changing as the sea
Is what the river is to me.

HOBART

I love the mountains and the river,
Love the tingly 'I'm home' quiver
That I feel when Hobart's lights
Sparkle 'Welcome' on the nights
When we wend our weary way
From a holiday away.
Hobart's small, but here we find
Friendly faces, peace of mind.

It isn't really cold, you know,
See the beauty of the snow!
Mount Wellington, protectively,
Looms above our small city;
The Derwent sparkles in the sun,
And offers fun for everyone.
It broke my heart to move away,
But now I'm back I'm here to stay
By it's beauty set apart,
Hobart, city of my heart.

TRUCKY'S LAMENT

Trucky's life is not much fun
Always going on a different run
I pack my bags and head for the truck
The job I'm doing, I know I'm stuck
The tanks are full, oil checked too
Nothing left to check or do
The load is secure and ready to go
We're on the road now, we can't go slow
The load is secure, the ropes are tight
Looks like I'll have a troublefree night
The rhythm of the diesel so strong and clear
Pure music to the trucky's ear
Feeling soft, feeling sore
All these troubles, pain galore
Stop at a road-house need a feed
Tummy is rumbling, I'm in need
Hunger satisfied, talked to my mate
On the road again now, don't want to be late
I need some sleep but I have to go
Can't stop now can't go slow
Get to my destination without much stress
Want to unload want to rest
Have a good feed have a good sleep
For a few hours now you won't hear a peep
I wake two hours later feeling a bit slow
Ring the boss, he says 'Are you ready to go?'
I love my truck I love my life
Sometimes I even think of my wife

Cecelia Harvey,
Trucky's wife,
Paruna,
South Australia

Jean R,
Hastings Point,
New South Wales

WHY I LIVE WHERE I LIVE

Almost by the back door
The tidal wave runs by;
Why am I so lucky?
Who's to answer why.

Sparkling green at high tide
Beckoning swimmers: fish to hide

Still mornings
Mirroring trees;
And as always, the welcoming breeze
For nearby is the pristine ocean
Still unspoilt, forever motion.

So, between the creek and sea,
Who wouldn't be me.

Heather Corfield,
Taroom,
Queensland

MY HOME

The sun rises above the ridge
And into the heavens above
Shining over hills and hollows
In this outback land that I love.

Out here in this far western land
Away from the city rat race
It's created by God's own hand
Out here, it's a quieter place.

The sun has set out in the west
Darkness in the sky around me
See the stars shine, some we know best
From my home with the family.

Some folks love being in the city
Others travel, they like to roam
Some enjoy living by the sea
I love living at my country home.

Out here in this open country
I don't want to travel, to roam
Here is my home and family
The place I want to be is home.

AN AUSSIE TAPESTRY

Across a canvas made of air
Each Sunday from the dawn
Our Macca weaves his magic threads
A tapestry is born.

The picture grows in size each week
Those more threads join the rest
Each new stitch added from its source
Fun, sadness, joy or jest.

Some stitches come from other lands
From Aussie types abroad
Some come from ships, from planes or trucks
From labourer or lord.

And children sometimes add their bit
To help the picture grow
With songs and poems or just a chat
To let the wide world know.

This land is quite a mix
Of nationalities
With tales to tell of good and bad
And trivialities.

Each varied thread with care combined
In unique artistry
The blend from this great land of ours
A wondrous tapestry.

Dorothy Watt,
Briagolong,
Victoria

WHY I LIVED WHERE I LIVED

Where the whisper of the hoop pines on a misty autumn morn
And the lilting call of whipbirds greet the dawn.
I see the wagtail dancing and the morning insects prancing
While parrots wing erratically and by their call I'm drawn.

Where the Blackbutt Ranges wake up to greet this breaking day,
The myriad voice of nature, in symphonic anthems say
There are better ways of coping and our Maker's heart is hoping
For my eyes to see the splendour as he points me in his way.

The haunting call of cat birds and the quietly grazing stock;
I'm awestruck at the winging of another distant flock
Of choughs who quickly gather, and ants work up a lather
To fulfill their call for service with no attention for the clock.

'Pastor Pete',
Peter Thamm,
Wamuran,
Queensland

The bettong slowly beds down in the safety of his lair
While the whiptail raises up his nose to proudly sniff the air.
The regent bower birds flashes, his dazzling colour clashes
Which makes mockery of the cheapness of the plastic everywhere.

I know the trusting glider has finished with his night,
No need to rush his routine, he keeps no schedule tight.
The creatures are competing while I seek wildly their defeating
In something I call progress, as I exercise my might.

The crow invites us listen to his mournful, plaintive cry,
And breaking tufts of fleecy fog are wisping 'cross the sky.
Fluttering lightly on the thirsty ground a feather speaks in silent sound
And pee wees sing their greetings with a wistful, warbling cry.

I could be in the city as the sun reflects in glass,
But I'd rather sit and play with the pine cones and the grass.
I cast my mind in wonder to this evening's coming thunder
When dusk brings light to closure in a symphony of brass.

I hear energetic youngsters from the noisy crowded streets,
Where computers hum and music blares, traffic drums and beats.
The never ending restless noise of artificial human toys
Make me wonder at our cleverness, but fearful of our feats.

But somewhere in the battling sound I hear another call
To hearken to the wildlife, which is rarely heard at all.
The haunting distant tinkling ring as bell birds once more start to sing
Bid me pause and ponder living, as another evening falls.

That bush call rings its message and is quicker to forgive
Me for the greed that bids me take much faster than I give.
Midst bunya tree and hoop pine, tangled bush and tropic vine,
It's home to me. I'm proud to say 'Yes, this is where I live'.

We lived in the city of Chelsea that has been changed to be part of the large City of Kingston. The area was built up on the Carrum Carrum Swampland that was part of the sea for thousands of years and a hunting ground for the Aborigines.

My wife and I are both ninety-three, been married seventy years and still enjoy your program, though we miss most of the early morning session as we sleep in!

Frank McGuire,
Edithvale,
Victoria

Chelsea is a beautiful town,
Where on a hot summer's day,
Hundreds of visitors travel down,
To enjoy our sun-warmed bay.
Yet those people, some from far-off lands,
Whose children play on our golden sands,
Perhaps fail to realise,

That to an earlier race of Australians
This was their seaside paradise.
The Aboriginal coastal tribe, the Bunurong by name,
Claimed the Carrum Carrum Swampland, teeming with game.
The call of the kookaburra was everywhere, laughter in the trees,
While the wedge-tailed eagle flew high in the air, gliding with the breeze.
The Aborigines had lived here for perhaps 30,000 years,
And then came us whites – civilisation, sickness and tears.
The white population had arrived,
In the year eighteen thirty-five,
Forty-two years later Jummy Dunbar, last of the Bunurongs, had died.
Now in a new century you may see the eagle fly,
Perhaps with the spirits of the Bunurongs as it glides across the sky.
The magpie still carols in the morning when the swans are still in flight,
While the white flowers on the tea-tree, signals, the schnapper's on the bite.
You can have all your big cities,
Wherever they may be,
But for me,
There is nowhere to compare with Chelsea by the sea.

WHY I LIVE WHERE I LIVE

Victoria Roberts,
Banks,
Australian Capital
Territory

In the wee small hours when I'm fast asleep
There comes a soft paddling of little feet
As I'm contemplating the day I feel so complete.
I have two beautiful children and husband who are very sweet
My days are not all smooth sailing
But who's complaining.

For at the end of the day, as I tuck them away
Little voices whisper I love you.
I have simple needs and am easy to please and my whole aim at the moment is values,
I'm a full-time mum to teach what's right and what's wrong
Is a tough job! Let me tell you.

It gets bloody cold where I live,
And the reeds dance a jig on the shores of Lake Burley Griffin
And the frost may not clear
Until noon through the year,
But when Floriade comes along, it's all forgotten
As the weather is grand where the daffodils and tulips stand
And other flowers too numerous to mention.

There's parliament sitting and maybe some spitting
Of words that may lack lustre and grace.
But the beauty is here for no other place holds dear
Canberra you're a great place.

I discovered you Macca and thought what a cracker
Your Sunday program on 2CN.
It sends shivers down my spine
When I hear the ballads, bird calls and rhymes
Of this beautiful place we call Australia.

A CITY TRAIN, WHERE I LIVE

Joan Caldwell,
Croydon,
Victoria

In this life you've got to have dreams
Even if you know the dream can't come true,
For while you have a dream
Nothing in life can hurt you
You can dream away your worry and woe,
Today a kingdom tomorrow a foe.
Dream of kingdoms and riches if you must.

But in the city I must dwell
So a dream of the country and the bush smells,
Of mountains, rivers and streams
The fauna and flora I never see,
Except in books of the library.
It's a dream that will never be!

For what in the city will get me there
And I hope with money to spare
A horse and a saddle I hope to bag.
To ride the high country is part of the dream
To drive the cattle down to drink at my stream.

So in the city I live to make this dream come true
And I work and I wish and I dream, do you?

WHY I LIVE WHERE I LIVE

Kay Carvan,
Rapid Creek,
Northern Territory

A large-bladed knife
Scabby with rust – or blood
On one side
Dull steel gleam
On the other

Poised on the sharp edge of the blade
Balanced between civilisation
And the raw power of the natural world

You shiver at twenty-four degrees Celsius
And wear sox to bed

And read in the morning paper
About the four-metre crocodile
On the beach
Opposite your front door

Where once in five years
You turn off the fans

Where yellow fig birds
Pure white Torres Strait pigeons
Bronze-shouldered doves
Rainbow lorikeets
White and black cockatoos
Bush curlews and several kinds of kite
Are daily visitors to your suburban home

And frill-necked lizards
Posture and dance
And dodge road-trains
On the highway

Darwin
Where you soon believe
It's unreasonable to travel more than twenty minutes
To get anywhere within the city limits

And if you can't park within twenty metres of the door
You might as well turn around
And go home

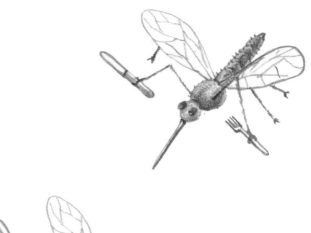

Where one day you're being eaten by mossies
And tormented by sandflies
Sitting cross-legged
Sweating and steaming
On the dusty red earth
Of Arnhem Land

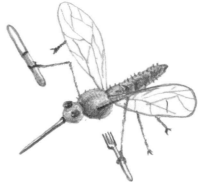

And eight hours later
Enjoying a glass of champagne
At an Eric Bogle concert
At the air-conditioned
Entertainment centre

Frances Kendall,
Wagga Wagga,
New South Wales

HOMETOWNS

Beside forgotten train tracks, along endless country ways
The little towns doze in the sun and dream of other days.
Remember when our world was here? Our hearts and hopes were high?
Barefoot favourites of the heavens, scruffy heirs of earth and sky.

'The bitumen' now covers up the dusty road of yore,
Past the little church our fathers built, the school of arts, the store
The schoolyard where we chanted rhymes or slogged a ball for six,
We climbed the sticky pepper trees and took a dare for kicks.

How we battled with arithmetic and spelling through the heat,
Till the clanging school bell sent us flying home on eager feet.
Past the cenotaph, the soldier resting gently on his gun,
His smile a blessing on us ever waiting in the sun.

The lilting of the river called to us to stop and play,
Among the she-oaks dappled shade we romped the day away.
Then in the evenings kindly light tired urchins homeward stray,
Soft grasses whispered as we passed and star shine lit our way.

Adventure seemed to call us and we didn't need a push
To let the city's glamour steal the children from the bush.
But amid the grimy clatter comes an old sweet memory,
And I know that up the country there's a town that waits for me.

Jan Collier,
Ben Lomond,
New South Wales

NEW HOME

In the land of the claret ash we are now found
Tending the cattle, guarding the ground.
Winter pipes are wrapped not to freeze
And the neighbour's son thinks I'm too old to bend at the knees.

We stack, unpack, move and remove
Contemplate positions, try to improve.
Furniture sited and the outlooks
Cupboards, shelves and still more books.

Gardening club stories are of the drought
They look wisely at me, eyes full of doubt.
Checking my knowledge of the climate here
Questions, interest and responses appear.

Jettisoned each morning from our warm bed
Weaners in yards, rowling to be fed.
Autumn brings maple leaves to the ground
In the land of the prunus tree we are now found.

Thanks for doing a great job reciting my last poem, 'Last Reflection'. Alex would have been proud of you. Apart from Alex Pike, we have another link which may be of interest to you, the *Montevideo Maru*. I lost two uncles on that ship, my mother's brother, Wilfred, and my father's brother Alex, both brothers-in-law and both perished together. What are the odds of that?

This year at Ballarat we were at the unveiling of a memorial to that terrible incident, and the attendance made our hearts swell with pride. There were so many relatives there of those lost, and still hurting.

Enclosed is another of my compositions. I reckon the sentiments and memories in this verse might have occupied the dreams of home of my uncles and their mates.

Geoff,
Central Victoria

HOME (OR DREAMS OF OZ)

There's dawning in the bushland
Of scarlet pink and blue,
Where bleeding skies turn amber
And greet life on earth anew.

The shadows quickly shorten
As the eastern ball ascends,
Whilst portly wombats shuffle
To the safety of their dens.

The sounds of bushland then begin
The sounds that reassure,
Magpies warbling from the heights
Ducks on swamp and moor.

The thumping of the wallaby
Through scrub and gullies dense,
Or parrots cracking seedpods
From their perch on tree or fence.

There's rivers with a majesty
That wind throughout the land,
Or gurgle through a mountain pass
With scenery wild and grand.

Where one might catch a fleeting glimpse
Of lyrebirds in the valleys,
Or platypus floating on their backs
Scratching furry underbellies.

There's colours of the spectrum
To dazzle and delight,
Of red claypans, lush green leaves
And reef quartz pink and white.

The brilliant showy splendour
Of the rainbow lorikeet,

Or the subtle yellow ochres
Of a waving stand of wheat.

There is fragrance of a ferny glade
Of bark and fallen trees,
Or that clean fresh smell of rain
On grass, carried on the breeze.

All these things and millions more
Will greet you without failure,
And 'Where?' you ask, 'Where else my friend,'
'Australia mate, Australia.'

Chris (Curly) Bradley,
Parap,
Northern Territory

I was wondering how long it would take to put pen to paper (or in this day and age, finger to keyboard). Only seven years! I was at sea when I first heard you, because that is all we could get from reception. But from then I was hooked. Anyway, what got me started on my letter was your mention yet again of the sea, and how people need to experience the wonder of it.

I am a teacher by trade and a gypsy by nature. I have had a few unique jobs like: working as a meter maid on the Gold Coast, fishing the waters of north Australia and training locals on the Tiwi Islands (when the barra farm was being established) and visiting pearl farms in the Kimberley.

In between these jobs and plenty of teaching I lived on a boat for four years (and intend to return to this) and sailed thousands of nautical miles around our coastline, and through Indonesia. It was during these travels that I wrote many poems that I'm sure you can relate to. They remind people that we have more than just country or city life, for there is life at sea too.

Currently I'm a student counsellor at a local high school. I'm also a proud grandmother with lots of living to do. Overall, I'm simply an ordinary Aussie girl who like many others has had some extraordinary Aussie experiences.

COUNTRY, CITY OR SEA

You can stand around the local club
Or even in an outback pub
But it won't be long before you hear one say
'Ah! A country life is the only way!'
Which then soon sparks a debate
When another will firmly state
'No way! The only place for me
Is life in the big city!
Then they continue to argue
About each other's virtues.
You'd think from the stress in their voice
that there was no other choice.

That's when I tell them this
A point they both have missed.
If they were like me and choose a life at sea
They would soon discover
A world with the best of each other.
Yes just like the city, you'd never be bored
As life at sea is exciting for sure.
There's plenty to do and folks to meet
Just as you find on the city streets,
Plus you're sure to find
Variety all the time,
Like the sight of the dolphin fin
And the taste of salt on your skin.
But then, you also have those starry nights
Like in the country, far from the neon lights.
And all that open space
Away from the hectic city pace.
There's the wind in your hair
And fresh air everywhere.
Kick back relax without a care.
And even if the folks aren't trendy
You can be assured they're awfully friendly.
So as you can see, it's the sailing life that I prefer
As it holds this perfect mixture.
You don't end up with a city country argument
As life at sea is simple heaven sent.

YOU ASK ME WHY I LIVE HERE

So, you ask me why I live here
Then let me tell you why
In this rugged wondrous place
Where the mountains reach the sky.

Here, where man is an intruder
Amid the forest and the ferns
Where sunshine into rainfall
So often, quickly, turns.

You ask me why I live here
When most would find severe
The mist-enshrouded mountains
And deep enchanted mere.

Tony Hosworthy
(Platypus),
Strathgordon,
Tasmania

Where the mist and fog will swirl among
The trees and button grass
Where sunshine and a windless day
Turn the lake to a looking-glass.

You ask me why I live here
When each new dawning day
Is never the same as the one before
In any conceivable way.

Where the sun caresses mountains
And changes every hue
A kaleidoscope of colour
From scarlet into blue.

You ask me why I live here
When the crimson sun does set
Upon the lakes and mountains
Ere night has cast its net.

Where the evening sky is bathed in light
Under red and yellow cloud
Then twilight settles in again
Before the night-time shroud.

You ask me why I live here
Where the birds and insects sing
When across the lake and mountains
Their joyous voices ring.

Where cries of cockatoo and currawong
Will often break the peace
Whose calling is a ritual
Which never seems to cease.

You ask me why I live here
When by the lake I stand
With rod and line and tackle
Gripped firm within my hand.

Where fishing is a pretext
For what I try to find
A peace and oneness with my world
And for me my peace of mind.

And you ask me why I live here.

11 – They Call It Progress

Listeners' concerns over the years have covered the development or over-development in cities, mining and land clearing in rural parts of the country, and more recently wind farms and the spread (sounds like a disease) of hobby farms.

Val O'Neill from Queensland put it succinctly:

'The only high-rise up here should be the Glasshouse Mountains and Blackhall Ranges'.

John Dynon's very amusing image of an outback dunny suggests little progress!

Lara Emerson,
Maleny,
Queensland

My name is Lara, I'm a teacher and been listening to your show for years. I have often planned to ring you to tell you about our beautiful town on your segment Why I Live where I Live. You may remember me as the girl who had a dangerous liaison with a five-metre amethystine python in the Daintree rainforest a few years back. You read my story to your listeners and included it in one of your books so I thought I'd update you on my latest encounters of a different kind.

I live on a 'Land for Wildlife' property on the banks of the Obi Obi Creek, so named after a revered local Aboriginal warrior. It's a very special piece of land with intact rainforest in our backyard along the creek. We've kept a lengthy list of wildlife sightings which includes plenty of pythons but none as big as that Daintree beauty! We've seen over one hundred species of birds on our property as well as rare frogs and even a platypus in the creek from time to time.

Maleny is celebrated for its rolling green hills of dairy farms, avocado and macadamia orchards, rainforest and waterfalls nestled in the Blackall Ranges, and for the famous folk festival that used to be held here. Now to my latest encounter, or 'war': Woollies want to come to our town! They study demographics to see where a new supermarket will be viable and then they go in with their stories of big employment opportunities and gullible councils invite them in. It happened right next-door to us in Buderim. The folks there say it destroyed their town through traffic congestion and businesses like the once-treasured bakery, greengrocer and butcher going broke. They protested to no avail. Now it's happening here.

Now, don't get me wrong, I'm not one of those BANANAS, Build Absolutely Nothing Anywhere Near Anything, and I don't hate Woolworths per se, but their demographic check didn't count on the backlash from angry residents who, like myself, are adamant that we don't need them. We came here because of the clean air, water and soil, and the rural feel. We shop at our local IGA which pours thousands of dollars into local schools and community needs, and it sells our fresh local produce, much of it organic. We don't want sprayed apples that have been sitting in a truck for who knows how long, or worse still, milk from Victoria. Deregulation of the dairy industry has damaged our town forever, with the large supermarkets shortchanging Queensland dairy farmers and sending them broke. No, our buck stops here in our small and thriving co-operative community where we grow our own produce and have our own brand of milk. It's healthy for us and healthy for the local economy. So we don't want Woolworths, 'the fresh food people', we grow our own.

But that's not the only reason people are willing to get arrested in protest. Our real plea is to save our Obi Obi Creek bank. It's incredulous to us that they would choose a site for the supermarket that will destroy a known platypus habitat. We have designed bumper stickers 'Woolworths – We Won't Shop There'. So that message is out there loud and clear!

Sandra and Ivan Kelly,
East Gippsland,
Victoria

I have listened to you ever since moving to East Gippsland nearly twenty-three years ago. When I first moved here we only had the radio as we had limited power. We never have hooked up to the power grid. I've often thought that I should write to tell you about where we live but have never got around to it. Now economics wants to destroy all the reasons why we chose this spot: peace, wildlife, distance away from built-up areas. We have this idyllic plot of ground that is ringed by a creek that flows, sometimes with ferocity when in flood, to the Gippsland Lakes. Our closest and only neighbours have had an offer that must be too good to refuse because they are going to allow a hard rock quarry on to their land which is no more than one hundred metres from our front boundary gate. Of course we are going to fight this all the way to the Supreme Court if we have too, but in the meantime our quiet life is threatened.

The local council has granted permission to the developer despite twenty objections, all based on sound environmental grounds, and still no environmental impact assessment has been done. The problem is that the government acts only come into force when something goes wrong. It's up to people like us to be the watchdogs. Two gravel pits located nearby are both erosion nightmares. When the rain is falling the silt flows into the creek and the fragile Gippsland Lakes. No-one wants to listen to someone who has been here for twenty-five years. I hope this letter might open up a can of worms in a lot of places where the checking mechanisms have been reduced by authorities needing to save money.

Developers have me perplexed. Thirty years ago Mandurah was a lovely sleepy little fishing town south of Perth with a lot of character, old pubs and buildings. The waterfront was lined with a mix of dwellings and caravan parks. But those days have gone. Developers had a dream of changing its character to make it look like the Gold Coast, and ensure the waterfront is only for the deserving (i.e. the very rich). Developers got their dream. Mandurah now looks like the Gold Coast and a playground for the rich. One restaurant sells fish and chips for $20.00 a serve! (That's another thing that has me perplexed. Why do fish and chips become more expensive the closer you get to the coast?)

Since then, 'Gold Coast-type development' became a euphemism for bad planning. The same developers then moved to Dawesville, just south of Mandurah, and realising people don't like Gold Coast-type canal developments decided to transform Dawesville into Venice! I don't know which Venice they were thinking of. Certainly not the one in Italy. In fact, it looks no different to the Mandurah that's supposed to look like the Gold Coast.

Now developers are set to change the face of Cottesloe Beach, a national icon, with high-rise apartments to have it look like 'The South of France'. The council wants to back these plans because of the money it will bring in and 'give Cottesloe a better image'.

What is wrong with the surfie-type image – going up to the Sunday session or having a burger after a surf? There won't be any pubs in this development. Just a line of taverns, a euphemism for expensive pubs where only the rich and well-dressed will be welcome.

Why did Mandurah have to look like the Gold Coast? Why does Dawesville have to look like Venice? And why can't Cottesloe just look like Cottesloe?

Francis Merchant,
Cottlesloe,
Western Australia

Eric Miles,
Boddington,
Western Ausralia

It seems the effort to conserve the magnificent heritage of our bush is more talk than action. I know there are people who put huge commitment into conserving natural bush, but they seem to be a tiny minority.

The reason I feel strongly on this issue is that I have a property I have resisted clearing even though I have had permission to do so. Always believing our bush had value other than as a stepping stone to farmland, I have spent years looking for alternative uses but have found none feasible. Now I would like to pass the land on to someone else, it is amazing how few people seem interested in putting their money and effort into a large area of bush. At almost 440 hectares (1100 acres) it is large enough to have better habitat ranges for plants and animals, but it loses appeal to individual buyers because of its size, and no organisation has expressed interest. If I don't clear it, state government will take control and demand that I continue to pay rates and insurances, control declared species, and provide fire management. Who said slavery had stopped in Australia?

It saddens me that while retaining the splendour of our natural heritage is a popular political catch-cry, it does not seem to represent the true feeling of the wider Australian electorates. If a significant number of people really want to retain our bush, why is there no allowance to share the cost across the whole community? I have come to see how little people value the intricate Australian bush compared to an inner city flat. And the clearing of bush for housing continues.

Out the window I can see a neighbour's dog has just travelled over a kilometre to pee on my shed post! It lightens an otherwise sombre reflection. I am going out to look at the wind in the gum trees, check out the birds and feel the space.

Joan Trenwith,
Renmark,
South Australia

I live where I live in Renmark in the beautiful Riverland of South Australia which is a renowned fruit growing area. My husband lived on a fruit block all his life and we bought our own block in 1970. We had some pretty tough times, but with extremely hard work and long hours we managed.

Our elder son, a fourth-generation fruit grower, has now taken over our block. He has pulled out apricots to plant wine grapes. Next, out will come the oranges to plant more wine grapes. The federal government doesn't care too much about the fruit grower. Brazilian orange concentrate and Turkish dried apricots come into Australia and we just can't compete with their prices.

But we love living on a fruit block, in a house nestled amongst the trees, and can't think of anywhere in Australia we would rather be. And I guess a few years down the track all the wine grapes will be pulled out and the oranges and apricots planted again, as everything seems to go in cycles.

Elizabeth Burrell,
Forrestfield,
Western Australia

Recently I read an article in an alternative newspaper which said that 'modern society is more about mastering nature than living as one within its beautiful chaos'. Well, I guess that just about sums it up. We created a new garden by mastering nature. We built a retaining wall and an irrigation network for the reticulation system; we established a lawn and we built a brick pathway through the garden beds.

The list goes on. The newspaper also states there is a loss of community values because 'people crawl inside their little box and turn on the television to escape'.

Well, I don't agree. While we were planning and building we met many people who were interested in what we were doing. During our breaks we sat in the shade of the pergola and shared many conversations with curious passers-by. We found a new sense of community. It was nice.

We think our garden is pretty good, too. We planted a host of Australian native shrubs. After two weeks renovating what formerly resembled the Great Sandy Desert we can sit back and watch it grow!

Having spent my childhood growing up in a semi-farming area less than fifteen miles from Sydney, in a loving community surrounded by family, I have always treasured my own space. Belrose, named after the gorgeous native rose and Christmas bells that grew up and I hope still grow on the neighbouring Lady Davidson Park, was an area prone to bushfires that provided so many nooks and crannies for young children to enjoy. We loved exploring the creek in the bush near the five waterfalls, and making cubby houses in the lower branches of the forest trees. Most of our families were involved in some sort of farming – chicken farms, piggeries, horses, goats, flowers, market gardens, nuts. You name it and it was going on in a quiet sort of way around Frenchs Forest, Belrose and Terrey Hills. Most had their own cows for milk.

As with most communities, in the name of progress our families were forced to move on as the rates were too high. Many of the families moved far from the city so they could continue the farm lifestyle. Some went interstate or were scattered all over New South Wales. They only saw one another at weddings and funerals or at reunions. It was a great era for letter writing and made us appreciate even more the closeness of our early childhood days.

Regardless of where we live our home is where our heart is. Many families in today's world will have to resettle their families several times as their work and circumstances change, and they may feel they have no true roots.

Wendy Kells,
Woolgoolga,
New South Wales

When I first wrote to your Why I Live Where I Live segment I was in the RAAF at Wagga Wagga. Well, things are changing all around I guess, and this time I'm the one who is deciding to change my location. I'm retiring from the RAAF after twenty years' service and am returning to Perth in just a few short weeks. I have to admit I'll miss Wagga. I have formed some wonderful friendships that will see me in good stead for many years to come, and have experienced country hospitality at its absolute best. During my stay I have been unlucky enough to suffer several bouts of ill health requiring hospitalisation, and some personal family tragedy, but my friends all rallied around in times of need.

I know that progress is something that one cannot stop and most times it's for the best. But I can't help feeling a twinge of sadness as I sit at my window on a cool but beautifully sunny afternoon and gaze across the park to the paddocks beyond.

Greg Carns,
Forest Hill,
New South Wales

I know full well that should I ever be lucky enough to return here that everything will have changed. The windmill is still there (and is still groaning for lack of oil) but some of the paddocks have been subdivided and new homes are already popping up like the new flowers of spring. I suppose people have to live somewhere, but it is a tad depressing to think that my lovely country view will soon disappear to one of bricks and mortar. Oh well, it's the price of progress I suppose.

I'll be leaving Wagga around 6 September and should be on the Nullarbor around the twentieth. If any of your listeners should spot my white panel van and covered box trailer give me a 'hoy' and we'll boil the billy for a while. I'd welcome the break!

➡ Jane Graham, Sandford, Tasmania

I live where I live because it is beautiful. My little home is quite close to Hobart, but it's near the water at Sandford which suits me very well because I'm a coastal person and an active volunteer for Coastcare.

What I love about this area is its unspoiled bays and beaches and the lovely views of the river and Mount Wellington. I especially love the birds and there are so many here; some of them travel from Siberia and North Korea to rest and feed in the waterways around my home. On one side of me is Frederick Henry Bay which has some of the clearest, cleanest water anywhere so the oyster farmers love it. On the other side is Ralphs Bay which is at the mouth of the Derwent River.

Sadly, everything seems to be changing. Now there is talk of a big developer buying our bay and filling it in with 800 canal estate homes and a marina. That makes a lot of people in my community very upset. We don't want to lose our bay and our birds, and it does all seem to be about the almighty dollar.

I wonder why anyone thinks beautiful, natural Tasmania needs any part of the Gold Coast on its shores? I live where I live because all the money in the world wouldn't see me living on the Gold Coast.

I live here because Tasmania is a little green jewel at the bottom of Australia, it is special and we'd like to keep it that way.

➡ Richard Harly (Big Bird), Crescent Head, New South Wales

As a kid growing up in Sydney near a golf course I scoured the bushland and liked it. I resolved to one day have a patch of my own. Five years ago I placed a deposit on one hundred acres of native woodland on the mid north coast. In April I turned thirty and I couldn't deprive myself any longer. With a few bob, I packed up my Datsun (you can read Holden) and a trailer with some second-hand corrugated iron, and did seventy kilometres an hour up the coast.

So, it is me, two kelpies, a gas fridge, kero lamp, a thirty-five dollar water tank that doesn't leak, and lots of frogs. I used to work at Taronga Zoo, but now I have my own zoo without the walls. My daily companions are wedgies, lace monitors, lots of snakes, 'roos, wallabies and there's also evidence of koalas, though I've not seen one yet. All kinds of small marsupials live here and so do I. I'd like to keep it that way but private landowners clear their land at a rate only they can keep up with. As a qualified horticulturist and an amateur naturalist, I'd suggest partial selective clearing be considered by them so the two worlds can live as one. So, up here I run my own race, am my own boss and enjoy watching life go by rather than traffic.

A few years ago a girl a few years younger than I couldn't believe it when I said I hadn't heard Macca. I'm hearing ya' Macca and that's why I live where I live!

Like two million other Australians I am a keen listener to your program. My parents, who live on a small farm in the southern tablelands of NSW, are also a part of your large audience. I'm writing to you about an issue that's affecting my parents and threatening the rural way of life They are Czech migrants who arrived in Australia in 1969 with nothing but the clothes they were wearing. They spoke no English and knew no-one. They've wholeheartedly adopted the Australian lifestyle of beaches and barbecues and my father, previously a ski instructor, has never skied again. He became the chief engineer on the new Parliament House in Canberra, and now works as a cattle and flock care auditor, visiting farms around southern NSW.

After educating their four children to university degrees, they opted for an active retirement on a 100-acre hobby farm forty-five minutes from Canberra. They keep a small herd of cattle and have planted hundreds of lavender bushes and Australian native trees, all of which my mother can name by species. I was married on the farm last year and it's a truly magnificent oasis in the dust.

It's become known that a local property owner plans to build a wind farm with sixty turbines, each ninety metres high with forty-five blades, that'll tower over hobby farmers like my parents. The locals, about 200–300 mostly retired public servants, will have to deal with constant noise, glare, the shadow and visual disturbance. In addition there's the loss of bird and animal life, erosion, the construction of an industrial road, the establishment of a quarry for building the turbines, and the building of large towers to connect the wind farm to the local electricity grid.

I'm a rural GP-in-training and have great concern for the health, especially mental health, of the affected people. The lack of sleep and constant background noise – by some accounts rather like a twenty-four hour motorcycle – and the glare and shadow could have a serious effect on them.

My research suggests that while wind energy is perceived as being 'green' and 'an alternative to fossil fuels', it's actually quite inefficient and only works at a certain speed. This is obviously unpredictable and fossil fuel is required as constant back-up. Despite the uptake of wind energy in Denmark, Germany, England, Ireland and Wales, there's huge dissatisfaction about both on- and offshore wind farms. No new wind farms are proposed in Denmark now that subsidies for their construction have ceased.

I know you receive loads of letters concerning changes in rural Australia, with many associated opinions. I hope you can 'air' this topic as I'm sure many Australians would like to contribute.

Judy Toman,
Canberra/New South
Wales

This letter from Tony Bailey describing his experiences with banks came in back in 1990. Fifteen years on he wouldn't be able to write such a letter would he? The banks have made so much 'progress' with their customer relations and friendly financial advisers . . . I wonder how Cuddles is going, or is Tony cooking his own tea?

Tony Bailey,
Cobden,
Victoria

I live where I live for one reason, my bank manager. Our last manager was a terrific bloke with very deep pockets. We got a new tractor and car out of him and were going to have another go when he got transferred. We think he's in the basement at head office counting two cent pieces!

His replacement was an accountant always wanting facts and figures. I went to see him about a winter overdraft and he wanted a cash flow budget. I said if we had plenty of cash I wouldn't be in his office! I filled in all the forms and went back only to find he was on holiday. So, I had to see the worst possible person, the relieving manager! They worry about everything. They don't like making mistakes so don't make any decisions – just put it in the too hard basket. I spent half an hour going through the horrible cash flow statement, the sweat running off me, with him just nodding his head up and down, looking really interested, when he suddenly said, 'How much do you fellows owe us? A hundred grand?' 'Cripes,' I said, 'Multiply it by three and you'll be much closer.' 'Oh,' he said, 'I can't handle this, I'll send it to head office and let them sort it out.' Relieving bank managers! I went down to the pub to recover.

Last year my son wanted a new milking machine. I said I didn't want to see Mr Scrooge the bank manager, so if he wanted the machine he'd have to fix it up. Knowing my son likes paperwork I reckoned it was goodbye milking machine. But he rang the manager, and about three weeks later we were in the back paddock when down the track in a cloud of dust came the bank manager and his boss. We talked about the crook weather and things for a few minutes, and then the manager said to my son, 'Now, about the forty thousand you want for the milking machine.' My son replied, 'Hang on, we only want twenty-five thousand.' 'Is that all,' said the manager (to impress his boss), 'Sign here.' We did, and off they went up the track in another cloud of dust. I sometimes wonder if he was sick that day!

So, I'm milking the cows and share farming for the bank. We have 239 black and white friesians and one orange and white one, Cuddles, the kids' cow. She's not much good, but every time I talk of selling her the kids cry and lie down on the ground and the missus won't cook tea. So, Macca, don't get a pet cow!

12 – And That's Why We Live Where We Live

Many letter writers wax lyrical when describing why and where they live on land, at sea, overseas – wherever. As you'll see, this chapter's full of lovely descriptions, but just enjoy this extract from Valerie J. Griffiths, Coffs Harbour, New South Wales.

I wonder where Jessica Kirkham in the picture is now?

A sun rising red from the ocean's horizon to greet the morning; a bushfire sunset over the roof of the darkening forest; a breaching whale in the bay below is an occasional winter delight; on pearl-grey days we can be entranced by mist rising from the forest gullies; on stormy nights dazzled by dancing lightning, leaping from the mountain tops or pirouetting on the sea. We are woken at dawn by birdsong and lulled to sleep at night with silence.

Graham Collins,
Glenden,
Queensland

My wife and I live in Glenden, a small town of about 1,000 people. It is 160 kilometres west of Mackay and is one of the coal mining towns in the Bowen Basin just to the west of the Great Dividing Range.

Being west of the Range means we are in a rain shadow. Mackay averages sixty inches of rain per year. Eungella Range and Mount Dalrymple, which are part of the Great Divide, can get up to 200 inches per year. Turrawalla Cattle Station near Glenden has been told by the weather bureau that they are in the best example of a rain shadow in Australia, receiving less than twenty inches per year.

The weather is ideal for coal mining. There are dozens of mines in the area with each one producing millions of tonnes of coal for export each year. I sometimes wonder if future generations will ask why we sold overseas so much of our country's valuable energy resource?

Have you ever been to a modern mining town? They are great places to live. We came here eight years ago, planning to stay just a couple of years. However, the people are so friendly, the job is so good and the town so nice. Eight years later we are still here!

From where we live we can see beautiful mountains all around. There are lots of trees in the town and we have bush nearby. Every morning we wake to the singing of birds and kookaburras laughing in the tall eucalypt trees near our house. Kangaroos often come right up to our house fence, and yet we are only a one-minute walk from the supermarket. Across the road are the swimming pool, a church and the tennis courts. So you can understand why we enjoy life here. And that's why I live where I live.

Anne Kent,
Serpentine,
Western Australia

I love the freshness of the air, away from the city smog and noisy traffic; away from the fumes. I love the abundance of trees and birds singing at my back door. The knowledge that blue wrens come to my garden along with kookaburras, magpies and many other birds. I love to hear the Australind go through, along with other Alcoa trains, and the occasional Hotham Valley train.

My family lived at Hopeland, six miles west of Serpentine from 1932–45. The farm life was good and although World War II was on we lived our lives happily enough, little realising how close Australia was to being invaded by the Japanese. Isobel, my sister, encouraged me to come back to live in Serpentine when my husband, Brian, thought he might have to go into a nursing home as he was suffering from asbestosis. When we did return in 1997 it was like coming home, as many of the local people still remembered me. Serpentine is a friendly town, and it's always interesting to walk up the street with my guide-dog Niddrie, and chat to different people.

Roger Frinsdorf,
Rostrevor,
South Australia

By mutual consent our backyard is a cat-free, pigeon-free, rat-and-mice-free zone. It is enforced by our aged German collie, Leroy, who has maintained this high standard for twelve years. This morning we had a crisis. Leroy appeared at the back door with a highly indignant, noisy and upset magpie held firmly by the wing in the mouth of the guardian of the backyard. What do I do, boss? It's not a pigeon or a rat or a cat, but it's not welcome. Let go Leroy! The tears welled in the old dog's eye as he knew the next step. It will peck me, boss. Drop Leroy! The obedient dog dropped and the noisy magpie immediately pecked him on the nose. Leroy retired hurt and sulked under the tank stand.

The magpie eyed the dog, then eyed me, and walked in a circle squawking and testing the wing. I put some water on my finger which it sucked then demanded more. It then tested the wing, jumped on the car then onto my shoulder. A great vantage point to observe Leroy the aggressor! The unlikely trio walked down to our long-time friend and neighbour Val who knows about these things. What to do Val? A little mince for the little fellow, not much as it's not good for them. Leroy watched attentively. Much refreshed, the noisy bird flew to the roof and called for mum and dad who arrived to a joyous reunion, and returned a bit erratically to a distant tree.

It's moments like this, and the koalas who come down on windy nights to shelter in our front yard, the black cockatoos who screech and destroy the pine cones and almond trees, the occasional fox, and very occasional eagle on the quiet foggy mornings that make this a paradise.

Yeah, let go Leroy!

We live at Rostrevor about ten kilometres from Adelaide on a hill next to Morialta Falls and Park. The views are across to the power station about twenty-five kilometres away on the coast, and smoke stacks tell me if I am going to get a call from my friend Mike. 'Good day for sailing today, Roger.' We can see the city at night with its colourful lights. But the main attraction is the wonderful neighbours we have had over the last thirty years.

We are getting old now and will have to find another haven a bit smaller. But we know that a new family will enjoy the beauty that exists here.

Bronwyn Hollis, Launceston, Tasmania

This is Bronwyn. She moved to Tassie, and this is the story of why she lives where she lives.

I'm originally from Port Macquarie, NSW. We lived there virtually all our lives. It's a beautiful part of the country.

How come you're in Carrick now?

We came down for a little holiday after we'd decided to put our house on the market, just to see how it'd go. Within a week it had sold! So we turned our holiday into an investigation, looking round to see what work there was and at real estate. We went back, packed up and resigned from the work places we'd been at for fifteen plus years. We thought this offered a new start in life, and within a month we'd bought a home and got work.

I know lots of people want to change their circumstances, don't they. But they, we, never do.

It was a big step for us. When we first got off the boat we thought, What are we going to do? Why are we here? But we're enjoying it thoroughly and working smarter, not harder.

It's a different climate.

When we first got here it was one of the wettest and worst winters they'd had. But we found it quite okay. We just put another log on the fire!

So you came down on a holiday, said 'This will do me,' and went home and packed up. What did your friends say?

They still think we're mad! But we've had friends and family come down and they're surprised at how pretty the place is. Both our mums are on their own and in their seventies, so leaving them was hard. But it's not the other side of the world. One of them has come over and the other's visiting next year.

The difference in real estate prices, was that a factor?

It was huge. But if somebody had said eight months ago that we were going to leave Port Macquarie and move to another state we would have told them they were crazy! But here we are and enjoying it.

That's great, Bronnie. Good luck.

Judi Cox,
Springfield,
Queensland

I live where I live because my mum and dad moved into a new house. At first I found it strange, but it's just the way things are. I am a pale-headed rosella, and before you tease me about being made into rosella jam, let me tell you I am a bird, though if you could see me, I'm more like the Toyota chook.

Many years ago my mum found me being a crow's breakfast, so rescued me. My feathers have never grown, so I'm completely bald except for some fluff down on my neck, and my skin is bluish. My name is Psycho because early on in the piece I threw a hissy fit when my mum was trying to feed me in my cage, and took a fair hunk out of her thumb. It didn't taste too good. I'm not a meat eater, and not into finger food.

I sleep in a shoe box wrapped in a tea towel to keep me cosy at night. Sometimes if the parents are a bit slack and don't get me up early enough I push my way out and have a little waddle and squawk around the kitchen floor.

Because I'm a bird with special needs (my mum teaches kids with special needs so she knows all about stuff like that) I have to go on holidays with the family. I've been sneaked into all sorts of high-rise holiday places, my cage and box covered by a beach towel. Dad says to be quiet because I have a very piercing (but extremely beautiful, if I might say so) call, a mix of parrot, phone ring and microwave sound, so usually I wait till we get inside before I start going off.

At my last home there were lots of big trees and other pale-headed rosellas used to feed in the branches and call to me. Mum and Dad thought I'd feel bad knowing that's what I was supposed to look like if I could see myself, so they never let me near a mirror, but I can guess by what visitors say when they see me. They all love me though and come and talk to me, and I chat to them if I'm in the mood. When the old house was being sold, mum put a sign on my cage that said what I was, and that I WASN'T a baby bird, or a sick one, and that I was really happy, and a picture of a pale-headed rosella (turned away from me), so prospective buyers didn't think I was mistreated or sad.

Where I live now, my cage is next to the door that opens into the garage. Boy, do I let them have it when they go and leave me too long. So that's my story. Fourteen years after my walk in the park with a hungry crow, here I am, and that's why I live where I live.

Written by my mum.

Christina Booth, Launceston, Tasmania

Christina, you've got an interesting job. You illustrate books.

Absolutely, it's the best job in the world. I've always been interested in drawing and I did a fine arts degree here in Launceston a few years ago. I'm also a teacher. A couple of years ago I met a lady who was starting to publish books and she liked my work. I was just in the right place at the right time.

You illustrate books for our good friend Max Fatchen, who writes lovely poems for the program.

Yes, I just illustrated his last book, which was really good fun. It's excellent poetry to work with.

I suppose it helps when you have good subject matter like that. It inspires you to come up with ideas.

Absolutely. The imagery just bursts out of it. My kids love it too.

Max has a poem about bread. Every time he looks at a loaf he sees waving ears of wheat.

Yes, it's 'Seas of Wheat'

When wind is dancing through the wheat
To shape each ripened head,
I seem to see not golden crops
But loaves of crusty bread.
And when I have a piece of bread
I think it's rather nice,
The wind, the sun, the dancing grain
Are there in every slice.

He draws pictures with his words and it makes it easier to draw.

And his Shakespearean one 'Get the to a cannery' probably wasn't hard either!

No it wasn't. I emptied the pantry and got out a few cans of peas and things! I just loved working on that one. I was a lot of fun.

Do you write yourself?

I've just started. I'm doing a picture book for children.

I know that unless you're with a big publisher it's very hard not only to get a book published, but also to sell it.

Yes. There's lots of really talented people out there and it's a very big ocean with a lot of fish in it. You have to have a passion and stick with it. I just spent a beautiful weekend with a heap of illustrators, writers and publishers, which was really good. But you realise just how many other people are trying to scrape a living out of this.

Tell me about living in Launceston. What's that like?

We live on an island and it's paradise! It's not very far away from beaches, it's a nice green city and the weather's great. We lived in central NSW for a while and came back here because we love it. It's a great place to raise children.

Good luck with your illustrations. Do you do painting?

Yes. I'm a landscape painter as well.

You've lots of material in Tassie for that. Lovely to meet you. I'll tell Max we met.

Charlie Booth, Stawell, Victoria

I talked to Charlie Booth right at the end of a program (from Stawell). He told me he was one hundred years and five months old. I only had a minute and a half left so I spoke to him afterwards about his long life. Here he is.

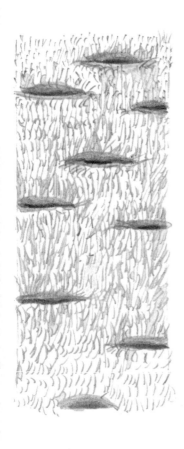

I have so much excitement. People ask me questions, which I love, because at 100 years old I'm able to answer them. Some of my stories are sad. I think the saddest was when I was eleven and outside my front door at Ascot Vale and as far as I could see there were soldiers on horseback. I asked, 'Where are you going with the horses?' They replied, 'We're going to war (the Great War) and won't be bringing them back. We'll have to shoot them.' Why do horses have to get killed? For an eleven year old that was a sad moment. Twelve thousand horses left Australia and not one came back. People are amazed when I tell them that. It's sad. What an awful way to fight a war, on horseback.

I have some stories about running. I met a man named Arthur Postle, who was known as 'the crimson flash'. He showed me a few tricks on how to get off the mark. He said, 'Races are won in the first ten yards.' I went in a lot of races but was never as good as Arthur. I ran in the Stawell Gift in 1925. It was before television and wireless and meetings were held in little towns like Bairnsdale and Warrnambool. The people thought it was marvellous. In those days every runner had a trowel to dig a hole for their start. I used to dig holes on my father's lawn and he went mad about it getting ruined! So he made me the first starting blocks invented. I took them to the Heidelberg Gift which was running before the Stawell. That goes back a long while! When I won the other runners complained that I had used mechanical means of getting off the mark. The stewards asked me what they were and I told them they were a great help. 'Great help,' they said, 'You're rubbed out for life!' Yes, I got life disqualification for using the blocks. I'd like Australia to know that. It flattened me.

I was living at Essendon and I went to see Eddie Tolan, a black American runner who was training at Carlton Football Club. I walked up to him and said, 'You're a champion. I want to race you over ten yards.' 'Why ten?' he asked. So, I explained about the starting blocks and he was happy to give it a go. I beat him by about two or three yards. Killed him! He said, 'You're the first man that's ever beaten me.' So, I gave him a chance on the blocks and made sure he won! He took them back to America with him.

I'm proud to tell you it was an Australian that first brought starting blocks into the world. I took out the patent rights. Cost me three pounds.

You've noticed and mentioned a couple of times that Canberrans are a bit sensitive to criticism of their town. It's true, but it's a good thing. For many years now Australians have enjoyed a great national pastime: bagging Canberra. In many ways it has been a uniting banner for Australians outside ACT.

Now I've learnt to live with the 'bagging Canberra' pastime. So have most Canberrans. But hey, we don't have to take it lying down. In increasing numbers Canberrans are now defending their town. During the 1960s when I was surveying in remote areas on large cattle and sheep stations, one of the toughest things about the job was having to tell the locals I was from Canberra. Having to put up with scorn. It wasn't until I knew we were moving camp that I was game to put up any kind of defence of Canberra.

But I like to think I had some success. The two main points I tried to make were:

1. Canberra is the capital city for all Australians, not just those that live there.

2. Apart from the few local ones, federal politicians are NOT Canberrans – they are sent to Canberra by the very people doing the bagging!

During the 1980s two pastoralists and their wives stayed at our place in Canberra. It was easy to convince them that Canberra was their country's capital city. Although Frank from the Pilbara seemed most impressed at the amount of grass in the local paddocks, Henry was almost starry eyed at the new Parliament House. As we came out of question time he said to me, 'Gee, I never thought I'd see anything like that.' I used much the same expression on seeing some camels lumber across his property.

*Russell,
Canberra,
Australian Capital
Territory*

Here is a little story for Why I Live Where I Live. I went to Wundowie in 1960 as a teacher and stayed for thirty years. I taught there for twenty years. Wundowie is a very interesting town. It was started back in 1944 to provide pig iron for WA during war times. The pig iron was to be produced using charcoal as the base fuel. There were huge hardwood forests surrounding, jarrah, wandoo and marri being the tree species. It was an exceptionally pure, high-grade pig iron produced. And it was sold world wide. Now that the forests have gone so have the charcoal furnaces. However, a big foundry is still there producing many iron and steel products. It produced the bollards used at the Sydney Olympics.

However, there are two further points of interest. It's here that the famous Sarich engine was developed. The town didn't receive any recognition of this fact when it

*Benjamin Seabrook,
Roleystone,
Western Australia*

was in the international news. A pity I think. Secondly it was the foundry that cast the anchors for *Endeavour II*. When I first went to Wundowie it was unbelievable with the smoke, dust and activity of the workers, and the mills slicing the trees. The industry worked twenty-four hours a day, every day of the year for forty years. The smell of charcoal was everywhere and the creek was polluted. Some 400–500 folk worked there at its high point. The mill produced some of the world's finest flooring. I can still recall coming over the hill into the town in 1959 to take up my first appointment. I can only describe it as a Dickensian horror scene. But now the furnaces are gone, going over the same hill into the town one is greeted by a well laid out town with a big footy oval in the centre, a swimming pool and a wonderful community hall. It has a spring-clean feeling.

One of the interesting aspects of the town is that it was built on a plan or scheme from Britain, the 'Garden City Plan'. Hard to imagine a town in the Australian bush being designed to meet an English plan. While I don't live there now I guess my forty-six years associated with it might qualify me to say so.

✿

Helen Taylor,
Cudgen,
New South Wales

5.00 a.m. Daylight Saving Time or Summer Time.

I take my cup of tea, sit on the front lawn and look up at the stars in the milky way. Total silence. Awe-inspiring.

Too early for our kookaburras. Too early for the roosters. Too early for the traffic noise. The dogs are still asleep. Only the rhythmic roar of the ocean.

It is pitch dark, no street lights. Just the magnificent stars.

I look at the Southern Cross that helped Captain Cook find Australia. He sailed right past here and named Mt Warning, Point Danger and Cook Island. He did a great job mapping everything for those that came after him.

This Tweed Valley with magnificent scenery, top beaches and a good climate is one of the best places on earth to live.

A rooster crows and breaks the silence. It is time to check today's diary and see what we are all doing today.

✿

Brian 'Rowdy'
McDowell,
Greensborough,
Victoria

I love listening to the people from all over Australia, in particular the people from remote areas. I have travelled extensively all through Australia and I love the places where solitude is paramount. But here in the suburban area of Greensborough there are plenty of trees and we are not far from the Plenty River, the life blood and source of Melbourne's water supply.

There are many species of birds in the area but a common link with yourself is the melodious warbling of our resident magpies. My wife, Deirdre, has been feeding them for many years and we see the new fledglings every year. We feed some by hand and Deirdre calls the original male magpie 'Brutus' because of the way he struts around the deck announcing that he is the boss.

At first light and in the evening 'Brutus' and now 'son of' walk up to the back door and sing for their meal. The magpie is an Australian icon and apart from the lyrebird I think its singing is one of the most melodious sounds in the suburban areas and even more so in the bush. I enclose a piece of poetry.

WHEN THE GOING GETS TOUGH

Well my boots are fairly buggered and my trousers are all frayed,
Strugglin' with bills but somehow gettin' paid.

There's food in the fridge we aren't starving yet,
I'll just keep on working I'm sure we'll get set.

Some days at sundown on a weather-beaten deck
I sit, have an ale and think what the heck.

Sure money's a worry, I think it's a curse
But it ain't all that bad, could be a lot worse.

I welcome the sunrise I breathe the clean air,
and the sky is still blue and the weather is fair.

Sunset's my passion, a joy to my eye, and my magpies
all sing when the evening is nigh.

My spirits undaunted when the going gets tough,
just to live in Australia surely that is enough.

Des, Port Lincoln, South Australia

Des is a horse trainer. Des, the horses like early mornings and the beach don't they.

Yes, they love the water and they love to have a roll. You can't beat the beach.

Are you based in Port Lincoln?

Yes, I've come from Clare. I came over last August with a few horses and I've been here ever since.

You grew up with horses?

I've been with horses pretty well all my life. I'm like everyone that had a pony when they were a kid. We were on a farm and it sort of went on from there. Eventually I got into show horses and then from there into racehorses. I've been training them for about forty years now.

Who's this fellow nudging you all the time?

This one is called Dee Jean. He won the other day up at Streaky Bay.

Do horses like racing?

Oh, yes. I think they get very keen, very excited and they know what it's all about. This horse here is a great old horse. He's a stallion called Jetway. He's very good for a stallion. Very easy to do anything with.

This horse, ladies and gentlemen, boys and girls, is rolling in the sand. He obviously likes it. Why did you move from Clare?

There are such terrific facilities here at Port Lincoln for training horses. Even though I love Clare, here we've got a sand track and a lovely turf track.

There seems to be something very humanising about being around horses.

It seems to grow on you a bit. I did try giving them up for a few months once, but it was just too hard. It was boring too. So I didn't take long coming back to them. It's particularly exciting if the horses are racing well.

It seems to get some people in one way or another, either the training or the gambling side. The adrenalin rush.

That's right. Also a great thing is when you break in young ones and then see them go through the stages and race as two- and three-year-olds.

Who is this young woman?

This is Rachel. She's our track rider.

Where are you from, Rachel? I saw you cantering along the beach.

I'm from Kimba. I've just moved here with my other half.

You grew up with horses obviously?

Yes. I'm a show jumper actually.

You're not a race jockey?

No, a track work rider. I train the horses in the mornings. I get up about five-thirty.

You enjoy that, obviously.

It's the best part of the morning I reckon. It's nice and quiet, especially along the beach. The horses like the gallop along the beach.

Nice to talk to you, Rachel, and Des, great to meet you.

You too, Ian. I've listened to your program on many a morning.

We get the occasional race trainer ringing up while travelling around the place. There was a bloke down in Melbourne last year who was taking a couple of his horses up to Hawker for the cup and ended up in Darwin. There's a lot of horse people listening out there. They must be up early!

Jim McCleod, Melbourne, Victoria

Jim McLeod was with the ABC for many years and his *Jazz Track* program was loved nationwide. He now lives in Melbourne. Jim, you've moved down to Melbourne from Sydney. Where do you live?

I live in Collingwood now. It's a great place.

Have they got a football team! Why did you move?

There are a lot of reasons. I certainly didn't move because I hated Sydney. I moved because there's a lot more jazz in Melbourne.

There is a lot more music isn't there, all sorts of music.

And I like working with the ABC people here. We also have an apartment that I like very much in Collingwood. The site used to be a distillery and we have a whole floor of big circular areas. As Barry Humphries once said, 'The thing about Melbourne is the sky,' and we see a lot of it with our 360-degree view.

You told me that you might be going to spend some of your retirement in Italy.

I live part of the year there now. We (my wife Gillian and I) bought a house in Montefagatesi, in Tuscany. The village has 160 people in the winter and about 600 in the summer. The Italian attitude to life is completely different; I can fly to London in a couple of hours or drive to Rome in five hours.

And I can be in Wamagama in fours hours! Jim, we often talk about the way cities are going on the 'Why I live where I live' segment. How do countries like Italy keep their little villages looking original, with no high-rises and home units.

There are lots of rules. Our next-door neighbour put up a plastic awning. The police came and told him it was illegal. And you can only have tiled roofs.

Is that one of the reasons you like living there?

Well, I have the best of both worlds. I have the city here and the country there. I'm growing fig trees and tomatoes, and I have grape vines.

I'm going to visit you! Will I have to bring along a trombone or a saxophone?

We're trying to get the village to buy a piano!

How long have you been going there?

For just over two years. The next time we go we're going to stay for a whole year because we want to see all the seasons.

So, in the future you'll live between Collingwood and Montefagatesi. Nice work if you can get it!

I'm very fortunate, sure.

Jim McLeod, lovely to see you and we all wish you well for your last program.

Which will be outrageously self-indulgent . . .

Just like this program every Sunday morning!

☼

I wanted to tell you about where we live in Western Australia. The farm is situated eighty kilometres north of Geraldton and eighty kilometres south of Kalbarri and, as the crow flies, twenty kilometres from the coast.

It was a complete sea change from gravel to sand, tall timber to low scrub, cooler to hotter and strong winds which finish blowing from one direction, turn and

Elaine Mauger,
West Binnu via
Northampton,
Western Australia

blow just as strongly from another. The first year we had several cyclones pass by — one dumped ten inches in two days and washed out all our dams of marron and left great gouges across paddocks, some over a metre deep.

We are thirty-eight kilometres from Northampton, our nearest town. It is a historic town, having been discovered in the bed of the Murchison River in 1848. Port Gregory on the coast was a convict hiring station, and Lynton Station is still a tourist destination today. The railway was opened in 1879. When lead prices slumped in the 1890s and the gold rush to Coolgardie/Kalgoorlie started, many miners turned to farming, which is the principal occupation around here.

This is the busy time of the year with the farmers cutting hay and starting to harvest. The Northampton district show is followed by the stud ram sale, and then in October the street facade is changed by quilts hanging on the verandahs from one end of town to the other. This is the annual Airing of the Quilts. Last year 305 quilts were flapping along the highway.

The low heathland-like scrub hides so many different flowers that you have to walk among them to really grasp the individual instead of the whole spectrum. At the moment our road is hedged by wattles overhanging with cream grevillea 'smelly socks' and underneath is smoke bush.

I am settling into this community, Macca, and just wanted to share it with you and the rest of Australia.

✷

Kathleen Devereaux,
East Devonport,
Tasmania

About thirty-two years ago we discovered Coles Bay, purchased a block of land in this quiet little hamlet and built a house in the style of a fisherman's croft. As we sit on the balcony overlooking the bay we realise how fortunate we are to have this place.

The road to Coles Bay is seventeen miles inland, passing a lagoon where swans and ducks make their home. Approaching the town the majestic mountains appear and you can pick out huge rocks along the top. These mountains form part of the Freycinet National Park, which is one of the first in Australia, and we are not pleased to have to pay a fee to enter!

We have two beaches to choose from and we can take the dog for a swim and long walks, which he loves.

In recent years others have discovered our sleepy town. A lodge has been built on the bay and we now boast a tavern, bakery, restaurant and supermarket. Fishing is a pastime the family enjoys. What can be nicer than fish caught in the morning and barbecued for lunch? Just cruising in the boat is fun, too. Of course, the seas are not always calm, and we even get snow on the mountains. But who cares when there is an open fire and a good book to read? Yes, this is our piece of paradise.

✷

Fred and John Koch,
Gosford,
New South Wales

I first saw Gosford during the war years. I moved here fifty years ago as it was a nice little country town just out of Sydney. Unfortunately it is not a little country town these days but there is still much to appreciate around Gosford. It is close to the hill and timber country and the ocean. What more could you want? My wife and I have travelled all over Australia in a caravan since 1990 and still find Gosford the most attractive area to live in.

We first heard Australia All Over in 1997 on a coach tour through Tibooburra, Innamincka, Birdsville and across the Gulf to Cairns and have listened ever since. Whenever an outback town is mentioned it is great to say we know the place. We have seen you in Darwin, Bendigo and Canberra, and hope to see you in Gosford soon.

Kaylene and Tom Corey, Georgetown, Tasmania

Kaylene and Tom grow tomatoes here and they are going to tell their story. Where are you from?

TOM: I'm a bit of a bastard child I guess. I'm a pom, but an African pom. I was bought up in Kenya and I travelled the world with business and what have you. Now I'm here in Tassie.

Kaylene?

KAYLENE: From Adelaide originally and then I travelled the world. Melbourne for fourteen years, and now here.

Why do you reckon you're here in Georgetown?

TOM: It's the best place to be!

Loud applause! I thought you'd all burst into applause!

TOM: I worked most of my life in the corporate world and had had enough. I came down to Hobart just for the weekend to see what Tasmania was all about and fell in love with the place. That was about two years ago and I then 'spat the working dummy'. We were surfing the net and came across Georgetown and the house and business. It was quite a challenge because it's something I'd never done before, growing tomatoes. I don't have green fingers.

It's interesting that you said, 'Spat the working dummy'. Cartoonist Larry Pickering used to reply, when asked 'What are you going to do?', 'I'm going to go and grow tomatoes.' So what is it like growing tomatoes?

TOM: It's bloody hard yakka.

I can imagine. It's cold here, not like tropical Queensland. How do they grow here?

TOM: Upwards! No, seriously. We've got a large greenhouse. We only grow in the summer months. Not in the winter at all. I never really understood tomatoes before I came down here. They were just green, then they went red and they were sort of round.

And then you ate them! Kaylene, is this your first venture with tomatoes?

KAYLENE: Yes, but I don't get time in the greenhouse as much as Tom does. I was talking to a lady who had done horticulture and she said that hydroponic tomato-growing was like feeding intravenously. She didn't believe it was the same as growing them in your garden. But we feed them nutrients and it's all very controlled. It's just a different way of doing it. It's lovely. It's not dirty. I don't have to dig in dirt.

It was about twenty years ago in Australia that the first rumblings about the taste and quality of tomatoes started. We talked about it on the program in the early eighties. A bloke rang up and said they're bullet tomatoes because they were really hard. Do you have tomatoes that actually taste like tomatoes used to taste?

TOM: Just like my grandfather used to grow, that type of taste? Absolutely.

Why is that?

TOM: Luckily we pick our tomatoes and sell them the same day. Our market is here. We can literally pick and sell them while they're still warm.

So you often wander round the greenhouse and sink your teeth into one?

TOM: Absolutely.

Did you think you would be growing tomatoes years ago?

TOM: No.

Do you recommend it?

TOM: Yes. It's a very rewarding lifestyle.

Not only financially but spiritually?

TOM: More spiritually than financially. Just ask the bank manager!

So you sell around northern Tasmania?

TOM: Just Georgetown at the moment. Although Kaylene is trying to get me to branch out. But I'm too lazy.

I should have asked you for a tomato recipe. I used to come home from school and my mum would cut slices of tomatoes, slices of onions, vinegar and sugar and she'd have sandwiches. I couldn't stand it!

Valerie J. Griffiths,
Coffs Harbour,
New South Wales

We live on Sapphire Mountain, situated in the northern beaches area of Coffs Harbour on the mid north coast of New South Wales. A jewel by name. A jewel by nature. Our small acreage is approximately 500 feet above sea level.

The front of our home faces the Tasman Sea and the Solitary Islands whilst the Orara East State Forest is our backdrop. To the north we view the disappearing coastline. A canopy of trees snuggles us into the ridge and protects us from the roaring southerly gales.

This environment provides us with an ongoing kaleidoscope of ever-changing scenes and light, a sun rising red from the ocean's horizon to greet the morning, a bushfire sunset over the roof of the darkening forest, or perhaps a silhouette of Split Solitary Island captured in a silver, moonlit sea. A breaching whale in the bay below is an occasional winter delight. On pearl-grey days we can be entranced by mist rising from the forest gullies. On a stormy night we can be dazzled by dancing lightning, leaping from the mountain tops or pirouetting on the sea. We are woken at dawn by birdsong and lulled to sleep at night with silence. Our acre of garden not only beautifies the home but provides employment in our leisure time. The harvest of flowers, fruit and vegetables is our reward. A walk along one of our many beaches or a stroll in a forest pathway our enjoyment. We share our oasis with visiting family and friends. All our neighbours with tails have visiting rights or find homes here.

Where else could we really live and have everything?

Peter Bain, Gladstone, Queensland

I was on board as Peter piloted a ship into port.

Good afternoon, Ian. I'm the Gladstone pilot. I'm on the ship to help the master come into the port at Gladstone.

Tell me about how you came to be a pilot. Were you a master first?

I used to be a master on the *Aurora Australis*, the old icebreaker down in Antarctica. She's a great ship. I've been up here since 1996 piloting in Gladstone and Bundaberg and Port Alma. I grew up on the Sunshine Coast – one of the originals from the Sunshine Coast. I live in Gladstone now.

So you're the pilot for Gladstone?

There are a number of us. I'm just one of the small boys. There are a lot of more senior pilots than myself here. There's eleven of us at the moment.

It's a busy port isn't it.

It's growing hugely and expanding very quickly. Typically there would be about twenty ships at anchor. There's about three or four there today. They're mainly exporting coal, wood chip, aluminium. There's a lot of potential around Gladstone for young people if they want to find a job.

When I was going to school I certainly didn't think of a life at sea. Why did you go to sea?

I ran away to sea. I had just read a book about South America and the old cargo ships. I had a vision of being a navigator, of taking a ship and looking at the stars from Australia to South America, and toddling off down the road with my surfboard. Unfortunately that never happened. Once you get into port you work harder than you do at sea! I was pretty lucky. Got to see the world. I think in the first four years I had been around the world about half a dozen times. Then I'd come back home and see my friends at university and teachers' college and discuss what they'd been doing. They'd been to a couple of parties and had a few surfs, but they hadn't been anywhere! I think going round the world is great for any young kid.

What do you prefer? Is being a pilot a natural progression from being a master? Is it better to be in charge of your own ship or helping to run the port?

Going around Antarctica was great on the *Aurora*. It's probably the last great sea voyage. You're going to the last place on earth. It was great going down there. Nobody had been there. It was almost like being a Captain Cook. The area was poorly charted. There was no set itinerary, no plan. There's a lot of science work going on and some really clever people working down there. I miss that a lot but piloting is still a very enjoyable job as you can see. It's tricky.

What's the Gladstone Harbour like?

It's very tricky. You have a sea passage coming in and then you have the berthing manoeuvre to get the ship alongside, as you'll see shortly. The tugs are over here in the distance – about a mile off – they will be coming along shortly and lashing up to us and then helping us berth the ship. These loaded ships are a lot more difficult to berth than the empty ones.

What can go wrong?

You can get sideways. They take a lot to stop. We are probably four miles from the berth and we are starting to slow down already. They just don't want to stop! You can't just put your foot on the brake. If we let go an anchor now the brake wouldn't stop it, the whole nine shackles would run out and just get left along the bottom. Even if we let go another, that wouldn't stop us either. You've just got to let the water friction slow the ship up. Going astern won't help us. We would just lose control of the ship. We just start slowing up gradually.

So you go out on the ships by helicopter?

Eighty per cent of the jobs here are done by helicopter. It's a little bit quicker for us. It's fifteen minutes by helicopter and about an hour by launch. It's a beautiful day today, but there is a lot of rough weather here. It's always windy in Gladstone and choppy seas. So the trip going out to the boat can be fairly rough. It's a long run and you'd need to run a least another pilot launch as well as the one we've got now, so the helicopter is a good option for us. With these large ships with clear decks it's quite safe.

A couple of months ago I was in Melbourne. I was talking to a bloke who worked on the wharves. He said Port Melbourne was the busiest port in Australia. This can't be far behind it?

It's catching up but probably not as busy as Melbourne. It's a different sort of cargo to the general containers and cars going in and out of Brisbane, Sydney and Melbourne. Gladstone is a bulk port. We take in coal. The ships that anchor here are 289 metres long, 47 metres wide. They're really big boats in a small area like Gladstone. Typically, 170,000 tonnes of cargo on board. Not as much as the ones in Port Hedland in the north-west; they're a bit larger again. Gladstone is a quiet achiever. There's a lot of economy generated for Queensland in this port. Unfortunately when you drive through the town you see the power station and the refinery. It's not a tourist town. But it's always great being on the water.

You love the job?

I love my job, but I wouldn't mind yours. I was listening last Sunday and thought 'What a great job you've got, Macca!'

It's like yours I guess — it has its moments. The trip down the coast was just brilliant. I've never done that before. I'm in love with our coastline and the maritime history we have. You can stare out at night and think Matthew Flinders was here. How did he do it without GPS or anything?

It's like us. You don't need the radars or the echo sounder. You just look out the window. See, the captain is bringing us round on the leads for the channel now. The GPS won't help us. The GPS would actually show us to be another couple of metres over here, whereas those leads are a hundred per cent accurate. If we're on those leads we're right in the middle of the channel. The same with the beacons in the water here. A pilot is pretty much eyeball mark one, a little bit of instinct and a hell of a lot of luck.

Peter, next time we come to Gladstone we'll talk more. Lots of people like to know about our coastline and hear from people like you who know what's going on.

After listening to you when you were in Darwin it prompted me to write to you for your Why I Live Where I Live segment. In 1970 my family and I left Sydney to live in Port Moresby as my husband had a transfer there. My five children were taken out of school to live in what was then quite an outpost. I really loved living there, it was different from Sydney. When the country prepared for independence we decided to leave, fearing uprising and riots. We went to Darwin in 1974 and we were very happy there. The population was not as big as it is now and we made lots of friends. On the day of Cyclone Tracy I had taken the youngest children to see *Born Free* at the local cinema. When we came out the palm trees were moving in the wind, which was getting stronger by the minute. It was Christmas Eve and all the presents were under the tree, the dinner was in the fridge ready to be cooked the next day and we were putting the finishing touches to the decorations. At 9.30 p.m. the big winds were getting worse and we saw a big fireball in the sky. We decided to move downstairs to a room in the basement. I was terrified at the noise of the wind and the sound of corrugated iron from the roof which took off and landed a couple of doors down. When the eye of the storm came the next door neighbour came in and invited us into his house. We were under the table with mattresses all around and there were heavy beams coming through the walls. It was terrible and a wonder we weren't killed. At 6 a.m. when it had all stopped we went back to our house and there was only a few walls standing. To this day, strong winds really upset me. Miraculously our car wasn't damaged and we decided to drive to Melbourne where my parents lived. My eldest daughter wasn't with us as she had moved to Canberra before the cyclone. She persuaded us to live in Canberra and I am still here. My husband died in 1987 and that is why I live where I live.

Val Thomson,
Banks,
Australian Capital
Territory

I live in East Doncaster, a suburb of Melbourne in a small 'court' of fun-filled angels! But I'm getting ahead of myself.

   Thirty-five years ago my husband and I bought our block of land on a new housing estate bulldozed from a pioneer's pear orchard. Other newly-weds bought the

Sandra Shaw,
East Doncaster,
Victoria

remaining eight blocks. I was able to welcome each new family with a plate of my shortbread. We all became friends as we built our homes and began to have children.

After a couple of years we realised how lucky we all were to get on so well together. The adults decided to go to a restaurant twice a year so the men could socialise somewhere other than over the din of their lawnmowers. We still enjoy our 'court do' thirty years later! A family that moved out of our 'court' still comes back to these gatherings.

When I developed cancer in 2000 our neighbours were very thoughtful in calling in with delicious meals to tempt my flagging appetite. After a short remission and another operation, I was having six months' chemotherapy, and once again neighbours were most generous with cooking gifts, and prayers. We have all supported each other in various ways over the years.

It is now 2003. Until three weeks ago I had enjoyed two years' remission and excellent health, including a glorious week hiking in the Canadian Rockies in summer. Suddenly the regular tests showed I needed another burst of chemo, and the angels in the 'court' have been appearing at the door with the most delicious and nutritious food you could imagine to ensure I bounce back as before.

So, you see that I live in the most caring and happy social environment anyone could wish for. While I am not near a beach or mountain vista, who cares? Long time wonderful friendships are why I continue to live where I live.

Bruce Green, Port Lincoln, South Australia

I'm talking to Bruce Green. Bruce what do you in town?

I run an abalone farm. We grow abalone, a land-based operation, pump sea water over them and the little critters enjoy it a lot.

So where's that from here? Out in Boston Bay?

Yes. Right out on the end of Boston Point. We have a wonderful view back to Port Lincoln looking at the silos and out to sea. We watch the tuna boats go out servicing the tuna rings. You couldn't have a better office. There's shipping coming in and out of the channel and never a dull moment.

Tell us about farming abalone. Is it hard?

It's interesting in that it's pretty new. We've learnt how to breed them and keep them going from the farm population so we don't have to go back to the wild each time to collect the adult stock. We induce them to spawn. Like all sea critters they tend to produce a mass of eggs and sperm at the same time. In our facilities we can make sure that just about all the eggs get fertilised. For the first five or six days they're free, swimming in the wild. They swim around and go through a couple of changes – metamorphoses – until they're ready to settle onto something that's growing algae. They're looking for a food source when their little egg sac runs out of energy. So we provide that by way of algae growing on sheets. The little fellows

settle on the sheets and from then on they're stuck to the bottom! They are like little suction caps and they spend their life moseying around grazing the algae.

What have you found out about abalone that has amazed you?

They're smarter than me at this point! They are a very interesting animal. They haven't evolved much for millions and millions of years, and if you were the king of the abalone you might think that that was a bit disappointing. You might say, 'Look at our mates, they've come out of the water and learnt to use computers!' But then you could look at it another way and say, 'I'm really proud of you. We've got a model that works and haven't had to change a thing.' They're tough little buggers. In the natural environment they live on rocks in heavy swells. They lift their little foot up (the muscle) and a bit of that is used as a hand to grab a bit of algae or seaweed as it runs past. If something comes along that wants to eat them they just suck down onto the rocks and they're very difficult to remove.

How did you get into this?

I was a pig farmer way back. So these are just aquatic, one-legged pigs!

Not sure they'd like that description!

They're not quite as communicative as pigs, which really let you know how things are going.

How did you get into abalone farming?

I chased a girl here. I think I've caught her, but you never know with girls! I just happened to have some expertise relevant to the abalone industry, which is really an intensive animal industry. So I transferred my skills across and I'm very happy here.

Where do you come from originally?

I'm a Queenslander. I love it here. It's a different sort of environment to Queensland.

Usually Queenslanders are rugging up and complaining about the cold!

I enjoy the cold. It's nice to have a change in season. Just now with autumn that bit of a nip in the air is just lovely.

Bruce it's great to meet you just walking along the street. It's funny how things happen.

Macca, it's good to have you in town.

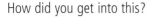

About twenty-five years ago we lived in an inner Melbourne suburb, now 'highly desired' by yuppies, in a weatherboard home with only two bedrooms. With an expanding family we needed a larger house. We looked around our suburb and at several of the adjoining areas but homes seemed to fall into two categories, too small or beyond our means.

At the time my work required frequent interstate flights, sometimes two a week

Ross Heathcote,
Keilor,
Victoria

(and no frequent flyer points then!) I seemed to be doing a lot of travelling to and from Tullamarine airport.

It was at this point that my wife said, 'Why don't we live near the airport?' Smart thinking. We looked at houses close to the airport but came up with the same problems – too small or beyond our price range. My wife, not to be deterred, suggested we look at a project home development at Taylors Lakes, about ten minutes from the airport. So, we selected one, bought a block and had it built.

At this time Taylors Lakes had very few amenities but the early residents were not to be denied. We all contributed to establishing good amenities. It was one of the first developments in Melbourne with all services underground.

To keep ourselves happy in our leisure time we founded a recreation club, which over the years has expanded to cover tennis, cricket, football, basketball, a garden club and a monthly social golf day. Every so often one or other of the groups has a dinner dance, trophy-prize giving night to which any residents are welcome.

This leads to the following story. I was on board the 6.00 p.m. flight back from Sydney one Friday evening. As we got close to Tullamarine I checked my watch and remarked, 'On time, thank goodness'. My neighbouring passenger asked, 'Why so interested in your arrival time?' 'I have a dinner dance to go to tonight. The moment I get off the plane I'll give my wife a ring and by the time I collect my bags from the carousel she'll be drawing up in the car. Quickly home, a shower and change of clothes and then to the dance.' He wanted to know how all this could be achieved, and I replied that Taylors Lakes was only ten minutes from the airport. I asked where he lived and he said Mount Eliza, and that it would take him close to two hours to drive home. I left him with the thought that as he was driving down the Nepean Highway he could visualise my wife and myself on the dance floor 'tripping the light fantastic' having already eaten our first course!

So, that is why we live where we live.

 Gwen Wilson, Wavell Heights, Queensland

I had set my alarm for an early start and all was quiet as I sat in the kitchen drinking a cup of tea. I then noticed a crackling sound from outside the house and thought one of my neighbours was pruning his shrubs.

I went out to the front patio to look but I couldn't see anyone. But the sound now seemed to be coming from the footpath. I went to the front gate but still couldn't see anything responsible for the sound which now seemed to be coming from above my head, in the bauhinia trees.

The trees had lost their leaves that were full of seed pods about six to eight inches long. As I looked up one of the seedpods burst open with a loud crack and many seeds floated to the ground. This was followed by more cracks as other seedpods burst open.

As I stood there with the seeds floating around me I wished I had a camera so that I could capture Mother Nature at work. I planted the trees about thirty years ago from seed when my son was at primary school learning about plants. This was the first time I'd heard the sounds but maybe I just haven't been there at the right time previously. I was just captivated by the spectacle of it all, and it lasted for about an hour. I felt like David Attenborough!

It was a great start to the day. It gave me such a lift. I'm so glad I was able to see it happening with my own eyes.

Lyn Bates, Weipa, Queensland

I'm a potter. I work at home. I play and play all day. Bruce has always worked in mines so we have moved around a bit. I came from Mount Carbine, which is down the road. From there to Telfer in WA and back to Maleny for a bit, and then Weipa came up. I learnt pottery here and that was it.

Were you artistic when you were younger?

Yes, I tried lots of things. I used to do heirloom sewing. White lace and materials far removed from mud. But I love it. I do functional ware but love the non-functional (sculptural) because it lends itself more to the bauxite and the kaolin that's here. I make a sheno glaze with the kaolin, that's my thing. And I use a bit of the local clay.

Do you like working with earth. Is that part of it?

Yes, that's the thing. I feel that part of your soul goes into each piece. That's what I love about it. The thing I wanted to learn here was how to use the local product. Before I came to Weipa I didn't know I'd be sitting on tonnes of clay. The potter's perfect paradise! And I like using the local product because it gives you a feel for the area. The total contrast between the wet and the dry here is just magnificent. And the sunsets! I walk Rocky Point beach every morning and it never ceases to amaze me the objects I pick up. I love this place. It's just so much a part of me. I think I could live and die here.

I love your program and I was so touched by your story about the little blue wren who was so alone in the big city. I love birds and we lived at the Gold Coast on a canal where we had lots of feathered friends in our garden. There I could handfeed a kookaburra, the pelicans, even a black swan. However, the birds I love the most are the blue wrens. A lady wren made a nest in a prickly bush in our garden. We didn't even know they were there until a friend found the nest carefully hidden. One day I looked out from my office and there on a branch of a bottlebrush were two baby wrens so tiny, gorgeous and fluffy. The mother was happily preening herself, and the daddy was hopping about looking for food for the family. Macca, I will never forget that little scene. How privileged was I at that moment to witness nature at its most beautiful.

We have moved from that bird haven now and would you believe that I think I am pining for them. People say to me, 'Thellie, get over it.' I didn't think I would miss them so much, but I do.

Thellie Norris, Tannum Sands, Queensland

Geoff Rogerson,
Denmark,
Western Australia

As a listener to your program for many years I always prick my ears up when birds are mentioned, especially the blue wren. I live out of town surrounded by bushland and these delightful creatures are never far away. Whenever they see me or hear the door bang they fly to the veranda to be fed with quickoats. There are about a dozen in the flock though they have now shed their brilliant nuptial plumage.

☼

Lenore Lomax,
Robina,
Queensland

I have families of little blue wrens which give me much pleasure. I counted eight of them today. When I work in the garden they hop along the top of the fence and don't seem at all worried by my presence.

My backyard is bounded by Robina Waters, with ducks, water hen of various sorts, pelicans, swans, cormorants and seagulls. The water hen had babies recently, as did the two beautiful snow-white ducks. I have planted some natives so I have rainbow lorikeets, willy-wagtails and honeyeaters. And of course there are some rowdy crows. At some times of the year hundreds of white cockatoos fly over on their way to their night nesting place in the gums on the other side of the waterway.

All this makes it a great joy to live here, but my greatest pleasure is the little blue wrens.

☼

Judith-Anne Tahir,
Tasmania

Spring in Tasmania literally takes your breath away. When this springtime experience occurs in your own garden, accompanied by choruses of birdsong, you know you're living in exactly the right place.

While I was gardening recently a female blue wren flew close by with a tiny bird in tow. Closer inspection revealed what I'd hoped for, a mother wren was teaching her baby to fly. The young bird was covered in soft, brown down and its tail was three centimetres at the very most. Its tiny wings had barely formed.

I stood stock still, scarcely blinking. The mother repeated her short flight pattern, the baby copying time and time again. They then flew to the lower branches of a dense berry bush.

When I looked closely I noticed there was a second baby perched there. The mother darted away and returned with tasty morsels for her young. Her rapid movements and intense manner clearly demonstrated the responsibly she felt. I was fascinated. This was motherhood at its heightened best.

Just when I felt I must withdraw from this family ritual and catch up with my chores, the mother wren flew across my path once again with another tiny bird in her wake – this was her third! It was getting late and I reluctantly had to leave. I didn't get back into the garden for several days. When I did, a tiny bird flew across my path and landed on the wire fence. It balanced there for a moment and then took off. Wings flapped violently as the small body was projected up, up and up. I held my breath, it was heading for the shed roof! Then just in time it lifted higher, clearing the roof and flying straight up into the hawthorn tree behind it.

What relief I felt. It seemed that yet another generation of blue wrens had been raised. The flying lessons had been successful – they'd passed with flying colours.

☼

Reverend Wesley Hartley at Busselton, Western Australia

I'm with the Reverend Wesley Hartley at Busselton in Western Australia. How long have you been with the Uniting Church? Is it the Uniting Church?

Yes, Uniting Church but originally Methodist. I was ordained thirty years ago in Melbourne. So it's been a long haul.

And where have you served?

In Melbourne and Hobart, and then the Kimberley and all that area of WA. I was at Manning, a Perth suburb, and Trinity in the centre of that city, and then with the conference of churches in Western Australia. I worked with the Aboriginal side of the Uniting Church and then almost by accident came to Busselton.

I suppose travelling around gives you a good idea what Australia is all about.

It does. I've worked in lots of places, and having worked with Aboriginal people as well I get a great insight into what a wonderful land we live in.

How do you think the Christian church is doing? Is it a difficult job, perhaps more difficult than it's ever been?

It is a difficult job. I'm actually hopeful for the church if not for its structure; I'm hopeful for what it is to be part of a faith community. I think the way we 'do' church in the future is going to be different. John Spong, for example, refers to the Church Alumni Association, 'those who are interested but not part of'.

Why do you think you became a minister? Is it in the family?

Yes, it was in the family. My father was a Methodist minister in Melbourne. He was mentioned in dispatches as a chaplain during the war, and was very well known in the early days of the peace movement. My mother was the first Presbyterian woman trained for the ministry. So it was in the blood. I just caught it I guess. But I'm glad I did.

Why are you glad?

I could have been a business person and made lots of money, but encountering people where life really matters is what counts; life's not what your position is but what you've done during it. I'd guess it's like yourself: you wouldn't change it for quids even though there are probably lots of other things you could do.

Yes, it's probably meeting people for me.

In ministry you encounter people in all sorts of different situations, in times of stress like death, and you become a link. It's a very privileged position to be in. I wouldn't change it for anything.

When you said you were overseas, what sort of things were you doing?

In the days when the iron curtain was still up I liaised with churches in Eastern Europe. I went to a lot of places meeting people surviving under very difficult cir-cumstances. It taught me not only the privilege of being an Australian and what a great country we have, but also that you can survive in any situation if you really set your mind to it. That's really reflective of what I understand faith to be.

Somebody said to me that Australians don't profess to be Christians or go to church. But it's amazing that at times of crisis, for example Bali, many go to church or get together, and faith is at the centre of their mourning.

Sure. I remember when I was young my father used to say that in New Guinea there was no atheist in a foxhole. I find Australians are very spiritual. I think the way we've 'done' church with them in the past has not been all that helpful. The church needs to be more genuinely with people rather than telling them what they ought to be; the nation and the church would be a much better place for it.

Wesley, nice to talk to you.

Reverend Warwick Humphries, Launceston, Tasmania

This is the Reverend Warwick Humphries' story.

I came here after the bush fires in 1967. Black Tuesday. I've been here ever since. I came for twelve months and stayed.

Why did you come after the bush fires?

Things didn't work out in NSW and I got an opportunity to do some work down here.

What work do you do, Warwick?

I'm an Anglican padre. Have been for thirty-nine years and enjoyed it. Lots of things I would have liked to have done differently, but it's been a good life.

Rewarding?

Challenging and hard. A lot of things we just aren't trained for. We're supposed to be experts in every area there is, but we're not.

The church it seems to me gets a lot of criticism from people with other agendas.

We get some bad press. We're not all perfect. We do the best we can with what we've got. There are a few fellows who've made wrong choices and it's tarnished us all.

What do you think you've got out of being a reverend?

I don't know what you get out of it. If I've done something that's made a difference. For instance I used to dislike intensely doing funerals because they are hard and sad. There wasn't much joy, but I realised that people need someone at that time so I found that to be quite fulfilling. I felt I could lift them up a bit. I enjoyed weddings. Sunday was always good to look forward to as people came together.

I like that about Sundays, too!

It's one of the reasons I haven't heard a lot of your program, Macca. When I do I really enjoy it. The last time was when I was at St Helens in Tasmania when we had the world veteran orienteering championships. It was a fantastic time. I thought you'd probably love to hear about it. We had Israeli generals, Norwegian doctors and professors. They couldn't get over the fact that they could walk freely in the bush. I can't remember what happened now, but I didn't ring. I was hoping somebody would.

Was your father a reverend?

No, he wasn't. He wasn't even interested. My mother was a great Christian soul. She encouraged us children. She didn't put any pressure on us. She was lovely like that. She just pointed us in the right direction.

I had one exactly the same.

My brother is also a reverend and I have another brother who is a bank manager. He's the wealthy one of the family.

You should hit him for a loan! It's lovely to talk to you. Keep up the good work.

Thanks Macca. It's lovely to come in here and share these few minutes with you.

We live in Sydney and I run a water taxi company on Sydney Harbour which isn't too bad a gig Mondays to Fridays. Great scenery and interesting people to deal with every day. But we really look forward to our weekends. We recently bought fifty acres at Wombeyan Caves which we try and escape to. It is a bush block with two creeks on which we built a two-storey cabin.

Daniel Purser,
Wombeyan Caves,
New South Wales

Every morning the kookaburras wake us up. We quietly wander downstairs and peer out the windows to find the local kangaroo family (mum, dad and baby 'roo) grazing amongst the frosted grass. Each week we tempt fate and edge closer to try and get them familiar with the human factor! We had to purchase a bird book to fulfil our curiosity about the numerous species that we admire from our bull-nose veranda. There are wombat holes everywhere but so far they have remained elusive. There have been a number of echidnas that are sometimes shy but at other times more interested in sucking the life out of the ant mounds.

On cool, clear nights we light a fire outside and watch in amazement as the evening sky comes alive. The stars are so bright and you can watch the satellites pass over the horizon. It feels so good when you are sitting around the fire with a group of people and the sky lights up with a shooting star. Everyone yells at the same time, 'Did you see that?' Weekends at the cave house are very basic and far enough away from the big smoke for us to feel we are a million miles away from it. This is just a 'why and where we go for our weekends' story I suppose!

Robert McAlpine, the Grampians, Victoria

I'm a property valuer and a farmer. The last time we spoke on air was during your 'Melbourne in the Park' program. My previous life was as a town planner for the government in Melbourne. I decided to give it away because I could see that what was coming was more and more, worse and worse. I've come to live in the Grampians as a lifestyle change.

So, are you responsible for what happens in Melbourne?

No, not any more! By the year 2015 Melbourne's traffic is estimated to double, which means more air pollution. I'm a fresh air fiend so I had to leave town and come and live in the Grampians.

I suppose it's the same for all the capital cities here is it?

Worldwide! You know in some countries they're in their second generation of children who have never seen the stars. Never seen the stars!

That's why I like doing outside broadcasts because you're out in the morning. It's the best time of the day I reckon. Do you still do any town planning?

No, just live in paradise in the Grampians.

It must be a fairly thankless task being a town planner because population pressure means earlier planning goes out of the window.

A lot of it's to do with money and real estate. Planners do the best they can, but in a scheme where private ownership of real estate dominates, the influences are really just too great.

Shirley Mealey,
Warrigal,
New South Wales

You had on your program from New Zealand a delightful man who gave his forthright opinion on the true value of the Bunya palm tree – as opposed to the eucalyptus and wattles as symbols of Australia – and said how great it would be to die after being rammed into the earth by a falling bunya nut! I would like to share with you my association with bunya trees and their nuts.

In the 1950s my mother owned a dairy farm in Picton, NSW. At the main gate were two enormous bunya trees planted probably a hundred years ago. She often warned picnickers to stay away from the trees and to watch out for falling nuts.

My husband and I and young family lived on a dairy farm in Kangaroo Valley. My eldest daughter returned from a holiday at her nanna's with several seeds from one of the nuts. We duly planted them and were rewarded with a small tree. When we relocated to the Shellharbour area I potted it, took it with us and planted it in the backyard. It's now forty feet high! Each March an average of thirty nuts fall off the tree, occasionally onto the veranda. My husband insists that when I mow the lawn (my job) in February and March I wear a helmet, and I enclose a photograph showing me in the helmet pushing a wheelbarrow full of freshly fallen bunya nuts. (See between pages 96 and 97)

I thought this would amuse you and can be added to your bunya memorabilia!

I could write 'why I live where I live' but I thought you would like to hear 'why I do what I do'.

This is my twentieth year of being a Telecross volunteer for the Red Cross. I joined because I was agoraphobic and hadn't left home for years. To cut a long story short I was asked to be trained and didn't have a panic attack. I adore all the Telecross members I have met over the phone each morning.

Telecross is a program which is free to elderly, frail or at-risk folk living alone in their own homes. There are exceptions to the living-alone rule, as in a case where one partner may be blind. Members receive a cheery phonecall every day of the year, including weekends and public holidays, between eight and nine in the morning. If they don't answer their phones the volunteer calls the regional Red Cross office and checks are made to ensure they're okay.

It is a most rewarding and humbling experience. I have shared a wealth of combined lifetimes. My problems are none compared to some of our heroic members. I have now been booked five times as a public speaker to promote Telecross, and my husband and I are in a Red Cross personal support team which is activated in times of disasters. No-one need feel alone. And you are always welcome to pop in for a cuppa!

Rhonda Cetta-Hoye,
Wyoming,
New South Wales

Dr Phil Hungerford, Tamworth, New South Wales

Here's Dr Phil Hungerford a local bloke who wrote 'The Bureaucratic Wriggle'. Why did you get the urge to write this song?

I've worked for the public service for over twenty years. I was sitting in an interminable meeting one day and thought I'd write a song. So, I put a piece of paper under the table and jotted down a few lyrics while pretending to listen, and there you have the song.

Tell me about yourself. You live in Tamworth and you work at the hospital. What sort of doctor are you?

I'm an emergency specialist at Tamworth hospital and work in the emergency department and also in the intensive care unit. We also do medical retrievals, which means we go out in ambulances, helicopters and planes and pick sick people up from small hospitals in isolated areas surrounding Tamworth.

How did you get into that?

I don't know. I kind of drifted into emergency medicine. I think originally I got into it because I was chasing the woman who was to be my wife. One thing led to another and I ended up doing emergency training. I've been a specialist for about twelve years and we're pretty settled and happy here in Tamworth.

You'd see life in the raw if you're working in emergency and intensive care?

You see a lot of amazingly inspiring things, people's strength and courage. In some ways it restores your faith in human nature. But you also see some terrible things and some absolute drongos. So it's good and bad and never dull.

This is the health centre for this region.

Tamworth is a base hospital so it's the hub of a really large area supposedly the size of Tasmania. We have recently amalgamated with Hunter Health and it remains to be seen whether our referral patterns and workloads stay the same.

Does the music keep you sane? Is that the purpose of music in your life?

I've always played music. It keeps me sane. I used to play when I was training at university to make money to make ends meet. I like writing songs. It's a kind of right side of the brain activity. A lot of doctors are pretty left-sided. I think some don't have a right side left!

You've lived here for twenty years?

I first came here in 1981 as a young, fresh graduate. I got sent on a country term from Sydney Hospital. That's when I met my wife-to-be. I came here permanently in about 1983–84, went away for three years to finish my emergency training, and returned as a specialist with wife and children in tow in 1991.

You've seen Tamworth change?

It's certainly changed. I think it's become more and more cosmopolitan. A lot of city people would laugh at this description, but I've seen the change from a pretty parochial country town to a town with cafes on the sidewalk. The population doubles during the music festival. It's great for the town.

What do you like about being a doctor? Have you ever thought about that?

I think about it all the time. It's a mixture. You can always get a job somewhere, make a bit of money. I think people mostly still like doctors, even if they like to whinge about them.

Do people whinge about doctors as much these days?

They're always whingeing to me about other doctors! There's the bad side. As I said before, you meet some great people and are humbled at what they are going through, and on the other hand you see a lot of horrible people. I guess it's the same with any job. Probably for you too, Ian!

That's another story! Back to your music. You've written a song about your daughter. You said she hates it and runs to her room every time she hears it.

I kind of hope one day when she has kids she'll like it. It's a song anyone with teenage kids will relate to. The sentiments are basically that you don't always like them but will always love them. It's called 'Fair Weather Girl'.

Noooooo!

N.M. Kelly,
Ravenshoe,
Queensland

I live on the Evelyn Tableland above the Atherton and at about 3,000 feet on the range for which I can find no name, but it's part of the Great Divide. It's 'Heaven in the Hills', away from the hustle and bustle that has become Cairns where I grew up. On the map we are really at the back of Ingham as the crow flies. It's an area of really good alluvial volcanic soil where lush paddocks produce fat cattle, about three crops of potatoes a year, and corn paddocks reach tasselled heads to the blue sky. Cyclones do hit with their edges at times, but mostly we get the beneficial rains; crystal streams feed the lovely Tully Falls and other falls abound in this moderate area in the tropics. We are on the edge of the drier outback, the cattle country begins at the edge of the lush area with an easily seen divide. The coast gets so very hot but up here we have moderate summers and sometimes really cold winters.

The swirling misted morn as the sun comes in furious colours over the farm mountains, the sunlight dazzling green paddocks at midday, and the cool, soft breeze that greets most evenings before the sun goes to rest with a flame of colour like a giant palette from a demented painter's studio.

Yes, it's 'Heaven in the Hills'.

Mark and Merryl Burdon

Mark and Merryl Burdon used to work in Oak Valley, an Aboriginal community, and Merryl was the nurse there.

MERRYL: Nursing work varies a lot. Sometimes you can be very busy and then it can be quiet when people from the community go away. But they will come at night if they're worried about themselves or their children, so you can have lots of disturbances. There aren't many emergencies at Oak Valley and generally it's very pleasant work. The people are lovely.

How do you like it out there, Mark?

MARK: I've loved the bush all my life and we've both spent most of our lives out there. I was the essential services officer at Oak Valley during the time that Merryl was the nurse there. I carted the water into the community and looked after the generators and the infrastructure generally.

What's your background?

MARK: I managed sheep stations for twenty years before I was dragged off them by my wife, who wanted to get back into nursing. We semi-retired to Ceduna, a place we'd always liked and where I originally met Merryl nearly forty years ago.

Merryl, the Aboriginal people at Oak Valley love their art.

MERRYL: Yes they do. There have been some newly discovered talents there just recently and they've got a lot of work on show in Adelaide at the moment.

That's obviously made a difference to the community.

MERRYL: Yes, they've become quite inspired by their artwork. It's really good.

Before at Oak Valley you worked at what they call the Pitt lands or the Pitjandjara lands. You're going back there soon?

MERRYL: Yes. We loved it up there. It's very grand, beautiful country, part of South Australia. A lot of people don't know about it and we're very happy going back to the communities. There's plenty of work to do there.

It's in the Musgrave Ranges?

MARK: Yes. In fact we're going to a place called Pipalyatjara where we were in 1997–98. It's to the west of the Musgrave Ranges in what's known as the Tomkinson Ranges.

Most of our listeners are living on suburban blocks. Explain to them what it's like and why you like it.

MARK: The country is absolutely magnificent. Grand, as Merryl just described it, with towering ranges and mountains interspersed with grassy plains, patches of mulga scrub and sand hills. It's situated just north of the Great Victoria Desert.

It's pretty isolated up there?

MERRYL: Yes. There's not very many medical personnel on the ground and we rely on the flying doctor to give us advice, and for evacuations when necessary.

You both live and work away from civilisation. Do you like that?

MERRYL: Yes, we prefer and enjoy it very much. I think we like the isolation and the bush.

Do you bird watch?

Mark: Yes. I also do a little bit of star gazing. I've got an interest in astronomy so it's a great place for clear skies and dark nights.

Give us a call some time from the Pitt lands.

MARK: Love to do that. You won't remember us, but we certainly will remember you, Ian!

Lidith Kerr,
Sunshine Bay,
New South Wales

When I was young I lived in George Street, Penshurst, Sydney. I was always on the front veranda and visitors admired me. Times were pretty good but then the Depression started. I was moved to Como, first to a brick house on a hill, still on the front veranda for people to admire. I was then taken to a house opposite Como School, once again on the front veranda. There a family of seven, who had been evicted for not paying the rent, moved in with us. Our family consisted of six kids and two parents so there were quite a mob of us. Of course, all were warned with a fate worse than death if they hurt me.

After a while I was taken to crown land at Lugarno. I once again had pride of place near the front door and was there for a few years. Next I was taken to a house on the Woronora River, again on the front veranda, and admired by people in boats as they rowed past. It was very cold there as the sun only reached the house for a couple of hours each day. The place was nicknamed 'Siberia' and I got pretty sick as I couldn't take the cold.

So off again, this time by punt under the Como Bridge to Green Point on the Georges River where I flourished for about twenty years. Then came a few more moves. Chittaway Point, back to Como, Sylvania, Cassilis, Gulgong, Nowra,

Miranda, and finally 'The Oaks' for over thirty years. There I was admired by lots of people, garden club members and aged pensioners would come by bus, and I took pride of place again.

Sadly that place was lost to bushfires but I was saved. I now live once again on a front veranda in Sunshine Bay, part of Batemans Bay.

I am now over ninety years old. My name is Cleopatra. I'm a rose begonia and parts of me have been given to dozens of admirers so they could grow one of their own.

Neville and Joan Ludke, Bunya Mountains, Queensland

Neville, we were talking earlier about the Bunya Mountains and the trees. You know them pretty well, don't you?

NEVILLE: Yes, we live up there. There hasn't been a bunya crop this year. We've had two good crops in a row, but because of the drought and the two good crops we can't find any at all. The cone is about the size of a man's head. Some of them get up to the size of a twenty-litre drum.

You can imagine one of them falling out of a tall tree! How high can a bunya tree grow?

NEVILLE: To about two hundred feet.

And there are male trees and female trees?

NEVILLE: Yes, the older trees definitely become more male and the smaller ones more female. The pollen evidently blows on the wind for a couple of miles. We have a whole lot of little trees near the house and I've never seen a male flower on them. They have nuts on them two years out of three.

I've got a little bunya at home. I've had it about ten years and it struggles in the pot but I don't want to put in the ground or it'll grow to two hundred feet! Not good in the suburbs where I live. Now, you were a park ranger at one time?

NEVILLE: Yes, we came up the mountains in 1972 and I was working for National Parks for five or six years.

Would it be fair to say that both you and Joan fell in love with the Bunya Mountains and trees?

NEVILLE: Yes. As I said, Bunya Mountains is home without a doubt. We lived up on the top for about five years. Joan likes walking in the fog. I can't handle it! You get fogs on the mountain that just sort of drip off you. They're really thick. When Joan got a spare minute out into the fog she'd go. It's not for me. I prefer to be down the bottom where it's not quite so wet.

Tell us all about it, Joan.

JOAN: I do love the mist on the mountains. When the mists and fog are around you don't know the rest of the world. It seems to coat and block out any pain or suffering in rest of the world. You can become free and know what a wonderful creation has been made. Just all enjoy this creation. It's out there for the taking.

I'm with you on that. I've walked in mist and fog. It's like you're on your own.

Barbara Grylls,
Kununurra,
Western Australia

I was listening to your program as usual when I heard the gentleman engineer from NSW saying that the Ord River Scheme was a white elephant. I could not believe my ears when I heard such balderdash. I have been a forty-one-year resident of the Kimberley region and can remember the situation quite clearly in the early days of the scheme. There were few residents, mainly pastoral stations employing Aboriginals who at that time were not paid award wages. There were few if any primary schools and no secondary schools.

The figures supplied to me by the WA Department of Agriculture state that for the last five years returns from agricultural crops have averaged between fifty and sixty million dollars. All these farmers pay taxes which return to the Australian community. Where there was minimal employment, now there are large numbers of employees in pastoral, tourism and agricultural industries. There are schools, primary, secondary and tertiary, employing teachers.

I love this region and have no desire to return to the state where I was born, Victoria, where on visits to family I find the residents have no desire to hear of anything outside their own backyard. My husband won't even go on a visit. Today when I looked out of my windows over the beautiful Ord River it was a lovely mirror, with the sound of many birds. The weather is glorious for approximately nine months of the year. We have a town where there is no dirty power station because of the benefit of hydro-electric power.

Yes, we are very fortunate to live in such a beautiful area. The Ord River and Irrigation Area and the Kimberley as a whole are definitely not takers but givers to the benefit of the whole Australian community. I hope you will let your listeners know that far from being a white elephant this area is one for the community to be proud of.

Reno Costa

This is Reno Costa who I met in Kempsey. We talked about fishing and living in Burrell Creek. He's a lovely bloke who came to Australia as a young boy with his family from Italy. It's amazing how things change when wars come, how security's much tougher. This is his experience.

Around about 1940 or 1941, when they were interning people like my Italian-born father, I remember he took me with him on his pushbike from Dunmore in NSW to Mr O'Brien's place at Minnamurra. He was my father's manager at the Dunmore quarry. I can remember Mr O'Brien saying, 'Listen Frank, I'll do everything I can to help you.' Looking through my father's papers, which we got from the archives, I saw he'd been contacted by a government department and told to report to Sydney with his suitcase packed. Perhaps to be sent somewhere like Hay and be interned. He'd made arrangements with a coal mining family at Coalcliff for mum and us three kids to move into their backyard and live in two tents if he didn't return from Sydney. Coal miners couldn't be interned. But he did come home from Sydney and they were really, really happy, I can tell you!

I can never forget Mr O'Brien. He was like an angel to us. We would probably have been without a father for five or more years. There was no talk of giving mum any help with the three kids. They were just taking dad. That's all there was to it. It was an insensitive system.

Now, this is still to do with dad's story. About two or three years ago I decided to register for working under the pension scheme. If you work from sixty-five to seventy the government gives you some money if you're eligible for the pension. I thought this was good idea and went to Centrelink. They asked what proof of identity I had. I passed over my naturalisation papers from 1943, but was still told to find out where I came into the country, and the name of the ship. I was going to give up, but my daughter phoned the local member of parliament. Centrelink rang half an hour later and told us not to worry, that it had all been fixed up!

So, it's always there, we don't feel it. But there's something. Like you said, if there's an upheaval, mate, you want to make sure you're on the right side.

The photograph (see between pages 96 and 97) shows the Barron Falls, or Din Din to give them their native Djabukai (Jab-oo-kye) language name, in flood. To make them flow with such force required Tinaroo Falls Dam to be running about a metre over the spillway, a very large private dam to burst, and finally a devastating cyclone to come across the coast!

The last time the Falls came close to looking like this photograph was in 1911. I took it the day Cyclone Steve hit. It entailed a thirty-five kilometre drive – the countryside was devastated, with trees down everywhere and most roads closed. When I got there I had to slide down a sodden hillside while keeping my camera dry – not easy. And I was all the time hoping no Joe Blakes'd come wriggling by – not funny. I leave it to you to judge whether it was worth it.

So, this is my why I live contribution. They say a picture's worth a thousand words. The next thousand words will follow as soon as possible!

Irene Shanks,
Mareeba,
Queensland

Ivan Gellie phoned from Bright, Victoria, on his own phone!

(See the photograph between pages 96 and 97)

G'day Ivan Gellie

I'm in Bright mate, in a phone box.

You can still find one!

No, I built it.

You've built your own phone!

I've built my own phone box, put it on the property and that's where I'm ringing you from.

Does Ziggy know about this?

Well, I don't know, but Telstra came to hook it up on Friday.

The little possums, that's good of them!

The fellow couldn't believe it when he saw this phone box. He said, 'You're kidding me.' I said, 'No, I need a site phone because I'm building a house here.' It's painted telephone red and is a genuine Ivan phone box.

Has it got a door on it like the old ones?

My word, oh yes.

Do you remember in what people used to call 'the bad old days' – I sometimes think they were 'the good old days' – when you could go into a phone box, close the door and have a private conversation. Now you're out on the street getting blown around, and the sun shines on you. What possessed you to build your own phone box, Ivan?

I suppose the fact that I needed a phone at the site. But I also thought, why can't I build something that's a bit unique. And seeing they're taking phone boxes away I've put one back!

It might start a trend. Did you find one from somewhere or did you build it yourself?

No, that's my game Macca, I'm a builder so I built the whole thing myself.

That's excellent. I'll have to come and see it, in Bright is it?

We're just a tad out of Bright, about five minutes, in the lovely tranquil state forest. Bev my wife's running around taking photos of me in the phone box at the moment!

I'd love to build a phone box in my front yard. I live in a suburb called Oatley and I can remember there used to be four public phone boxes on the west side. There's one up the shops now, but the others have all disappeared. You're reversing the trend. I think it's a wonderful thing Ivan.

DEPHNE MADYARA

The Art of Being Private

BUILDING IN SILENCE

Other Books by Dephne

Incorruptible Beauty

Breaking Soul Ties

A Woman's Body Is A Temple

A Woman's Body Is A Temple: Study Guide & Self
Reflection

Copyright

Dedication

This book is dedicated to the Author and Perfecter of my faith, Jesus Christ, the risen Son of the living God, Firstborn over all creation, Who is the beginning, was with God and is God. The WORD that came down from heaven and became flesh. I love You forever!

To God the Father who loved me before I was born and formed me in my mother's womb and put inside me treasures and a voice, calling me to salvation through Jesus Christ to live a life worthy of the calling He has given me. To Him be the glory forever!

To the Holy Spirit my Teacher, the very power of God who raised Jesus Christ from the dead and now lives in me; empowering me, helping me, counselling me and leading me into all Truth daily. Amen.

Honour and glory be to You O God, my all and my everything, be glorified forever and ever, Amen.

Contents

CHAPTER 1

The Art of Being Private as a Godly Lifestyle

About three years ago, the LORD Jesus said to me, "build in silence" as I was studying the book of Luke in chapter one. This chapter speaks about Elizabeth, who hid for five months when she discovered she was pregnant at her old age, with her first child—John the Baptist. You see, before this life-changing encounter and revelation, I had developed a trivial nature and mental attitude of speaking without using discretion. I was not applying this kind of wisdom, concerning anything and everything I was building, planning, trialling, thinking or executing in certain areas of my life. The passage of scripture that transformed my life that day is taken from the book of Luke, saying:

The key focus scriptures are underlined

There was in the days of Herod, the king of Judea, a certain priest named Zacharias, of the division of Abijah. His wife was of the daughters of Aaron, and her name was Elizabeth. And they were both righteous before God, walking in all the commandments and ordinances of the Lord blameless. But they had no child because Elizabeth was barren, and they were both well advanced in years. So it was, that while he was serving as priest before God in the order of his division, according to the custom of the priesthood, his lot fell to burn incense when he went into the temple of the Lord. And the whole multitude of the people was praying outside at the hour of incense. Then an angel of the Lord appeared to him, standing on the right side of the altar of incense. And when Zacharias saw him, he was troubled, and fear fell upon him. But the angel said to him, "Do not be afraid, Zacharias, for your prayer is heard; and your wife Elizabeth will bear you a son, and you shall call his name John. And you will have joy and gladness, and many will rejoice at his birth. For he will be great in the sight of the Lord, and shall drink neither

wine nor strong drink. He will also be filled with the Holy Spirit, even from his mother's womb. And he will turn many of the children of Israel to the Lord their God. He will also go before Him in the spirit and power of Elijah, 'to turn the hearts of the fathers to the children,' and the disobedient to the wisdom of the just, to make ready a people prepared for the Lord." And Zacharias said to the angel, "How shall I know this? For I am an old man, and my wife is well advanced in years." And the angel answered and said to him, "I am Gabriel, who stands in the presence of God, and was sent to speak to you and bring you these glad tidings. But behold, you will be mute and not able to speak until the day these things take place because you did not believe my words which will be fulfilled in their own time." And the people waited for Zacharias, and marvelled that he lingered so long in the temple. But when he came out, he could not speak to them; and they perceived that he had seen a vision in the temple, for he beckoned to them and remained speechless. So it was, as soon as the days of his service were completed, that he departed to his own house. <u>Now after those days his wife Elizabeth conceived; and she hid herself five months,</u> saying, "Thus the Lord has dealt with me, in the days when He looked on me, to take away my reproach among people."
Luke 1:5-25 (NKJV)

I went on to teach about this revelation and Rhema Word via my online ministry, but at the time, I didn't quite grasp what "building in silence" really meant in my day to day life. I had merely understood one side of the coin to what being private entailed. I only understood it to be only a silent weapon of warfare in context to the warfares I had gone through for the most of my childhood into adulthood; concerning my plans and ideas.

In my case, the Holy Spirit had shown me people who were fasting against the plans I had shared with them but were pretending to support me. Concerning my love life, I had come across guys who were trying to divert my love life. For example, my friend and brother in Christ who happened to be a minister of a church told me that God was telling him that I was his wife. Now, at the time I was in courtship, and when I reminded him that I was already with someone, he didn't flinch but gave me a scripture that God "supposedly" gave him. It's unfortunate when a believer is convinced that they are hearing from God but are hearing from their mind or will. In that situation, the Lord assured me that He didn't tell him that, but he fell in love and was "driven" by his feelings!

Moreover, I've had friends and acquaintances studying my life, concealing their obsession, witchcraft, envy and jealousies with smiles, pretence and unity. Thanks be to God, who in His mercy has revealed the hidden truth on all those occasions! He is the God who can show you and I the thoughts of the heart, so as not to be blindsided by corruption. Beloved, being so public and open over the years, giving access to specific individuals who were not called to have access to me, did not always prove wise.

It's not until early 2019 that I received clarity, more so, clarity about the other side of the coin of "being private". I had been pondering about what being private really looks like in my day to day life. The Holy Spirit answered me with a vivid vision of what happens when I share my private life with others. He showed me people gathered in the living room of my house, some sitting on the sofas, some standing and still, others couldn't even fit because the room was crowded as they all faced and looked at me. I was shocked! He said to me, "you have invited them all." "They all come inside your home when you share your life". From then on, I understood that being private is not just about protection like in the case of Elizabeth, who hid, but it's also about wisdom and humility. It's similar to how Christ lived His life on earth in the context of prayer, the Bible says:

The key focus scriptures are underlined

Now when it was day, <u>He departed and went into a deserted place</u>. And the crowd sought Him and came to Him, and tried to keep Him from leaving them; but He said to them, "I must preach the kingdom of God to the other cities also, because for this purpose I have been sent."

Luke 4:42-43 (NKJV)

From that visual revelation and encounter, I was enlightened and had to ask myself some hard questions. "Am I prepared to invite everyone in my house concerning A, B or C"? From then on, I needed to learn from Christ, the art of being private.

Some months later, my Pastor started a teaching series titled "the art of following", and I chuckled within when I heard the title because the LORD had been teaching me about the art of being private! This was simply a confirmation of what God was telling me in the secret place. You see, there are days I want to share my happiest private moments, my new breakthroughs, my plans and goals but then I remember, is it necessary, what is my motive, what is the purpose, what will I achieve? Am I seeking man's applause?

The heart of this book is to show you the truth, that you may know the Truth of Christ on being private and building in silence. The reality of Christ that scrutinises and challenges attitudes of the mind, exposing behaviours and deceptions that defraud us of God's will for us all.

If you struggle with being private, don't understand the reality of privacy or seek man's applause as you hide behind the things you share with people, this too will be ministered in this book. Depending on who you are, there's a price to pay for your identity. You are valuable in God's eyes, and there's a cost for the anointing on your life, your destiny and your blessings. There is a demand on your life purpose and calling. Does this make you extra special or better than other people? Absolutely not. It just means that if you know your value, you will need a level of grace and wisdom to live your life more effectively. For example, the eyes need a different level of grace compared to a mouth; all are equally valuable, but their functions require different levels of capacity, power and wisdom for "total" effectiveness.

Beloved, we live in a world and society that influences you to be outspoken and freely pour out every emotion and thought hidden inside of you. A world that highlights the importance of baring diverse facets of self-image and self-expression. For example, on social media, if you log onto Facebook, the first post staring at you on the top front page asks "what's on your mind (insert your name)?". Twitter says, "what's happening?". Furthermore, despite your education qualifications or work experience, almost every job application wants to know what your hobbies and interests are, as part of their recruitment policies.

Moreover, in your day to day relations, be it with co-workers, student peers, acquaintances, family members or friends; they will at one point or another want you to share details about your personal life. It may not be very apparent, but the truth is, information is being somewhat besotted almost at every turn! The world system and its people seek you and me to speak more about ourselves; our thoughts, our plans, our fears, our lifestyles, our happy and sad moments, and more!

So then, if the world is heavily driven by information, whether the information is relevant or irrelevant, necessary or unnecessary, futile or profitable, edifying or damaging, life-changing or life distorting; where then does one lay their boundaries in such a climate and generation? With this universal phenomenon of extra transparency and lack of boundaries, self-control and ability to restrain oneself from too much exposure; how does one defer from what is expected and what is abnormal? What should be spoken and what shouldn't? When is the right moment to share information with outsiders and when is the wrong moment?

Being private in the 21st century comes with a stipend of humility and wisdom that promotes preservation and godliness. It takes a certain level of humility to be private and within that humility is a substance of wisdom, confidence that thrives outside of people approval. Confidence, whether hidden or open, built on righteousness. Indeed, some beautiful qualities and virtues are confounded in the act of being private. I pray that as you read this book and discover these qualities, the Holy Spirit of God will help, teach and empower you to put to practice these qualities and wisdom shared in this book, in your day to day life, finding the inner peace and joy through Jesus Christ as you make the decisions, steps and choices, Amen.

CHAPTER 2

The Art of Exclusivity

The key focus scriptures are underlined

Then God said, "Let Us make man in Our image, according to Our likeness; let them have dominion over the fish of the sea, over the birds of the air, and over the cattle, over all the earth and over every creeping thing that creeps on the earth." So God created man in His own image; in the image of God He created him; male and female He created them. Then God blessed them, and God said to them, "Be fruitful and multiply; fill the earth and subdue it; have dominion over the fish of the sea, over the birds of the air, and over every living thing that moves on the earth."

Genesis 1:26-28 (NKJV)

From the passage of Scripture above, we learn a very vital life strategy and method from God Almighty during the creation of man; you and me. That when it came to creating human beings, the idea, vision, goal, the objective was being discussed amongst God the Father, Son and Holy Spirit. The matter of creating humanity was conveyed, deliberated and concluded into action within the triune God. The Bible says:

"...let Us make man in Our image according to Our likeness..."
Genesis 1:26 (NKJV)

If we begin to dissect this grand plan that God the Father, Son and Holy Spirit had, we can start to see that there are levels of exclusivity that were adhered to, when the information was being shared. The plan of making man was exclusive to God alone; God the Father, God the Son and God the Holy Spirit! Only He is capable of executing this grand plan and seeing it through for His glory and purpose. God is Father, Son and Spirit, and in this context, God's plan, idea and motive for humanity was deliberated within the Trinity. Beloved, each time you make a plan, set up a goal or constitute life-changing decisions, what is your will and who do you release information to about those plans and decisions? Is there an element of exclusivity in how you communicate or execute individual choices in life? Look at your life today, how many essential plans, ideas, strategies and decisions are you blurting out, that still need to process in your heart until your mind and strength catch up with the tune of your heart's beat concerning the matter? Are you aware that some of your plans, ideas and strategies need to be concealed in your heart and thoughts? Do you know which plans still need to remain on the shelf of your heart until it is the right time to share with others?

There are matters of the heart that still need to be cooked in the inner man, your spirit or your emotions before you release them into this earthly atmosphere. Beloved, how many times have you discussed an idea with people you were not exclusive with or who were not exclusive to that idea? How many times have you told your plans to people who were not in your inner circle?

YOU CAN BEGIN TO PUT EXCLUSIVITY TO USE TODAY

Cambridge dictionary defines exclusivity as **"the quality of being available only to a small number of people who are rich enough or considered good enough"**. Similarly, another reference goes on to define exclusivity by stating the following, **"the state of being the only person, group of people, or organisation that is allowed to have or do something"**.

Beloved, can you see how the parallel ethos of exclusivity through both definitions is grounded on setting boundaries and defining your relationships?

Often times, through ignorance, there can be an enigma that connects and associates exclusivity with riches and fame; as laid out by the Cambridge dictionary. Perhaps this may be due to the rich and famous being fostered by their positions in society to master how to use exclusivity to their advantage? Beloved, in God's kingdom, exclusivity is wisdom you can master in your own life. Being exclusive or making a particular area of your life exclusive can become a practice or even a trait that exudes a behaviour that works for you in every mould of your life. Today you can begin to use exclusivity in areas of your life by simply training yourself to know the position of everyone around you. This is only effective when you become aware of your surroundings and the relationships you have with the people in your life.

Awareness or in better terms—perception and godly discernment, play a vital role in your behaviour within the bracket of "exclusivity" leading to being private. It is not so much about how much you share but more so, "whom" you share "how much" with! The is due to the fact that applying exclusivity effectively in your life is determined by perceiving "the position" of everyone around you. Below are nine different levels you can begin to be aware of when applying exclusivity. In no particular order:

- Yourself

- Friends

- Pastors, mentors, therapists, counsellors and advisors

- Social media

- Family and relatives

- Acquaintances

- God

- Spouse

Now let's look at each of these levels in greater detail:

SHARE WITH YOURSELF

There are many desires in our hearts to share certain information. These burning desires can spring up fashioned as questions, concerns, ideas, memories, stories, dreams, visions or general day to day narratives. However, with all that internalised information bursting at the seams of our hearts and souls we can end up missing out on the virtue of "pondering" to self. Sometimes the urgency to share information comes through applied forms of pressure such as culture, upbringing, childhood backgrounds, religion, friendships and family values. However, through the Bible we can learn how to tame these urgencies. One of the most famous biblical figures who mastered the art of pondering about information was Mary, the mother of our LORD Jesus Christ. It's written:

The key focus scriptures are underlined

Now there were in the same country shepherds living out in the fields, keeping watch over their flock by night. And behold, an angel of the Lord stood before them, and the glory of the Lord shone around them, and they were greatly afraid. Then the angel said to them, "Do not be afraid, for behold, I bring you good tidings of great joy which will be to all people. For there is born to you this day in the city of David a Saviour, who is Christ the Lord. And this will be the sign to you: You will find a Babe wrapped in swaddling cloths, lying in a manger." And suddenly there was with the angel a multitude of the heavenly host praising God and saying: "Glory to God in the highest, And on earth peace, goodwill toward men!" So it was, when the angels had gone away from them into heaven, that the shepherds said to one another, "Let us now go to Bethlehem and see this thing that has come to pass, which the Lord has made known to us." And they came with haste and found Mary and Joseph, and the Babe lying in a manger. Now when they had seen Him, they made widely known the saying which was told them concerning this Child. <u>And all those who heard it marvelled at those things which were told them by the shepherds. But Mary kept all these things and pondered them in her heart.</u>

Luke 2:8-19 (NKJV)

Beloved, there is certain information conceived in us that is meant to be birthed only in the confinements of self; it was never meant to trespass outside of the safety of your heart and soul. Mary kept certain vital information in her heart regarding the prophetic Word which the shepherds had conveyed to her as declared to them by the angel; concerning our LORD Jesus Christ.

If you were being told these great words about the great destiny of what you are carrying inside of you, would you have found wisdom in keeping this to yourself or would you have told your relatives, friends, social media followers or co-workers? Ironically, the same scenario of Mary, the shepherds and the angel happens to you and me more often than we know. We hear extravagant and awe-striking news about the thing we are about to give birth to. Be it a new ministry, a business deal, a wedding, an educational degree, a plan, a spiritual gift or a new house. Regrettably, so many of us are being robbed because we tell the news too early to individuals who cannot discern (at that moment) the revelation, condition and value of what we are about to birth—people who have no capacity to believe in nourishing what we have just birthed.

Beloved, each time you are anxious to tell people sensitive information that is still meant to be concealed in your heart, you must always search your heart and find out where the motive and source of pressure to speak, is coming from.

Nowadays, we live in a very modern world that has access to tools that can compliment keeping information to self. These are tools such as journals and diaries. Are you someone who just can't keep things inside for long due to excitement or a personality that loves sharing your heart and mind with others? There's nothing wrong with your enthusiasm or your blessed ability to convey information so freely by being transparent. However, this is whereby you can utilise journaling. Diaries and journals are outlets if taken full advantage of, that can help us to release certain information bottled up inside that no one else needs to know or hear. Journaling and dairy-writing help not only to keep your thoughts organised but also aides you to record your ideas and plans and relieve stress. Allowing you to self-reflect and even manage personal changes!

Additionally, renown kings like king David used the method of speaking to self as a way of releasing information with the objective of self-encouragement. It's written:

> Why are you cast down, O my soul?
> And why are you disquieted within me?
> Hope in God;
> For I shall yet praise Him,
> The help of my countenance and my God.
> **Psalm 42:11 (NKJV)**

Beloved, what's your objective when you release information? There may be people in your life that feel obliged to your transparency before they offer encouragement, but you must know that you can speak encouragement to yourself and save yourself from expectations and demands of man! Having this attitude like David shifts you from relying on the wrong people speaking into your life who can steal, kill or destroy what is conceived inside of you! Like king David, we can give pep-talks to ourselves. Let's pray!

PRAYER

Father God, give me the understanding to know the difference between what to share with people and what I need to store inside until the right time. I know this requires self-control which is a fruit of the Spirit, and I ask that by Your Spirit You help me cultivate it and give me wisdom on how to exercise it through my words, thoughts and behaviour. Father, by Your Holy Spirit empower me to withstand the pressure of oversharing my life, dreams, plans and heart with people. Please teach me how to take captive the thoughts that ought not to share with anyone else except me by utilising tools such as journals, diaries and self-talk as I grow in the lessons of exclusivity. This I request in the name of Jesus, Amen.

SHARE WITH FRIENDS

The man of too many friends [chosen indiscriminately] will be broken in pieces and come to ruin, but there is a [true, loving] friend who [is reliable and] sticks closer than a brother.
Proverbs 18:24 (AMP)

Defining what a friend is, is the first step in knowing "whom" to share "how much" within the sphere of friendship. One of the most significant challenges we can face, when manoeuvring through life is defining who our friends are and who isn't our friend. Many a time, out of desperation for solidarity through friendship, some hand out "friendship" titles to spectators whom they have warmed up to in their hearts. They settle for mediocrity friendships. Spectators are people whose role in your life is to watch you. Your life is their show, and they have no capacity to add any value to it. Such individuals are nowhere to be seen when you are in severe, dark and dry seasons because they are programmed to only stick around for the highlight reels of your life; those moments are their entertainment.

Beloved, are you telling spectators and acquaintances your ideas, plans, thoughts and not getting back the words, reactions and behaviour of a "friend"? Does it seem as if your expectations are too high in certain friendships in your life? Are you not getting the harvest of what you are planting in your friends? If you answered yes, it's important to remember that no matter how great of a friend you are to him or her, a spectator's purpose is to spectate, he or she simply cannot play the role of a friend. You and your life are their show, and their part is to observe, add a few opinions here and there, then go. Hence why, when you tell your "friend" about your business idea, promotion, new venture, new relationship, new engagement or new plan; he or she cannot support you. Your "friend" cannot comprehend it! As a result of this, you may find that you are rummaging through your so-called friendship managing their negativity, jealousy, insecurity, envy, bad moods, outbursts or irritation. Your friendship seems to now be like an academic essay assignment! You can no longer casually mention the great things happening in your life, lest you offend him or her. If this is the kind of friendship you have, it is dysfunctional, and you are settling!

Sadly, some of us Christians have gone into dangerous territories of abuse, bitterness, unforgiveness and hatred simply because we expected too much from individuals who are not capable of being a friend. Beloved, do not allow a lousy friendship to cause you to accommodate sin in your heart. The Bible lays a foundation of what friendship is. We see throughout the Bible that God had a standard when it comes to friendships. Do you have a standard for your friendships? God takes friendship so seriously such that He calls three types of people in the Bible, His friend:

1.   Abraham

Was not Abraham our father justified by works when he offered Isaac his son on the altar? Do you see that faith was working together with his works, and by works, faith was made perfect? And the Scripture was fulfilled, which says, "Abraham believed God, and it was accounted to him for righteousness." And he was called the friend of God. You see then that a man is justified by works, and not by faith only.
James 2:21-24 (NKJV)

2.   Moses

So the Lord spoke to Moses face to face, as a man speaks to His friend. And he would return to the camp, but his servant Joshua the son of Nun, a young man, did not depart from the tabernacle.
Exodus 33:11 (NKJV)

3.   Christians (disciples) who do His commands

"I am the true vine, and My Father is the vinedresser. Every branch in Me that does not bear fruit He takes away; and every branch that bears fruit He prunes, that it may bear more fruit. You are already clean because of the word which I have spoken to you. Abide in Me, and I in you. As the branch cannot bear fruit of itself, unless it abides in the vine, neither can you, unless you abide in Me. "I am the vine, you are the branches. He who abides in Me, and I in him, bears much fruit; for without Me you can do nothing. If anyone does not abide in Me, he is cast out as a branch and is withered; and they gather them and throw them into the fire, and they are burned. If you abide in Me, and My words abide in you, you will ask what you desire, and it shall be done for you. By this My Father is glorified, that you bear much fruit; so you will be My disciples. "As the Father loved Me, I also have loved you; abide in My love. If you keep My commandments, you will abide in My love, just as I have kept My Father's commandments and abide in His love. "These things I have spoken to you, that My joy may remain in you, and that your joy may be full. This is My commandment, that you love one another as I have loved you. Greater love has no one than this, than to lay down one's life for his friends. You are My friends if you do whatever I command you. No longer do I call you servants, for a servant does not know what his master is doing; but I have called you friends, for all things that I heard from My Father I have made known to you.

John 15:14 (NKJV)

If we study these three types of people, we will find some common ground. They all had to prove something by paying the price of trust. Be it through their loyalty, motives and vision; in alignment with God's. Abraham's proof is through believing in God. It's only after passing the test of faith that God began to call Abraham His friend! Beloved, do your so-called friends believe in you?

Moses' proof is through his humility and obedience to God. His relationship with God is one of a kind, emblemed by transparency, whereby God speaks to Moses face to face! Beloved, how soon do you hand out a "friend" title before testing if they can handle your real face? Your true face behind the bright smile, the calm eyes and steady countenance?

Lastly, we who believe in Jesus Christ are His friends when we walk in unison with God. Those whom you are defining as friends in your life, do they have faith in you, is there a friendship system in place that regulates good obedience and is their walk with you in unity or disagreement?

On the contrary, what kind of friend are you to others? Jesus Christ is our blueprint and is the standard of a true friend. We should all learn from Him! While on earth, He was amiable, compassionate, down to earth and humble. The LORD Jesus is a friend to the sick and the healthy, the poor and the rich, the influential and the unknown, the sinners and the saved, the weary and the strong. Beloved, you too can practice compassion, humility, friendliness to those who deserve it and those who don't deserve it. As Christians, you and I have the grace to love all.

The King of kings would get invited into different homes for lunch, dinner and fellowship by different kinds of people. He is truly the light of the world and fitted in everywhere! Yet, He had three disciples He was close to; Peter, John and James. He entrusted them with secrets, responsibility and revelations. Child of God, your purpose will require you to shed certain friends, forcing you to discern whom you can entrust with your secrets, defined responsibilities and aspects of you within your friendship circle. Just like Jesus was friends with many people, but His purpose demanded a certain level of transparency to only three of those many people. It would help if you too used this same wisdom. When you discover your mission in life, you will no longer speak anyhow to anyone.

Hence, when you know your purpose, your friendships become like a two-sided coin. One side resembles the friends that see your face. These are they who understand you and whose thoughts of you are conditional to your behaviour towards them. For example, if you are a natural giver, these kinds of people will like you, but if your finances are affected and you can no longer be as generous, these kinds of people will disappear.

Then the other side of the coin of friendship resembles the friends that see and know your symbol. These are they who know your mission, your purpose, your mind, your heart; the real you veiled behind the face. For example, they know that you are a giver, and if for some reason, you are unable to be as generous, they understand your heart and won't be offended if you don't give a birthday or Christmas present. So then, you can be everybody's friend but yet have a few friends. Discover those few friends today. Let's pray!

PRAYER

Father, I thank You that you have poured out Your love in my heart by Your Spirit. You have made me a candidate of love to others, and I pray that You teach me by Your Spirit how to talk, behave and think in this love towards others whether they are my friends or not. For those whom I have labelled as my friends reveal to me their hearts. Help me distinguish between friends and spectators in my life. Protect me from pretenders and bad company masquerading as friends. Expose and deliver me from every friend in my life right now who is assigned by Satan. Bring into my life individuals who can be valid and authentic friends, for Your glory. Amen.

SHARE WITH YOUR PASTOR, MENTOR, ADVISOR OR THERAPIST

The Word of God encourages counselling to the point of warning us of the predicament of a downfall if there is little to no counsel. Moreover, it highlights the inevitability of success when there is a multitude of counsellors. Unfortunately, some Christians and people, in general, have been conditioned to assume that advise, counsel, therapy and mentorship should be on an "if it is not broke don't fix it" basis. Yet, you will find some of these same individuals running to their family members, friends or spouses with questions, problems, confidential conflicts and trauma that only a Pastor, Counsellor, Mentor, Advisor or Therapist is equipped to handle, listen to and help solve.

Knowing the purpose of a Pastor, mentor, advisor, counsellor, or therapist can help us define many of the relationships that have become displaced in our lives. Relationships can become dislodged when we are no longer aware of what defines them. Many a time, people are turning their friends into their therapists and as a result, fail to achieve the results they need because the friend cannot provide the kind of empathy, patience and discretion that a trained therapist can provide. Beloved, are you expecting your friends to tackle the trauma you are still carrying from your childhood? Friendships can become overbearing and somewhat imbalanced, especially in seasons when the friend in need is seeking therapy from an unqualified but great friend. You see, no matter how great your mother, friend, best friend, husband or manager is; are they qualified spiritually, mentally or physically to be your Pastor or mentor? Can you discern if there is capacity in the individuals in your life whom you seek counsel and advise from, to tackle your issues?

This is where the art of exclusivity can become efficient, starting with correctly identifying the need. Is your need one for financial advice? Perhaps, it is marital or relationship counsel? Maybe spiritual clarity for a significant life decision? Is it mentorship for personal growth? Is it something you need to ask the Holy Spirit? Now, look around your life and outside your sphere of influence, with soberness. Check who is equipped to step in the shoes of your need; according to God's will.

On the other hand, there is precise insight, wisdom and direction that can come from those who are not necessarily qualified by a degree, a title or experience but are qualified by God to help you. Yet, it's just up to you to "discern" these kinds of people. The Bible illustrates such relationships through the life of Ruth and Naomi, her ex-mother-in-law. Ruth had suddenly become a young widow with no children. She was now living with her mother-in-law, who was also a widow but in her old age. Ruth decided to believe the God of Naomi, to follow her failure of a mother-in-law (failure according to society and logic) and to marry into her people if the opportunity arises; illustrated through her words here:

The key focus scriptures are underlined

Then she arose with her daughters-in-law that she might return from the country of Moab, for she had heard in the country of Moab that the Lord had visited His people by giving them bread. Therefore she went out from the place where she was, and her two daughters-in-law with her; and they went on the way to return to the land of Judah. And Naomi said to her two daughters-in-law, "Go, return each to her mother's house. The Lord deal kindly with you, as you have dealt with the dead and with me. The Lord grant that you may find rest, each in the house of her husband." So she kissed them, and they lifted up their voices and wept. And they said to her, "Surely, we will return with you to your people." But Ruth said: <u>"Entreat me not to leave you, Or to turn back from following after you; For wherever you go, I will go; And wherever you lodge, I will lodge; Your people shall be my people, And your God, my God. Where you die, I will die, And there will I be buried. The Lord do so to me, and more also, If anything but death parts you and me."</u> When she saw that she was determined to go with her, she stopped speaking to her.

Ruth 1:6-18 (NKJV)

Ruth had a marital need, but the person who positioned her to receive a breakthrough in that area of urgency did not look qualified nor relevant. God used an unusual situation and woman to lift and prosper Ruth. Indeed, Naomi gave Ruth marital advise that changed her life forever! She told Ruth where to meet her husband, what time to arrive at the place of appointment, what to wear when she goes, what to notice once she sees him and where to go when she sees him. It's written:

The key focus scriptures are underlined

Then, Naomi, her mother-in-law said to her, <u>"My daughter, shall I not seek security for you,</u> that it may be well with you? Now Boaz, whose young women you were with, is he not our relative? In fact, he is winnowing barley tonight at the threshing floor. <u>Therefore wash yourself and anoint yourself, put on your best garment and go down to the threshing floor; but do not make yourself known to the man until he has finished eating and drinking. Then it shall be, when he lies down, that you shall notice the place where he lies; and you shall go in, uncover his feet, and lie down; and he will tell you what you should do.</u>" And she said to her, "All that you say to me I will do." So she went down to the threshing floor and did according to all that her mother-in-law instructed her. And after Boaz had eaten and drunk, and his heart was cheerful, he went to lie down at the end of the heap of grain; and she came softly, uncovered his feet, and lay down. Now it happened at midnight that the man was startled, and turned himself; and there, a woman was lying at his feet. And he said, "Who are you?" So she answered, "I am Ruth, your maidservant. Take your maidservant under your wing, for you are a close relative." Then he said, "Blessed are you of the Lord, my daughter! For you have shown more kindness at the end than at the beginning, in that you did not go after young men, whether poor or rich. And now, my daughter, do not fear. I will do for you all that you request, for all the people of my town know that you are a virtuous woman. Now it is true that I am a close relative; however, there is a relative closer than I. Stay this night, and in the morning it shall be that if he will perform the duty of a close relative for you—good; let him do it. But if he does not want to perform the duty for you, then I will perform the duty for you, as the Lord lives! Lie down until morning." So she lay at his feet until morning, and she arose before one could recognise another. Then he said, "Do not let it be known that the woman came to the threshing floor." Also he said, "Bring the shawl that is on you and hold it." And when she held it, he measured six ephahs of barley, and laid it on her. Then she went into the city.

Ruth 3:1-15 (NKJV)

Child of God, God can do the same for you if you train your eyes to see people the way He sees them. Can you discern who around your sphere of influence has the key to a locked door in this season of your life? Though not qualified, there are people God can use in your life right now to correctly place the right pieces on the puzzle of your season right now. They can help you discover:

- How to define your breakthrough

- Where to meet your breakthrough

- What time to arrive at your breakthrough

- How to behave in the vicinity of your breakthrough

- How to dress for your breakthrough

- How to speak towards your breakthrough

There are people in your life who have the capacity to invoke a marital miracle, a financial miracle, a healing miracle or a spiritual breakthrough; by their counsel, advise, guidance, leadership and mentorship. Your awareness of these kinds of people is critical! Let's pray.

PRAYER

Heavenly Father, help me by Your Holy Spirit to discern the areas in my life that need therapy, counsel, advise and leadership that is beyond what my friends, family and acquaintances can offer me. Like Naomi positioned Ruth, LORD God lead me to the right people who can position me to my place of relevance, deliverance, healing, breakthrough and true-identity. Help me to discern the treasures in the lives of those who are around me, just as Ruth noticed the treasure in the life of her mother-in-law Naomi so that I don't miss out on what You want to do in my life through these individuals. Father God, I commit my eyes, ears and mouth to You; empower them with Your counsel, wisdom, understanding and truth, Amen.

SHARE WITH SOCIAL MEDIA

There is a saying that goes, "once you post something on the internet, it stays there forever even if you change your mind and delete it later on." To a certain extent, this is a faithful saying seeing as the internet is like a time capsule. One simply can't delete small fragments from their computer because the world wide web can keep a record of deleted posts, pictures, messages and so on through various websites and applications. With that in mind, social media is a powerful and innovative tool of the internet that allows you and me to share different types of information and content instantly publicly. So then, we are all faced with the dilemma of how much or how little of our lives, we ought to share on social media.

> In the multitude of words sin is not lacking,
> But he who restrains his lips is wise.
> **Proverbs 10:19 (NKJV)**

We are living in the height of an internet culture that makes it challenging to foster restraint due to how "social media" is engineered. For example, applications such as Twitter, Instagram and Facebook readily employ access to your photographs, microphone and camera on your device. They give you an informed choice to instantly post a piece of your life in the form of words, pictures or videos!

Hence, it is essential in this generation, more than ever, to establish the purpose of social media in our personal lives. Beloved, what is the goal of social media to you? Is it to keep in touch with family and friends? To minister the gospel? To share highlight reels of your life? To grow your brand? To intentionally make people jealous and envious of you? To stalk other people? For malice in the form of gossip, abuse, scorn and bullying? Why do you log on, browse and post on social media? Establishing the purpose of why you use social media is the first step in defining the relationship you have with social media. This is vital to evaluate how you express yourself on social media. Without discovering the primary cause for social media in your life, you can end up making a caricature of yourself on social media.

Secondly, what is the motive behind what you say and how you use social media? When our motives are impure, ungodly and displaced, we can lose track of the purpose of social media as we feed an unhealthy obsession or need for attention— for example, telling social media the things that need to be shared with a best friend, spouse or counsellor.

Beloved, are you turning social media into your best friend, lover, counsellor or diary; in your head? Have you lost sight of the reality of social media being a digital social space with a collective number of individuals? Indeed, the reality is that everyone on social media is not your best friend or in as much, your friend, even if you are perfect, sinless and overflowing with unconditional love like the LORD Jesus Christ Himself! Putting social media on a pedestal of "best friend" is distorted and if I may say, a flawed definition of a best friend.

Therefore, the need for attention, if not controlled under the fruit of the Holy Spirit named "self-control", breeds delusion. If one is not careful, that delusion can soon turn into idolatry. Whereby an individual uses social media as a form of therapy, as a substitute for a friend, as a void for loneliness or as a boost for low self-esteem. In fact, without prudence and awareness, it is easy to fall into the derision of making the collective space of social media into a person, title or a god. This almost always becomes mentally and emotionally taxing to the one who has misplaced his or her priorities.

Beloved, the Holy Spirit wants to teach you today how to use social media in a healthy and non-deviant way that will work for you and not against you. The Holy Spirit is able to counsel and lead you in how to express yourself on social media in a practical, constructive and non-competitive way. Will you involve the Holy Spirit in your social life on the internet? He wants to lose the chains that are holding you addictive to social media to the point where you share things that are only appropriate for a spouse. Today, you can have a complete makeover from inside. Let's pray!

PRAYER

LORD Jesus, Your Word says that in the multitude of words, sin is not lacking, but he who restrains his lips is wise. Help me to keep my life, sanity, contentment, peace and authenticity in a world that is mesmerised by likes, comments, statuses and followers. Father, help me by Your Holy Spirit to be wise in how I portray and express myself on social media. Grant me Your wisdom, understanding and peace. Help me to use discretion in what I say and how much I share on social media. By Your Word and Holy Spirit, fill the voids within me so that delusion, dependency or social media idolatry; won't find room in my heart. LORD Jesus, from today, sit on the throne of my heart and transform my personality, spirit, character for Your glory, Amen.

SHARE WITH A FAMILY AND RELATIVES

There is a saying that goes " blood is thicker than water", meaning that family relationships and loyalties are the strongest and most important ones. Unfortunately, that is not always the reality. Just because you are related to somebody does not mean that they have the same mindset as you, same understanding as you or the same desires for you. We see a classic example that dismantles this popular family ideology through the life of Joseph and his eleven brothers below:

The key focus scriptures are underlined

Now Joseph had a dream, and he told it to his brothers, and they hated him even more. So he said to them, "Please hear this dream which I have dreamed: There we were, binding sheaves in the field. Then behold, my sheaf arose and also stood upright; and indeed, your sheaves stood all around and bowed down to my sheaf." And his brothers said to him, "Shall you indeed reign over us? Or shall you indeed have dominion over us?" So they hated him even more for his dreams and for his words. Then he dreamed still another dream and told it to his brothers, and said, "Look, I have dreamed another dream. And this time, the sun, the moon, and the eleven stars bowed down to me." So he told it to his father and his brothers; and his father rebuked him and said to him, "What is this dream that you have dreamed? Shall your mother and I and your brothers indeed come to bow down to the earth before you?" And his brothers envied him, but his father kept the matter in mind.

Genesis 37:5-11 (NKJV)

Joseph shared information with his brothers in the hopes of getting back some encouragement, positive affirmations, confirmation, interpretation and support concerning his dreams, but unfortunately, this only triggered envy, hate, undermining and questions. Beloved, just because they are your blood, it doesn't guarantee their loyalty to you. Just because they grew up with you doesn't ensure their support for you. Can you discern when to share, how much with, to your relatives? There is a danger with sharing information with relatives that are not on the same page as your words, dreams, vision, decisions and plans. Sharing this kind of information can conceive contempt, envy and jealousy in them. The Bible sheds light on families for Christians who choose to live for Jesus:

"Do not think that I came to bring peace on earth. I did not come to bring peace but a sword. For I have come to 'set a man against his father, a daughter against her mother, and a daughter-in-law against her mother-in-law'; and 'a man's enemies will be those of his own household.'
Matthew 10:34-36 (NKJV)

As you may know in the case of Joseph, everything was God's will and Joseph ended up as a ruler in Egypt just as he saw in his dreams. On the contrary, you are not Joseph, you are (insert your name). How do you know that you will make it like Joseph, when you share information with relatives who don't understand God's plan for you? When it comes to what we share with family and when we share what we share with family, it's important to discern who to speak with about your plans, ideas, breakthroughs, success, vision, dreams and goals. Share these with a relative or family member who speaks the same language as you! When Mary had a visitation from the angel Gabriel, she didn't go to her parents who were organising her wedding to her soon husband-to-be. Mary was led to speak to her cousin Elizabeth about her extraordinary encounter, her prophetic

Word and future plans! At that time, Elizabeth was now pregnant, carrying John the Baptist who would be the messenger who prepares the way for the LORD Jesus. As soon as Mary greeted Elizabeth, the babe inside Elizabeth's womb leaped and became filled with the Holy Spirit, Elizabeth also began to prophesy. This was not about blood being thicker than water but about Elizabeth understanding the language of Mary! It's written:

The key focus scriptures are underlined

Then Mary said to the angel, "How can this be, since I do not know a man?" And the angel answered and said to her, "The Holy Spirit will come upon you, and the power of the Highest will overshadow you; therefore, also, that Holy One who is to be born will be called the Son of God. Now indeed, Elizabeth your relative has also conceived a son in her old age; and this is now the sixth month for her who was called barren. For with God nothing will be impossible." Then Mary said, "Behold the maidservant of the Lord! Let it be to me according to your word." And the angel departed from her. <u>Now Mary arose in those days and went into the hill country with haste, to a city of Judah, and entered the house of Zacharias and greeted Elizabeth. And it happened, when Elizabeth heard the greeting of Mary, that the babe leaped in her womb; and Elizabeth was filled with the Holy Spirit.</u> Then she spoke out with a loud voice and said, "Blessed are you among women, and blessed is the fruit of your womb! But why is this granted to me, that the mother of my Lord should come to me? For indeed, as soon as the voice of your greeting sounded in my ears, the babe leaped in my womb for joy. Blessed is she who believed, for there will be a fulfilment of those things which were told her from the Lord."

Luke 1:35-44 (NKJV)

Mary spoke to Elizabeth, her cousin, she didn't go her husband-to-be Joseph because he wouldn't have understood what God was saying and doing in that season of her life. Sometimes even our closest family, in the form of our children and our spouse; may not be the right people to tell certain things that God is doing. This needs God's wisdom and maturity because He may require you to not tell anyone about what He is saying to you, until the right time and season.

Similarly, in the case of Abraham when God told him to sacrifice his son Isaac. Abraham had to use wisdom and did not tell anyone what God was saying in his season of being tested.

The key focus scriptures are underlined

Now it came to pass after these things that God tested Abraham, and said to him, "Abraham!" And he said, "Here I am." Then He said, "Take now your son, your only son Isaac, whom you love, and go to the land of Moriah, and offer him there as a burnt offering on one of the mountains of which I shall tell you." So Abraham rose early in the morning and saddled his donkey, and took two of his young men with him, and Isaac his son; and he split the wood for the burnt offering, and arose and went to the place of which God had told him. Then on the third day, Abraham lifted his eyes and saw the place afar off. And Abraham said to his young men, "Stay here with the donkey; the lad and I will go yonder and worship, and we will come back to you."

Genesis 22:1-5 (NKJV)

Beloved, in your season of testing, if you tell certain relatives what God is saying or doing in your life, will they truly understand? Would Sarah have accepted Abraham's direction and understood his test, especially since Isaac was her only child that she waited ninety years to have? We must allow the Holy Spirit to direct us on who to share certain things within our families. Beloved, as God continues to usher you into new seasons of life, discern who to speak to in your family, when to speak and what to speak. Let's pray!

PRAYER

Most High God, You are the creator of the universe, everything in it and everyone in it. You know the hearts of all humanity, including my very own relatives and family. Father help me to discern who in my family is for me and who is on the same page as me. Joseph told his family the dreams You gave him, and instead of affirming and supporting him, they plotted to kill him but you protected him. Protect me Father. Do not allow me to tell my dreams to family members who will steal, kill or destroy those dreams, ideas and plans You give me. Lead me as You lead Mary to Elizabeth, to the right relatives and family members who speak the same language not only with me but also the same language as You! LORD God, I pray You deliver and protect me from the mistakes I made in the past, telling things rashly to my relatives, things I should not have told them. This I pray in the name of Jesus, Amen.

SHARE WITH ACQUAINTANCES

The Cambridge dictionary describes acquaintance as "a person that you have met but do not know well". Unfortunately, out to convenience, many people often define people they have met but don't know very well, as friends. Convenience in the form of how nice they are to you, how generous they are to you, how successful they are, how popular they are, how you grew up in the same neighbourhood or how you both attend the same church, school, job or events. Being nice, popular, successful, attending the same functions and being in the same places is not a conduit for friendship.

Beloved, do you share your secrets, plans, life and ideas that are exclusively fit for friendship circles with individuals who are not yet proven friends even though they are very nice? The Bible warns us through the life of king Hezekiah about the dangers of being overly open with people who are only acquaintances. It's written:

The key focus scriptures are underlined

At that time Berodach-Baladan the son of Baladan, <u>king of Babylon, sent letters and a present to Hezekiah, for he heard that Hezekiah had been sick. And Hezekiah was attentive to them,</u> and showed them all the house of his treasures—the silver and gold, the spices and precious ointment, and all his armoury—all that was found among his treasures. <u>There was nothing in his house or in all his dominion that Hezekiah did not show them.</u> Then Isaiah the prophet went to King Hezekiah, and said to him, "What did these men say, and from where did they come to you?" So Hezekiah said, "They came from a far country, from Babylon." And he said, "What have they seen in your house?" So Hezekiah answered, "They have seen all that is in my house; there is nothing among my treasures that I have not shown them." Then Isaiah said to Hezekiah, "Hear the word of the Lord: <u>'Behold, the days are coming when all that is in your house, and what your fathers have accumulated until this day, shall be carried to Babylon; nothing shall be left,</u>' says the Lord.

2 kings 20:12-17 (NKJV)

The son of the king of Babylon was kind and giving when he heard Hezekiah was sick. In life, there will be people around your life who are not necessarily your friends, but they carry a kind personality, loving character and giving nature but this does not mean that you know them enough to be your friends. Hezekiah allowed presents and words via letters from Berodach-Baladan to beguile his judgement and open up not only his home but the secrets of his house to an enemy! Beloved, do not allow presents and flattering words to provoke you into revealing the treasures of your heart to people who are not your friends! The Bible warns us of flatterers and puts them in the same category as gossipers saying:

He who goes about as a talebearer reveals secrets;
Therefore do not associate with one who flatters with his lips.
Proverbs 20:19 (NKJV)

Have you allowed similarities and personalities to mesmerise you into revealing pieces of silver and gold attached to your destiny to people whom you do not know very well? Is that work colleague that you tell all the latest news about what's happening in your love life; meant to know all that information? That church brother or sister that you are trying to force a friendship out of, would this still be the case if you didn't go to the same church? Is this forced friendship a classic case of convenience?

The prophet Jeremiah laments to God concerning his acquaintances whom he discovered to be frauds! At his lowest season they were planning to denounce him by throwing him under the bus to see him fall! It's written:

For I heard many mocking: "Fear on every side!" "Report," they say, "and we will report it!" All my acquaintances watched for my stumbling, saying, "Perhaps he can be induced; Then we will prevail against him, And we will take our revenge on him."
Jeremiah 20:10 (NKJV)

Now, not all acquaintances are like the acquittances of Jeremiah. However, as with all relationships, character is the focal point to the demise or success of a friendship. Understand that acquaintances are not friends. Are the people in your life genuine friends, or are they just acquaintances? Today is an opportunity to look around your life soberly and put in place the misplaced relationships that accurately fit in the category of acquaintance. You can begin to practice exclusivity by simply setting boundaries which will require you to scale back in how open you are with people you do not know very well. Let's pray!

PRAYER

Father, by Your Holy Spirit, help me to discern between acquaintances and friends. Empower me to evaluate every friendship that I have formed in order to distinguish those who are acquaintances and those who are indeed my friends. Help me to be patient in growing genuine friendships that are not built on convenience but on loyalty, trust, love and goodness. Teach me how to conduct myself with acquaintances, give me wisdom in how to express myself with acquaintances whilst being true to the character and personality that you gave me. King Hezekiah gave too much of himself to acquaintances that did not have his best interests, and this harvested trouble in his kingdom. Father, protect me from acquaintances who seek to do me harm and who add no value to my life. In the same way, create in me capacity to be an authentic and godly acquaintance to others. This I pray in Jesus name, amen.

SHARE WITH A SPOUSE

Marriage comes with a manual that only the Holy Spirit can help a couple to adhere to, in order to harvest a reality of seasons of enjoyment, peace, joy and happiness in their marriage. Those who choose to become married can benefit from having the mind of Christ as they live and build their marriage. One of the most critical sections in the unique manual of a couple's marriage is adhering to the exclusivity of a marriage covenant. Exclusivity that calls a couple to perceive that besides God, there is no one more important to a husband than his wife, likewise, there is no one more important to a wife than her husband. This is why it's written:

The key focus scriptures are underlined

But if you do marry, you have not sinned [in doing so]; and if a virgin marries, she has not sinned [in doing so]. Yet those [who marry] will have troubles (special <u>challenges</u>) in this life, and I am trying to spare you that. But I say this, believers: the time has been shortened, so that from now on even those who have wives should be as though they did not; and those who weep, as though they did not weep; and those who rejoice, as though they did not rejoice; and those who buy, as though they did not possess [anything]; and those who use the world [taking advantage of its opportunities], as though they did not make full use of it. For the outward form of this world [its present social and material nature] is passing away. But I want you to be free from concern. The unmarried man is concerned about the things of the Lord, how he may please the Lord; but <u>the married man is concerned about worldly things, how he may please his wife</u>, and his interests are divided. The unmarried woman or the virgin is concerned about the matters of the Lord, how to be holy and set apart both in body and in spirit; but <u>a married woman is concerned about worldly things, how she may please her husband</u>.
1 Corinthians 7:28-34 (AMP)

Problems begin to arise in homes, marriages and the personal lives of couples who don't apply the exclusivity of marriage and the boundaries of oneness that the title "husband and wife" carries. When spouses comprehend that their parents, pastors, children, relatives, friends, business partners or any other human being; are not more important their spouse, that understanding will regulate how they convey and handle information outside of the confinements of their marriage. For instance, you can't tell a best friend things that you need to speak with your spouse about. This is due to the seemingly apparent reason of differing relationship heights between a friendship and a marriage; though somewhat interchangeable in the sense that a spouse can be a best friend too.

Now, one might argue that they speak more to their best friend and are closer to their best friend than they are to their spouse. This may be very true for incompatibility reasons such as different perspectives, lack of transparency, past or present trauma, infidelity, unfaithfulness, financial illiteracy, lack of loyalty, uncomplimentary personalities and so on; in a marriage. So you find that the best friend is filling that void that the spouse cannot fill. However, despite the valid differences, weakness, flaws and transgressions in a marriage, one cannot substitute their spouse with a best friend. As Christians, we ought to define our relationships according to God's standard. The standard of God establishes the covenant of marriage as closer than friendship, as expressed here:

"Therefore a man shall leave his father and mother and be joined to his wife, and they shall become one flesh".
Genesis 2:23 (NKJV)

A husband and wife are one. Married couples are one flesh with their spouse; they are not "one flesh" with their best friend whom they are not married to, no matter how faithful and close the best friend is to them! Beloved, perhaps you are not yet married, but you can start renewing your mind today in how you speak and behave towards marriage. Is there past trauma, hurt, unforgiveness, weaknesses, cultural differences, financial mistakes, traditional practices; that can potentially hinder you from the transparency that is required towards your future spouse? Remember, biblically, a spouse is your first priority once you are married. Then together as a team of husband and wife, your child(ren) will be your first priority. Is there a possibility that the position of a future spouse can become displaced? Maybe you are already married? Is one or more of the issues mentioned hindering you from experiencing the joy and peace that exclusivity brings in marriage? The Holy Spirit is present and ready to usher you into a peaceful place which begins inside of you and overflow into your marriage. Let's pray!

PRAYER

Father God, I thank you for my spouse and that you have called me to display your glory of oneness in marriage even as the Church and Christ are one. Help my marriage / future marriage to clearly demonstrate the revelation of unity. Teach me by Your Spirit to put my spouse first before anyone else. Teach me not to make him / her an idol. Show me where I have neglected the lines of communication by being transparent with other people in a way that is only appropriate with my spouse. Holy Spirit power of God, deliver me from trauma, sickness, idolatry, sin and error that was blocking me from trusting, loving and being completely open without shame according to Your original standard of marriage in the garden of Eden. Show me the mysteries of transparency in marriage. Help me and teach me by Your Spirit to discern when my transparency with people or the internet becomes threatening and detrimental to my marriage. This I pray in Jesus name, Amen.

SHARE WITH GOD

While there may be issues with oversharing our lives with the wrong people or with social media, the real common problem we have in Christendom is that many of us don't have a lot to share with God! God Almighty is pushed into the corner of many people's hearts. For example, when an individual has a breakthrough or an answered prayer, quite often, some individuals run to social media to announce the breakthrough, one may immediately call a close friend, another tells their spouse, while others exalt the Pastor who helped them to pray about the breakthrough. God is suddenly kicked out once we begin to glory in the answered prayer. Sadly, the LORD God has been perverted into a magician with a wand; in the lives of many Christians. Some only go to Him when they need something. Beloved, have you distorted the loving-kindness, power and grace of God into a mockery?

The bible speaks of ten lepers who were healed but only one out of ten went back to Jesus to thank Him for the healing. Likewise, how many of us Christians practice sharing themselves selflessly to/with God by going to Him in worship, thanksgiving or praise?

The key focus scriptures are underlined
Now it happened as He went to Jerusalem that He passed through the midst of Samaria and Galilee. Then as He entered a certain village, there met Him ten men who were lepers, who stood afar off. And they lifted up their voices and said, "Jesus, Master, have mercy on us!" So when He saw them, He said to them, "Go, show yourselves to the priests." And so it was that as they went, they were cleansed. <u>And one of them, when he saw that he was healed, returned, and</u>

with a loud voice glorified God, and fell down on his face at His feet, giving Him thanks. And he was a Samaritan. So Jesus answered and said, "Were there not ten cleansed? But where are the nine? Were there not any found who returned to give glory to God except this foreigner?" And He said to him, "Arise, go your way. Your faith has made you well."
Luke 17:11-19 (NKJV)

On the other hand, Some who desired marriage and waited for marriage, when they finally got married, they abandoned God and made their spouse their god. The spouse has become their life bible and oxygen. They hardly speak to God about things that only God deserves to hear. No longer do they tell Him their worries or fears. They are too busy to thank Him for their day to day wins! Jesus has become a past time in their lives. Beloved, how much do you share with God? Do His Sovereignty and omnipotence cause you to neglect transparency on your part? No matter how God-fearing, God-loving, thoughtful, humble, kind and loving the one you love is, no matter how beautiful your garden of Eden (your marriage in private when God is the only audience) is, remember, the one you love is not your saving grace. Jesus Christ is your "only" saving grace. Jesus is the worthy and proven "True Love". Jesus is the One who brings true happiness and joy that no amazing boyfriend/girlfriend, fiancé/fiancée or husband/wife can ever deliver. Jesus touches areas of the heart, spirit and mind that no man or woman can ever reach. Let the LORD Jesus be enthroned at the centre of your heart; yes, as your first love!

God is greater than all things and all people, and there are just some situations, circumstances, seasons and types of information that He alone can carry. There are things God wants to speak with you about, spiritual experiences He wants to show you, signs and wonders He wants to reveal to you, but He needs you! God requires the real you! He longs to have day to day encounters with you! The Holy Spirit of God is a Person and now lives in you when you believe in the only Begotten Son of God; He wants a relationship and fellowship with you!

PRAYER

Father God, You are seeking true worshippers. I repent of reducing Your kind and loving nature into a microwave system for my immediate needs and wants. I repent of talking to You, seeking You and spending time with You the most; when I need something. I have been selfish, and from today I repent and ask that You help me by Your Spirit to appreciate You, to worship You in spirit and truth. I choose to follow Your leading in all seasons of my life. Show me by Your Spirit the lengths, width, depths and heights of Your love for me so that I will not be afraid to tell You anything, whether big, small or irrelevant. Before I run to my friends and acquaintances, before I run to social media, before I run to relatives, before I run to a therapist, before I run to my Pastor and before I run to my spouse; please enlighten me by your Holy Spirit to run to You first! Draw me close by Your Spirit so that I may have a growing and deeper relationship with You. Teach me the secrets of making You my first love, in Jesus name I pray, Amen.

CHAPTER 3

The Art of Knowing When To Speak and When To Be Quiet

The key focus scriptures are underlined
To everything there is a season,
A time for every purpose under heaven:
A time to be born,
And a time to die;
A time to plant,
And a time to pluck what is planted;
A time to kill,
And a time to heal;
A time to break down,
And a time to build up;
A time to weep,
And a time to laugh;
A time to mourn,
And a time to dance;
A time to cast away stones,
And a time to gather stones;
A time to embrace,
And a time to refrain from embracing;
A time to gain,
And a time to lose;
A time to keep,
And a time to throw away;
A time to tear,

And a time to sew;
A time to keep silence,
And a time to speak;
A time to love,
And a time to hate;
A time of war,
And a time of peace.
Ecclesiastes 3:1-8 (NKJV)

To every time in our personal lives, whether looking at the time through the lens of a country, generation, an era, lifestyle, family background, particular culture, an economic climate, a day, a month or a year; there ought to be exercised times and moments of keeping silent and those of speaking.

A TIME TO BE SILENT

The Hebrew word used in the Bible for silence is **chashah** which means:

- to be silent,

- quiet,

- to be still,

- to rest,

- inactive,

These five expressions of silence can be applied on a day to day basis as wisdom within the foundations of being private. In your personal life, have you mastered times and moments of being silent and of speaking? Have you understood the beauty, importance and wisdom of exercising such moments? Be it to colleagues, friends, relatives, a Pastor, family members, opportunities or social media platforms? Sometimes people assume that being private is characterised by being secretive but being private is vaster than that. It can be as simple as taking time away from social media and friends by being inactive or resting. The word silent in Hebrew when translated has one of its expression as "inactive". This can be applied to today's social media era.

Some individuals cannot go two days without being inactive on their Facebook, Twitter or Instagram account. They are active daily and have not yet trained themselves to exercise seasons of being inactive. Being active is just as

crucial as being inactive on social media, and it's so vital for individuals to

practically apply this wisdom concerning the purpose of social media. Beloved,

your life and time are essential, hence, don't use your time wastefully, consumed

by spending hours a day scrolling, browsing and posting information on social

media, when that time could be used to be more productive. When was the last

time you were inactive on your social media platforms just to rest mentally or

emotionally?

One of the expressions of silence, when translated from Hebrew, is rest. Ask

yourself, "how can I apply more rest in my life? Sometimes due to the demands of

life such as caring for children, working a job, ministry, education, careers, daily

needs and wants, financial constraints, health problems and so on; how we relate

to rest can become obscured. Perhaps you are one of the many individuals who

has ruled out rest because your current circumstances can hardly accommodate it?

Cambridge dictionary defines rest as "to (cause someone or something to) stop

doing a particular activity or stop being active for a period of time in order to relax

and get back your strength". Rightly so, your body and mind need rest from time

to time to regain strength. I want to bring to your attention that not giving

yourself "a time to rest" can be detrimental, even causing your body and mind to

spiral into exhaustion, depression, stress, mood swings, burn-out or body deficiencies. Remember that God Himself, who is all-powerful, rested from all his work!

The key focus scriptures are underlined
Thus the heavens and the earth, and all the host of them, were finished. And on the seventh day God ended His work which He had done, and <u>He rested on the seventh day from all His work which He had done</u>. Then God blessed the seventh day and sanctified it, because in it He rested from all His work which God had created and made.
Genesis 2:1-3 (NKJV)

Beloved, is there stillness, rest and quietness in your life? Could you use more rest, quietness, stillness and moments of inactivity in your social life, love life, financial life, emotional life or even your spiritual life; without feeling guilty, ashamed and doubtful? For instance, could your finances be screaming for some rest from your spending? Saving may be a way of stillness and rest to your financial life! Take a moment and ponder on how those five expressions of "silence" can transform and change an area of your life for the better. How can areas of your life benefit from more privacy, more stillness, more quietness, more rest, and de-activating?

A TIME TO SPEAK

Furthermore, the Hebrew word used for speaking is **dabar**, which means:

- to speak with one another,

- talk,

- declare,

- converse,

- command,

- promise,

- warn,

- sing,

Looking at these expressions of "speaking", many of us can recognise and have seen the reality of each of these expressions on a day to day basis, except in cases of health conditions and certain restrictions. Otherwise, many of us know how to talk, declare, converse, command, make promises, warn others and how to sing! Yet, how many of us know when to do each of these things? You see, the problem is not with you talking, but issues begin to arise when you talk too much. Discipline and boundaries distinguish the difference between two kinds of people; the wise from the simple. This is because when you set boundaries for your mouth, you will know when to talk and when to stop talking. As you master this, you will soon begin to notice the words you speak. Assuredly, talking in itself is beneficial, and in fact, there is nothing wrong with it, however, not knowing when to stop talking can soon expose folly, as it is written:

Do you see a [conceited] man who speaks quickly [offering his opinions or answering without thinking]? There is more hope for a [thickheaded] fool than for him.
Proverbs 29:19 (AMP)

The essence of knowing when to speak and when to be quiet is answered in Ecclesiastes 3:1 as written:

To everything there is a season,
A time for every purpose under heaven:
Ecclesiastes 3:1 (NKJV)

Child of God, can you see how the answer of "a time to speak" is confined to a season and a purpose? The reason why you must be silent and why you must speak is confounded in your season and your mission! It is no wonder why when we are not sure or aware of our seasons in the calendar of God, and we end up speaking recklessly.

If you knew that you were about to enter a season of earth-shattering breakthroughs, would you not be more careful in how you talk, what you declare, what you sing, whom you converse with, what you command, the promises you make, how you warn yourself and others? Understanding your season plays a great deal in how you behave, think about yourself, speak to yourself and others! So many of God's children have been robbed of their promised lands, birthing their right Isaac, meeting their spouse, attaining their crown of honour; simply because they didn't know when to be silent and when to speak! They didn't practice the art of being private in their talk in a crucial season of their life!

Other times, children of God cower down in seasons that require them to speak, to declare and to command; they become silent instead. Child of God, does doubt, worry, heartbreak and fear silence your voice box in seasons that need you to speak up? Despite your personality, your likes and your comfort zones, there is a season that requires you to speak life just like grass that needs to be watered.

Thus, purpose and seasons ought to be the two directives for why you and I speak or remain silent. Your mission and the purpose of everything connected to you will help you to know when and how to speak or be silent. The Hebrew word used for season is **zĕman** which means:

- a set time,

- appointed time,

- time.

As a result, there is a level of understanding for your times and appointed times that is needed along with the wisdom to know when to speak or when to be quiet. This understanding is crucial regarding events, situations, life journeys, conversations, relationships and decisions in life.

The Hebrew word used for Purpose in Ecclesiastes 3:1 is **chephets**, which means:

- pleasure;

- hence (abstractly) desire;

- a valuable thing;

- a matter (as something in mind)—acceptable,

- delight(-some), desire, things desired,

- matter,

- pleasant,

- purpose,

- willingly.

MASTERING WHEN TO KEEP SILENT AND WHEN TO SPEAK

Child of God, at times life may not allow you to be quiet or to speak, so you end up being ruled by what life presents to you instead of ordering life through principles of wisdom. Indeed, life may not even afford you the balance of speaking and being quiet, but you have the power to create that balance, that mindset and that moment. That power comes from the Holy Spirit. The Holy Spirit of God can counsel, help and lead you into all truth concerning your times, seasons and purpose on earth. The Bible urges us to live our lives according to our calling:

> So I, the prisoner for the Lord, appeal to you to live a life worthy of the calling to which you have been called [that is, to live a life that exhibits godly character, moral courage, personal integrity, and mature behaviour—a life that expresses gratitude to God for your salvation], with all humility [forsaking self-righteousness], and gentleness [maintaining self-control], with patience, bearing with one another in [unselfish] love.
> **Ephesians 4:1-2 (AMP)**

Unfortunately, if you don't know who you are, the treasures hidden in you, the seasons God is walking you through, your future, your authentic gifts and your calling; you may not be in a position to tune your voice to conform to your future through your speech. If you knew that you are a prophet, would you still speak carelessly about yourself and others? I'd like to believe that you would be more careful because you understand that a prophetic office carries different weight when it comes to spoken words. If you knew you were an evangelist, would you still be working for a company that causes you to always lie in order to make a sale? Child of God, is your real job interfering with the purpose and seasons of your life that demand silence in order for you to inherit God's promises? Perhaps it's your friends?

Today, everything can change if you are ready to allow the Holy Spirit to lead you! He can guide you and me through His wisdom on how, why and when to apply the action of speaking or remaining silent. You are not alone but God the Holy Spirit is in you! You can ask Him to give you the daily ability and power to create a window of opportunity whereby you can rightly and correctly apply the moments of talking and moments of silence. The LORD Jesus mastered the times to keep silent and the times to speak on several opportunities. We can learn from Him and begin to practice that in our day to day lives, as written:

1.   The LORD Jesus urges His disciples to go away to rest

Then the apostles gathered to Jesus and told Him all things, both what they had done and what they had taught. And He said to them, "Come aside by yourselves to a deserted place and rest a while." For there were many coming and going, and they did not even have time to eat. So they departed to a deserted place in the boat by themselves.
Mark 6:30-32 (NKJV)

As you can see above that people were coming and going, and the disciples barely even had time to eat. Yes people needed to be healed, they needed advice and they needed to be counselled, but Jesus still told his disciples to leave and go rest for a while. Likewise, life can begin to put a demand on us such that we will not find enough time to eat and sleep! There will always be someone who needs you, who is calling your phone for an emergency or who is asking for help. Child of God, sometimes it's okay to say no to the demands of life and to say yes to self-care and rest! Are you burnt out and stressed out? Are you nutrient deficient? Perhaps you can begin to be a disciple who goes away and rests? From today you can start taking short breaks, holidays and time-off regularly to simply rest! Did you know that the art of being silent also involves rest? When your body relaxes, your mind begins to recharge, and your body refuels.

2.   The LORD Jesus ignores His accusers.

Now Jesus stood before the governor. And the governor asked Him, saying, "Are You the King of the Jews?" Jesus said to him, "It is as you say." And while He was being accused by the chief priests and elders, He answered nothing. Then Pilate said to Him, "Do You not hear how many things they testify against You?" But He answered him not one word, so that the governor marvelled greatly.
Matthew 27:11-14 (NKJV)

The LORD Jesus teaches us a fundamental lesson on answering back to harsh critics, accusers, undercover bullies, fruitless debates, cynicism and day to day hate! There is wisdom in not always having the last say. Indeed, it's okay to not always answer back! The internalised "stillness" within you gives you a posture of mind and heart to not feel like you have to defend yourself to rumours, hatred, lies, fallacies and debates. The slander and entitled questions find no bridge to your heart to conceive worry, anger, nor defensiveness because you are at rest! Child of God, what's popular is not always what's true. Jesus was at rest in His truth and in that moment didn't need to explain His truth. He is the King of the Jews despite how many testify against Him. Beloved, it wasn't the question that the governor asked that mattered, it was why he asked the question. As you grow to be still, at rest and silent within, you will begin to hear the "why" behind words spoken to you, more clearly. Discernment flourishes in hearts that are at peace.

3.   The LORD Jesus tactfully answering back His haters.

Now it happened on one of those days, as He taught the people in the temple and preached the gospel, that the chief priests and the scribes, together with the elders, confronted Him and spoke to Him, saying, "Tell us, by what authority are You doing these things? Or who is he who gave You this authority?" But He answered and said to them, "I also will ask you one thing, and answer Me: The baptism of John—was it from heaven or from men?" And they reasoned among themselves, saying, "If we say, 'From heaven,' He will say, 'Why then did you not believe him?' But if we say, 'From men,' all the people will stone us, for they are persuaded that John was a prophet." So they answered that they did not know where it was from. And Jesus said to them, "Neither will I tell you by what authority I do these things."
Luke 20:1-8 (NKJV)

When the chief priests and scribes came to challenge the LORD Jesus and were being confrontational about His assignment and mission, He spoke back! Remember, there is a time to speak and a time to be silent. Jesus knew when to speak, but this "knowledge" was verified by what He spoke. Beloved, it's not so much about when you speak but much more so, how and what you say, that leaves an impact. What Jesus spoke had an impact on the scribes and chief priests such that the purpose of their confrontation, which was to challenge His authority, was dismantled. Likewise, when you get an opportunity to speak back, to defend yourself, to command things and to declare a matter, make sure that it is worthwhile. Use your time to speak productively! Say, "Holy Spirit, help me to speak back wisely on every opportunity and in every season that requires me to speak during challenges and trials, amen."

4. The LORD Jesus not retaliating after being insulted and abused.

He committed no sin, nor was deceit ever found in His mouth. While being reviled and insulted, He did not revile or insult in return; while suffering, He made no threats [of vengeance], but kept entrusting Himself to Him who judges fairly.
1 Peter 2:22-23 (AMP)

The LORD Jesus did not seek revenge at the Cross as He was suffering and being insulted. The LORD of lords did not threaten back those who were abusing and scoffing at Him! This does not mean that He was weak, but His vision and mission had to override the insults of man and their abuse. Christ's vision was Salvation, and His mission was accomplishing John 3:16 by taking on the sin of the world as the sacrificial Lamb of God and rising from dead! It took 30 years for Jesus to start His ministry and began to fulfil His mission after water baptism. When you know your mission in life and are on a mission towards that vision, you will afford to overlook certain kinds of noise, distractions and disturbances. The external storms of life will not be able to upset the internal stillness and peace within you! When we don't know who we are, what we have and where we are going in life; storms get the best of us because our pillars of peace and quietness were already dismantled. Hence, know your vision and be on a mission! The art of being private expresses itself through the keeping of your inner peace as you focus on your mission, goals and vision.

PRAYER

LORD God help me to know my purpose and my seasons that I may correctly apply my heart to understand when to speak and when to be silent. I repent of speaking carelessly and also of not speaking up when I should have! Father, by Your Spirit, empower me with wisdom and an attitude that is slow to speak but quick to listen. Reveal to me strongholds that I have built through my words and teach me to build what is right from this day forward. Deliver me from fear, worries, low self-esteem and doubt so that I can speak up boldly and loudly in every season that requires me to speak. Give me boldness like a lion to never be silent in a time to speak. This I pray in Jesus name, Amen.

CHAPTER 4

The Art of Keeping Private Victories Low Key

The key focus scriptures are underlined

Now David was the son of that Ephrathite of Bethlehem Judah, whose name was Jesse, and who had eight sons. And the man was old, advanced in years, in the days of Saul. The three oldest sons of Jesse had gone to follow Saul to the battle. The names of his three sons who went to the battle were Eliab the firstborn, next to him Abinadab, and the third Shammah. David was the youngest. And the three oldest followed Saul. But David occasionally went and returned from Saul to feed his father's sheep at Bethlehem. And the Philistine drew near and presented himself forty days, morning and evening. Then Jesse said to his son David, "Take now for your brothers an ephah of this dried grain and these ten loaves, and run to your brothers at the camp. And carry these ten cheeses to the captain of their thousand, and see how your brothers fare, and bring back news of them." Now Saul and they and all the men of Israel were in the Valley of Elah, fighting with the Philistines. So David rose early in the morning, left the sheep with a keeper, and took the things and went as Jesse had commanded him. And he came to the camp as the army was going out to the fight and shouting for the battle. For Israel and the Philistines had drawn up in battle array, army against army. And David left his supplies in the hand of the supply keeper, ran to the army, and came and greeted his brothers. Then as he talked with them, there was the champion, the Philistine of Gath, Goliath by name, coming up from the armies of the Philistines; and he spoke according to the same words. So David heard them. And all the men of Israel, when they saw the man, fled from him and were dreadfully afraid. So the men of Israel said, "Have you seen this man who has come up? Surely he has come up to defy Israel; and it shall be that the man who kills him the king will enrich with great riches, will give him his daughter, and give his father's house exemption from taxes in Israel." Then David spoke to the men who stood by him, saying, "What shall be done for the man who kills this Philistine and takes away the reproach from Israel? For who is this uncircumcised Philistine, that he should defy the armies of the living God?" And the people answered him in this manner, saying, "So shall it be done for the man who kills him." Now Eliab his oldest brother heard when he spoke to the men; and Eliab's anger was aroused against David, and he said, "Why did you come down here? And with whom have you left those few sheep in the wilderness? I know

your pride and the insolence of your heart, for you have come down to see the battle." And David said, "What have I done now? Is there not a cause?" Then he turned from him toward another and said the same thing; and these people answered him as the first ones did. Now when the words which David spoke were heard, they reported them to Saul; and he sent for him. Then David said to Saul, "Let no man's heart fail because of him; your servant will go and fight with this Philistine." And Saul said to David, "You are not able to go against this Philistine to fight with him; for you are a youth, and he a man of war from his youth." But David said to Saul, "Your servant used to keep his father's sheep, and when a lion or a bear came and took a lamb out of the flock, I went out after it and struck it, and delivered the lamb from its mouth; and when it arose against me, I caught it by its beard, and struck and killed it. Your servant has killed both lion and bear; and this uncircumcised Philistine will be like one of them, seeing he has defied the armies of the living God." Moreover David said, "The Lord, who delivered me from the paw of the lion and from the paw of the bear, He will deliver me from the hand of this Philistine." And Saul said to David, "Go, and the Lord be with you!"
1 Samuel 17:12-37 (NKJV)

In life, there are great battles, tricky challenges and needed light bulb moments that we can walk through in victory, but ironically we can go through these things when no one is watching. Again, there are winning moments we blaze through at the right time, that deserve applause but remain inconspicuous. Have you ever experienced a time of overcoming a significant obstacle in a season of your life when no one was watching? Have you gone through a challenge that was presented to you and through divine strategies and strength, you defeated that challenge, but there was no audience to clap for you and no witnesses to testify on your behalf regarding that successful transition?

Beloved, how content are you with winning private battles? How comfortable are you with winning battles in the absence of an audience without having an urge to shout it on the rooftops of social media, friendship circles, family dinner tables and business meetings; minutes, hours, days or weeks later? Assuredly, God presents to His children certain challenges for the sole reason of strengthening, preparing and training them for a more significant or different challenge ahead. There are some battles that God had sent you when there was no audience to protect you from distraction as He trains you! Yet, when you start being idle, talking too much by disclosing these private victories that the Holy Spirit is not leading you to uncover, this slows down the purpose of what God is trying to teach you. When we choose to side with our desire to be praised and cheered on, we can put ourselves in a place of vulnerability because some private victories are meant to be secret until your season to fight a more prominent and public battle, arrives! This is why we must understand the "why" before the "how" of every battle we are facing.

Can you discern that some of the private battles you've won still need to be kept private until the time of your next public promotion? Do you understand that when you promote yourself by revealing your private victory that is meant to be kept private, you are removing a stepping stone to your next public promotion? Hence, if you find that you are winning in secret, fighting battles in secret and that there hardly seems to be an audience to lift you, cheer you or recommend you; could it be that God is still training you for public battles?

In the quoted passage of scripture, we see the young man David, being sent by his father to give his brothers food. In the past, David would pop in and out to see his brothers, seeing the battles they were fighting, but this day was different. This sending from his biological father was really not about food for his brothers, but it was an orchestrated sending from God his spiritual Father! This was a God-led assignment and appointment for David to hear and see Goliath. On that day and that hour, God was appointing David to be positioned as a solution to a similar problem that he faced with his biological father's sheep! David had faced similar battles when an outsider would try to steal, kill or destroy his father's sheep. David discloses these private battles below:

> Your servant has killed both lion and bear; and this uncircumcised Philistine will be like one of them, seeing he has defied the armies of the living God." Moreover David said, "The LORD, who delivered me from the paw of the lion and from the paw of the bear, He will deliver me from the hand of this Philistine." And Saul said to David, "Go, and the LORD be with you!"
> **1 Samuel 17:36-37 NKJV**

This time, it wasn't a battle with lions and bears for his father's sheep, no, David was now needed by God to be a solution to God's sheep (Israel) and fight the outsider who was an uncircumcised Philistine, named Goliath. One would imagine that David had heard the sound of a hungry growling lion before it attacked his father's sheep. Indeed, he probably was aware of the pitch of a growling bear when it intruded his space with the intent to attack his father's sheep. Now God was sending David under the guise of his giving food to his brothers, to actually hear the sound of a giant's boastful growls before attacking

God's sheep; the nation of Israel. David listened to the speech of Goliath, he saw the height and built of Goliath but was not moved because in private, he had fought creatures just as bold, boastful and high! Beloved, can you recognise that some of the private battles you faced were positioning you to identify a public battle that you need to step up to and fight? The lessons and skills you learnt in secret gave you boldness to approach bigger lessons in public. Can you perceive how your private battles, experiences and skills were positioning you to become bolder? To be more courageous and fearless when society, financial markets, a world pandemic, a family crisis, and life demands need you to be a solution to a problem? Why ruin the process by telling everyone your private battles and lessons before reaching the pivotal battles that you have been training all along in secret, to fight?

One of the challenges of individuals who win a private battle and want to tell everyone immediately is not discerning and recognising the differences between a private victory and a public victory. Beloved, can you discern that every victory you've ever won in life, doesn't necessarily need to be shared? Can you recognise how some of your winnings still need to go on a time-out shelf in your heart until your external environment can sustain your victory's testimony? Understanding the difference between a private and public victory testimony puts you in a position that demands you have to foster care, intelligence, wisdom and vigilance because you now understand the sensitive connotation that comes with your battle.

David knew when to share the victory that was on a time-out shelf after his environment had changed in a way that sustained his report! After forty days and forty nights of Goliath presenting himself to Israel, the atmosphere shifted for David to step in! David fought a lion and a bear in private, but now he was putting himself forward to fight a public challenge in the form of Goliath. However, before David could face Goliath he needed to meet his discouraging brother who was making unsolicited accusations:

> Now Eliab his oldest brother heard when he spoke to the men; and Eliab's anger was aroused against David, and he said, "Why did you come down here? And with whom have you left those few sheep in the wilderness? <u>I know your pride and the insolence of your heart</u>, for you have come down to see the battle." And David said, "What have I done now? Is there not a cause?"
> **1 Samuel 17:28-29 (NKJV)**

Secondly, David also had to face being undermined by king Saul, as written:

> And Saul said to David, "<u>You are not able to go against this Philistine to fight with him; for you are a youth</u>, and he a man of war from his youth." But David said to Saul, "Your servant used to keep his father's sheep, and when a lion or a bear came and took a lamb out of the flock, I went out after it and struck it, and delivered the lamb from its mouth; and when it arose against me, I caught it by its beard, and struck and killed it. Your servant has killed both lion and bear; and this uncircumcised Philistine will be like one of them, seeing he has defied the armies of the living God."
> **1 Samuel 17: 33:37 (NKJV)**

Lastly, David had to face the intimidating words of Goliath, as written:

So the Philistine came, and began drawing near to David, and the man who bore the shield went before him. And when the Philistine looked about and saw David, he disdained him; for he was only a youth, ruddy and good-looking. So the Philistine said to David, "Am I a dog, that you come to me with sticks?" And the Philistine cursed David by his gods. And the Philistine said to David, <u>"Come to me, and I will give your flesh to the birds of the air and the beasts of the field!"</u> Then David said to the Philistine, "You come to me with a sword, with a spear, and with a javelin. But I come to you in the name of the Lord of hosts, the God of the armies of Israel, whom you have defied. This day the Lord will deliver you into my hand, and I will strike you and take your head from you. And this day I will give the carcasses of the camp of the Philistines to the birds of the air and the wild beasts of the earth, that all the earth may know that there is a God in Israel. Then all this assembly shall know that the Lord does not save with sword and spear; for the battle is the Lord's, and He will give you into our hands."

1 Samuel 17: 41-47 (NKJV)

Child of God, private challenges come with the sweetness of not arousing distractions from people in our lives and our circumstances. Public challenges, victories and lessons on the other hand, have a stipend of invoking further distractions. So then, before you announce things publicly, be prepared to face discouragement from people and situations, like David did that day on three different occasions before slaying Goliath. Hence, when you pre-maturely announce things without sufficient confidence, trust and boldness that was built up inside you during private lessons, battles and victories; your assignment can be diverted! Now because David's faith, self-esteem, courage and skills were forged in the private place during his private victories; he could not be easily discouraged when his brother tried to stop him from petitioning himself to king Saul. Moreover, when King Saul tried to undermine David's age, stature and life experiences; this was the perfect time for David to begin to herald his private victories and testimonies in king Saul's presence. Then, when Goliath tried to intimidate David, the young man was not moved because he knew how to respond without fear!

Therefore, the purpose behind David stating his private victories was not to show off, but it was to reassure and earn the vacancy for the job of fighting Goliath! Nowadays, many of God's children aimlessly boast, dabble and pipe up about their private victories to anyone who has ears. Perhaps out of low self-esteem or maybe a need to feel important? With information-driven platforms on social media, the need to "boast" is astounding! Those who aimlessly speak about things they ought not yet to speak, are not strategic in their thinking and have little substantial vision when they reveal their private victories so carelessly.

Beloved, we can both learn from David! He didn't need to tell his successes at the family dinner table. Ponder on that for a minute.

This young man's responsibility was to look after his father's sheep, each day he came home afterwards, perhaps his father or one of his eight brothers would ask him how his day went, yet, in all those years, he never revealed to anyone, according to biblical scripture, that he had fought lions and bears. That, beloved, ought to show you how David, though he was young, was mentally strategic and spiritually wise. The art of being private comes with a stipend of being strategic and wise! This is were some fail! They fail to be private by not knowing how to behave wisely and how to be strategic in behaviour and speech. The Bible says:

Be sober [well balanced and self-disciplined], be alert and cautious at all times. That enemy of yours, the devil, prowls around like a roaring lion [fiercely hungry], seeking someone to devour.
1 Peter 5:8 (AMP)

David was very low-key, keeping his lips sealed until the right opportunity to speak presented itself! An opportunity that demanded him to elaborate on specific credentials and life experiences. Indeed, to prove, assure and be accepted by king Saul for the role of fighting Goliath. Sure enough, if you study the rest of the story, you will see that the same power that came upon David in secret when he faced his adversaries in the form of lions and bears, came upon him again and rescued him from Goliath! David put his confidence in the LORD and killed Goliath. Beloved, these private victories are not for you to brag about but for you to use them as stepping stones to your next big battle, your upcoming season, your next lesson, your future investment. Indeed, these private victories are for you to gain strategies and use wisdom on whom to speak to about them, including when and why to do so.

PRACTICAL WISDOM TO APPLY

• Ask yourself, "what victories do I still need to keep on the time-out shelf of my heart?"

• If there is a particular victory or battle that you won, ask yourself, "why am I sharing this testimony?" Is it because you want claps and cheers from people? Is it because you genuinely want to encourage others by telling the world what God has done for you?

• If your motives for sharing things that are not yet meant to be shared are self-centred, egoistical, self-esteem boosters; could it be that there is a void inside of you that needs to be filled? Perhaps there is a need for attention that you are not receiving in your personal life, and you are compensating for that by over-sharing or pre-maturely sharing things to feel more accepted, more content, more confident or happier?

• Be honest with yourself and look within, does your confidence come from people, or does it come from God? If you were to share your ideas publicly, but your relatives discouraged you like David was discouraged by his brother, would you abort those ideas and bow down to discouragement? Would you thwart your goals if those who seem more mature, experienced and knowledgable told you that you are not good enough, like when Saul told David that he was too young to fight Goliath? Would you abort your plans if a situation threatened those plans via intimidation, just like Goliath tried to intimidate David? If you answered yes to any of these, it might be time to be developed in the secret place a little bit more until you can practice resilience!

• Scrutinise the private battles you have faced so far. Whether you won or lost, what have those lessons, struggles, and challenges taught you? Count one by one the skills you have developed from them and note them in your journal to pray over them.

• Begin to recognise and sharpen the skills, developments and lessons you received from your past battles and put this to practical use in your speech, actions, conduct and way of thinking in different areas of your life. For example, if losing a job and being financially limited has taught you to save the little that you have and manage your money more carefully; use those skills actively in your financial life despite having little or plenty. In turn, teach and invest in others to do the same.

CHAPTER 5

The Art of Letting Others Praise You

The key focus scriptures are underlined
Let another man praise you, and <u>not your own mouth</u>;
A stranger, and not your own lips.
Proverbs 27:2 (NKJV)

Although the entire Bible is the wisdom of God for teaching, reproof, correction and instruction in righteousness, the book of Proverbs is one of the 66 books in the Bible widely known as the book of wisdom. It reveals the simple and yet profound intelligence of God that can be applied in all walks of life. The highlighted scripture is an instruction that can be used in business environments, family communications, work relations, dating and love relationships, marriage and more.

We are being exhorted to "let another" person praise us instead of us as individuals praising ourselves! This proverb is correcting the posture of our hearts and renewing our mindsets because, in our fallible human nature, it is easy to slip into subtle but corrupt expressions of self-praise.

The type of praise the Bible is speaking about here isn't about giving a testimony or being transparent about a new blessing in one's life. It is the kind of praise that has a connotation to boasting. The word praise is originally written in Hebrew as **halal**. Halal is the same word used throughout the Old Testament in the Bible concerning praising God, and when it is translated to English, it means:

- to shine (figurative of God's favour)

- to rave about

- to flash forth light

- to praise

- to boast

- to be boastful

Can you see how this type of praise carries a criterial motive and an emblem that defines its true nature? This is not ordinary praise! In other words, let other people flash forth light on you, let others rave about you instead of you raving about yourself, let others boast about you instead of boasting about yourself, let other people shine you instead of shining yourself to others.

The Word of God is counselling us to exercise some level of self-control and humility through our speech and conduct. It is so easy to talk about how great we are but can what we say about ourselves live up to the expectations of others? For example, in television talent shows such as X-factor or The Voice, there is usually scenarios whereby a contestant is being interviewed before they perform in front of the judges. Some contestants begin to talk about how great they are and how angelic their voices sound only to let out a diabolical screeching sound! The extremely underwhelming voice singing in front of the judges exposes all the pomp that the contestant was masquerading as talent or confidence. He or she praised themselves but couldn't live up to their praise!

Beloved, when the Word of God is counselling us to let other people praise us, it is seeing beyond the speech and words being said because sometimes letting other people praise you, keeps you from embarrassment and living up to self-expectations that you can't afford to reach. None the less, if you are adamant about praising yourself to others, at least make sure that you live up to it.

Furthermore, the Bible expresses this kind of praise (halal) towards God, in the following scripture:

> Praise the Lord!
> Praise, O servants of the Lord,
> Praise the name of the Lord!
> Blessed be the name of the Lord
> From this time forth and forevermore!
> From the rising of the sun to its going down
> The Lord's name is to be praised.
> **Psalm 113:1-3 (NKJV)**

Can you see the essence of what praise means and how it is convenient when given appropriately? When praise is done out of context, it ceases to become praise, but rather it presents itself as self-glory and flattery. There is a difference between those who praise themselves and those who are praised by others. When you praise yourself, it "may" come off as self-glorifying and flattering yourself, on the other hand, there is more weight added when other people authentically boast about you, rave about you or give you shine.

No doubt, there will be times that you will incorruptibly rave about your hard work, talent, gift, strides, achievements, goals and so on but remember, when you "allow" others to do the raving about you, it witnesses more about your value in the ears of the hearer. An exceptional man named Job is described in the Bible as blameless and God-fearing to the extent of God Himself boasting about him (not in him) to Satan!

The key focus scriptures are underlined

Now there was a day when the sons of God came to present themselves before the Lord, and Satan also came among them. And the Lord said to Satan, "From where do you come?" So Satan answered the Lord and said, "From going to and fro on the earth, and from walking back and forth on it." <u>Then the Lord said to Satan, "Have you considered My servant Job, that there is none like him on the earth, a blameless and upright man,</u> one who fears God and shuns evil?"

Job 1:6-8 (NKJV)

Now let's say that Job started praising himself to the angels and people that he is blameless and God-fearing, though he would be correct, would his boasting hold more weight over God boasting about him? Likewise, child of God, it's not your truth that always matters to people but how and why your truth is communicated! Will you begin to allow others to praise you rather than you praising yourself to others?

We live in a generation that has catapulted boasting almost as a form of freedom of speech! With phenomenons such as face-timing, tweeting, blogging and vlogging; these engaging platforms can make it is easy for one to slip into boasting of oneself. There is nothing wrong with expressing ourselves, our styles, our gifts, our faith, our passions, our hobbies, our businesses, our families and homes through photography, writing and videos. We are all created to be productive, to shine and reflect God's glory even through our creativity. However, there is a small print of social media that if not discerned, one will use social media as an entertainment stage where he or she puts on the best show of their life for the world. As charming, lucrative and trendy as it is to use social media platforms to boast, on the bigger scale, this can potentially birth an indiscreet culture. A culture given a microphone when connected to the internet, to curate a facet of themselves without accountability. Now, there is nothing wrong with you and I curating an aspect of ourselves to the world, however, unless self-control and wisdom are exercised and instilled in us, our future generation could be in serious trouble! An advanced, privileged and fast-paced age that has no discretion is dangerous. Consequently, our lack of discretion begins to undermine the privilege of technology that we have now and the generations after us.

As a ring of gold in a swine's snout,
So is a beautiful woman who is without discretion [her lack of character mocks her beauty].
Proverbs 11:22 (AMP)

Beloved, self-control, humility, discretion and wisdom can start with you today in how you communicate, whether it is digitally, written or orally! There are ways to boast in wisdom and propriety. The Bible shows us about boasting through the lives of ordinary people who decided to set themselves apart for God's glory and also through ordinary people who on the contrary, sought after their own glory, as per below:

1. Apostle Paul chooses to boast in his weaknesses rather than his strengths:

If I must boast, I will boast of the things that reveal my weakness [the things by which I am made weak in the eyes of my opponents].
2 Corinthians 11:30 (AMP)

If I wish to boast, I will not be foolish, because I will be speaking the truth. But I abstain [from it], so that no one will credit me with more than [is justified by what] he sees in me or hears from me.
2 Corinthians 12:6 (AMP)

2. David boasts in the LORD before he fought Goliath:

And Saul said to David, "You are not able to go against this Philistine to fight with him; for you are a youth, and he a man of war from his youth." But David said to Saul, "Your servant used to keep his father's sheep, and when a lion or a bear came and took a lamb out of the flock, I went out after it and struck it, and delivered the lamb from its mouth; and when it arose against me, I caught it by its beard, and struck and killed it. Your servant has killed both lion and bear; and this uncircumcised Philistine will be like one of them, seeing he has defied the armies of the

living God." Moreover David said, "The Lord, who delivered me from the paw of the lion and from the paw of the bear, He will deliver me from the hand of this Philistine." And Saul said to David, "Go, and the Lord be with you!"
1 Samuel 17:33-37 (NKJV)

3. People in business or any career profession who boast in their plans and goals:

Come now [and pay attention to this], you who say, "Today or tomorrow we will go to such and such a city, and spend a year there and carry on our business and make a profit." Yet you do not know [the least thing] about what may happen in your life tomorrow. [What is secure in your life?] You are merely a vapour [like a puff of smoke or a wisp of steam from a cooking pot] that is visible for a little while and then vanishes [into thin air]. Instead you ought to say, "If the Lord wills, we will live and we will do this or that." But as it is, you boast [vainly] in your pretension and arrogance. All such boasting is evil.
James 4:13-16 (AMP)

4. A spirit of boasting (narcissism) that will sweep the world in the last days:

But understand this, that in the last days dangerous times [of great stress and trouble] will come [difficult days that will be hard to bear]. For people will be lovers of self [narcissistic, self-focused], lovers of money [impelled by greed], boastful, arrogant, revilers, disobedient to parents, ungrateful, unholy and profane, [and they will be] unloving [devoid of natural human affection, calloused and inhumane], irreconcilable, malicious gossips, devoid of self-control [intemperate, immoral], brutal, haters of good, traitors, reckless, conceited, lovers of [sensual] pleasure rather than lovers of God, holding to a form of [outward] godliness (religion), although they have denied its power [for their conduct nullifies their claim of faith]. Avoid such people and keep far away from them.
2 Timothy 3:1-5 (AMP)

Beloved, can you see the different motives of boasting? The question we can begin to ask ourselves when we boast is "why am I praising myself?" and "what is the result I am trying to get by boasting?" There is an underlying motive behind every form of boasting, be it in self or in God, and it's essential to explore this to avoid deception.

DO YOU "NEED" LOTS OF ATTENTION?

Have you ever seen in family dynamics, a child who is yearning for the attention of their parents? Regardless of the attention-seeking behaviour being negative, positive or healthy, attention is a basic need for every human from a very young age. From the time you were given birth, you needed attention one way or the other in the form of care, love and protection. Unfortunately, not everyone grows up to experience healthy care, sincere love and sufficient protection. Perhaps you were the child who didn't get enough attention growing up? Maybe you didn't experience consistent support, love, empathy and care in your childhood? It could be that you did not grow to know what affirmation sounds like, what praise and rewards from those you love and trust look like? Beloved, thankfully, you have the greatest Father who formed and fashioned parenthood! His name is Jehovah Elohim! He designed good parenthood, and He always sees you even when those close to you can't. As related by the Psalmist David:

O Lord, you have searched me [thoroughly] and have known me.
You know when I sit down and when I rise up [my entire life, everything I do];
You understand my thought from afar.
You scrutinise my path and my lying down,
And You are intimately acquainted with all my ways.
Even before there is a word on my tongue [still unspoken],
Behold, O Lord, You know it all.
Psalm 139:1-4 (AMP)

If you didn't receive enough attention growing up, the Father is there for you as your parent, and He will never leave you nor forsake you! You can always go to Him for refreshment as you enter His presence through prayer and praise. You are welcome to enter His throne room and tell Him all that is in our heart even though He sees it all; you have access to His everlasting peace, love and joy through Jesus Christ.

Child of God as you manoeuvre through different life experiences such as childhood, adolescence, education, career, relationships, marriage, parenthood, business and so on; the human nature's need for attention in the form of approval heightens. Hence, due to that human nature of needing attention, our egos, heads and hearts can cunningly implode as we go through these seasons of life. Even the most secure individuals can become attention-seeking if they do not anchor their heart on God's Truth whose understanding sets the soul and mind free.

> And you shall know the truth, and the truth shall make you free."
> **John 8:32 (NKJV)**

The Holy Spirit wants to teach and counsel you from the foundation of God's Truth. There is a humility, assurance, confidence and identity that can begin to be carved in your heart as you discover what God thinks about you through the Holy Spirit.

Often, our life experiences can carve out elements that hide underneath the surface of our souls, until dealt with. Aspects of fear, insecurity, pride, arrogance and low self-esteem. People who are insecure in themselves or have low self-esteem lean towards seeking "constant" praise, assurance and adoration for the express need of feeding barrenness that is concealed inside of their hearts. The low self-esteem is a mindset of doubt and fear. A person may look and speak confidently, but the fear, worry and doubt inside their heart is speaking another language. Such people who depend on applause are often in survival mode as their oxygen masks attach to the words of people. Their security is in the approval of man. Hence, the closer you get to know them, the facade of confidence seems to wither away as their mask slips off when you discover that the confidence is flawed and counterfeited self-praise.

How laborious it is to pretend consistently, only for people to get close to you and discover the real you that you were concealing behind self-boasting and self-praise. It is tragic when people realise you weren't as bold, confident, talented, intelligent, skilled, affluent, educated, beautiful, anointed or whole as you claimed to be but instead, you were playing the "fake it till you make it" game positioning yourself to receive accolades of attention. Here's an illustration of what that behaviour looks like. Sometime during the ministry of the LORD Jesus when He was out and about, He became hungry. He then saw a fig tree from afar off, looking lush, green and promising of food. However, the closer He got to it, the more disappointed He became! It's written:

Now in the morning, as He returned to the city, He was hungry. And seeing a fig tree by the road, He came to it and found nothing on it but leaves, and said to it, "Let no fruit grow on you ever again." Immediately the fig tree withered away.
Matthew 21:18-19 (NKJV)

Child of God, are you always telling everyone how green your leaves are? Is your confidence from your speech louder than the faith in your heart? Do you live up to the self-praise you herald? Unfortunately, you can only put up a facade for so long before those close to you begin to see that your constant self-praise is only a tool you are using to fish for praise. They will soon discover that you are only trying to appease the lack of authentic fruit in your life. It's only a matter of time before people become exhausted with the constant need for attention and praise. Understand that those who are great, do not tell people how great they are. Instead, their greatness is recognised by others. Real authentic confidence should become a fruit that others in your life can enjoy. So then, ask yourself, what is the drive and motive behind your self-praise and attention for praise? What is the source of your confidence? Is it from people or from God's Truth that sets you free?

The problem with fishing for praise and adoration from people is that the results are often short-lived, causing the attention seeker to walk and live in a cycle of pleasing people. Seeking attention and praise from people can dangerously lead an individual to over-sharing, overexposure, over transparency and unrestraint openness to people and environments that are not called to see facets of that individual's life.

YOUR GREATNESS WILL SPEAK FOR ITSELF.

It's intriguing how our LORD Jesus, the most famous Man ever, would often heal people in the Bible, then tell them to tell no one about Him or about what He has done. As written here:

The key focus scriptures are underlined
When Jesus departed from there, two blind men followed Him, crying out and saying, "Son of David, have mercy on us!" And when He had come into the house, the blind men came to Him. And Jesus said to them, "Do you believe that I am able to do this?" They said to Him, "Yes, Lord." Then He touched their eyes, saying, "According to your faith let it be to you." And their eyes were opened. And <u>Jesus sternly warned them, saying, "See that no one knows it." But when they had departed, they spread the news about Him in all that country.</u>
Matthew 9:27-31 (NKJV)

As you can read above, this didn't stop these two healed men from telling other people about Jesus! There is a way that praise from other people spreads quickly as compared to self -praise! Nowadays, people are hungry for praise and adoration to the point of shouting their good works from the roofs of the house! The LORD Jesus did not have to tell people how great He is, constantly. The Anointing continually witnessed this on His behalf! Child of God are you in ministry, in business, in the corporate world or a competitive career? Let others praise you instead of praising yourself to others!

Correspondingly, businesses, companies, brands and innovative leaders have long caught onto the wisdom of letting other people praise them according to Proverbs 27:2! They call it "word of mouth" advertising or marketing. They have discovered how the power of allowing other people to praise their business models, employment structures, products and customer services can grow their influence, power and wealth! What a tragedy when Spirit-filled believers turn the blind eye and don't maximise this concept but business heads who are not necessarily Christian, apply it! Applying the concept of "letting others praise you" in business has become one of the most potent forms of marketing a brand or company. The only catch is that the brand or business must genuinely be outstanding lest the "word of mouth" becomes negative free-marketing.

Hence, when looking at some of the world's most successful brands or products, you will often find that their work speaks for itself. Have you ever seen a Bentley commercial on your favourite television channel? You will barely see Bentley commercials advertised. Beloved, if you master your craft, your gifts, talent; to grow and develop over time, whatever that is produced out of them will spread like fire through word of mouth and recommendations. Remember, those who are really great, do not go around telling people how great they are, rather, their greatness is recognised by others. King Solomon was one of the most wisest man on earth, and because his wisdom was so exceptional, people would travel from remote parts of the world just to hear him speak!

"Now all the earth sought the presence of Solomon to hear his wisdom, which God had put in his heart."
1 Kings 10:24 (NKJV)

Beloved, people will seek you when they discover your value! It's not so much about what you say about your value, but the value people put on you, when they find out about you. In this context, Solomon's value to people is clearly seen by the demand of visitors to his life. What has God put inside you? Do you know the treasure He has buried in you? Are you willing to really invest your time, resources and energy into developing that treasure, such that people will begin to honour and boast about you?

PRACTICAL WISDOM TO APPLY

It's not too late to shift areas of your life by analysing and applying Proverbs 27:2. Today you can start here:

- **Don't compare and compete with others**. The posture of comparison and competition is often laden with frustration, panic, fear, anxiety and paranoia. Some today are battling with inadequacy, low self-esteem, anxiety and all sorts of unnecessary money spending simply because of acts and thoughts of competing. Beloved, be "still" in your own story and identity. Stop watching what so and so is doing now, next or tomorrow. Let Christ form in you entirely! There is great peace that comes in knowing that you are "fearfully and wonderfully made." There is confidence in knowing that your Father in heaven has unique plans for you that are for peace and not disaster, plans to give you a future filled with hope. Remember, your power is in discovering you, the you that no one else can ever be, the you that is one in billions of the world's population, the you that will never be replaceable! Your true identity is your inbuilt power!

- **Discover yourself!** Often, we end up praising ourselves out of fear, doubt, low esteem and emptiness because we don't have authentic confidence and a true identity but are looking for co-signers. Other times we get so caught up in planning for the future, wishing we had something we don't have today and working to accomplish specific dreams such that we don't make time to live in the moment and learn about who we are "at the moment". Who are you today? Can you focus on that first? When it comes to discovering certain aspects of yourself, be patient as you grow in the LORD because this is a "process" that can take weeks, months or years before coming to the surface of your life. Allow yourself to change, shift and let go of the old for the new. Change is part of your growth.

- **Accept who you are!** Usually, people who are whole and know who they are rarely feel the need to boast about themselves. Their wholeness and fulfilment are from within. Their joy, peace and happiness is a fruit of the Spirit that external forces and influences cannot drive out. This is why it is important to discover every aspect of you as much as you can; what you like, what you don't like and what inspires you. Then take steps to live out those things you want and are inspired by because just as there are moments of self-discovery, there is also a part of self-acceptance to that self-discovery, that you need to embrace. Do you accept the person you are becoming? Do you accept the growth, changes and edification taking place in you or are you boasting about yesterday and comparing yourself to people who are at different seasons than you? Did you know that after you accept yourself, you now need to learn how to be content with who you are and what you have? Contentment is the start to accepting yourself and has the power to drive out boasting, facades and unrealistic expectations.

• **Fuel your growth.** Learn to fuel the passion you have for your hobbies, skills and talents to develop yourself and your craft, using diligence to live out the "you" in this now moment of your life. Therefore, if you spend your time, resources and energy in becoming the best version of you, you will not need to compete nor feel the need to tell people how great you are because sooner or later your life will emulate your greatness. You won't need to log onto Facebook or Instagram to parade your greatness, but people that have experienced your greatness will log onto Facebook and Instagram to talk about their experiences concerning your gift, talent, skill or ability! The Spirit of God can help, teach and counsel you to become the best version of yourself. Ask Him daily to help and guide you be the real authentic you.

CHAPTER 6

The Art of Living a Quiet Life and Minding Your Own Business

"...But we urge you, brethren, that you increase more and more; that you also aspire to lead a quiet life, to mind your own business, and to work with your own hands, as we commanded you..."
1 Thessalonians 4:10-11 (NKJV)

In our daily lives, we are given the maximum power of choice in how to behave, systematically think and curate our experiences. Indeed, we are continually being afforded moments of conducting ourselves in a way that is worthy of honour and admiration, especially as individuals who are called to be saints in Christ.

Beloved, the principle of living a quiet life is a doorway that gives room to a staircase of knowledge—knowledge in minding one's own business. No matter how you have been conducting yourself in the past, today you can choose to live your day to day life in such a way that accommodates quietness while applying the principles of minding your own business.

In today's culture, countless things are being curated by society, the economy, technology, systems and more in our day to day living; pulling you and me against these two critical coping strategies! The methods of the world push us further and further away from understanding what quietness and minding one's own business resembles. Many individuals are left feeling short of, uninspired and too empty to make it an aim to lead a quiet life and mind their own business because that is against current trends, lifestyle and conducts. Beloved, in a staged world of Instagram, Tik-tok, Facebook and Youtube, are you left feeling insecure, confused, discouraged and dampened about aspiring to live a quiet life with family, friends, colleagues or acquaintances? Do you find yourself unable to mind your own business because of pressure?

We live in a generation where drama is marketed as a trend and injected into our daily lifestyle and culture. An age that capitalises on sexual immorality, impurity, debauchery, idolatry, witchcraft, hatred, discord, jealousy, fits of rage, selfish ambitions, dissensions, factions, envy, drunkenness, orgies and the like. Hence, a quiet and private life becomes rarer and somewhat of an unorthodox way of living.

Think of how unique "star rubies" are. They are beautiful, mesmeric in colour but very rare. You too are like that precious jewel in God's eyes and His Spirit is calling you and me in this generation to be set apart and display His beauty as rare jewels of His Kingdom and power. Being a treasure that defines a different magnitude of quietness, just like a multifaceted ruby stone that displays its clarity, rarity, beauty and shine. Hence, people may not understand the hidden depth of what living a private and quiet life really entails. Yet, living a quiet life shows an overlooked character of peace that you and I need to create for ourselves perpetually. A character represented by you protecting the volume of noise you will allow into your life.

When you become acquainted with adjusting the volumes of external noise in your personal life, it means you don't engage in drama, online clapping back, arguments, petty discussions, prying and gossip! For example, you just became friends with a new person, but they are full of insecurities, drama and conflict; their dysfunction is starting to spill uncontrollably into your own life. What do you do? You set boundaries! Those boundaries are your ability to adjust the noise in your friendship-life. Child of God, the ability to tune out the noise in your life to create more peace and quietness is not personality-based but is an essence of wisdom, vigilance, class and excellence. For example, Daniel was an exceptional man with an excellent spirit in the government sector. His work ethic, looks and diligence began to invoke extreme jealousy in his insecure peers, attracting drama even as he minded his own business. Never the less, Daniel had learnt the concept of adjusting external noise and decided to put on the volume of "ignore" towards the evil antics and jealousy inspired threats; as seen in this account.

The key focus scriptures are underlined

Then this Daniel distinguished himself above the governors and satraps, because an excellent spirit was in him; and the king gave thought to setting him over the whole realm. <u>So the governors and satraps sought to find some charge against Daniel concerning the kingdom; but they could find no charge or fault, because he was faithful; nor was there any error or fault found in him. Then these men said, "We shall not find any charge against this Daniel unless we find it against him concerning the law of his God."</u> So these governors and satraps thronged before the king, and said thus to him: "King Darius, live forever! All the governors of the kingdom, the administrators and satraps, the counsellors and advisors, have consulted together to establish a royal statute and to make a firm decree, that whoever petitions any god or man for thirty days, except you, O king, shall be cast into the den of lions. Now, O king, establish the decree and sign the writing, so that it cannot be changed, according to the law of the Medes and Persians, which does not alter." Therefore King Darius signed the written decree. <u>Now when Daniel knew that the writing was signed, he went home. And in his upper room, with his windows open toward Jerusalem, he knelt down on his knees three times that day, and prayed and gave thanks before his God,</u> as was his custom since early days.

Daniel 6:3-10 (NKJV)

Beloved, it takes the wisdom of God to know when and how to respond to noise! As you may know, Daniel was persecuted, thrown into the lion's den but he came out without a scratch! **He was kingdom-focused not hater-focused.** You too have power to stop the noise or to allow noise into your home, your marriage, your relationships, your spiritual walk, your job and career but you need God's wisdom and direction to implement that maximum power of choice by being kingdom-focused.

Therefore, quietness will demand you to design "it" for yourself. The Spirit of God has indeed equipped you to do this if you are willing to pace through His design-plan with Him and allow Him to teach, help, empower and counsel you in how to do this. Remember we are all unique to God, and every individual faces different levels of distractions, noise and battles according to the life plan God has written for each one of us. It is the Holy Spirit who can help you, and I curate and mirror God's perfect will.

People often mistakenly attach this biblical quietness and minding your own business to personality. They look at it from an introvert or extrovert perspective. Unfortunately, our personalities simply don't have enough capacity to house God-inspired principles of "living a quiet life". Let me illustrate that to you through John 15:1-2. The LORD Jesus says:

"I am the true vine, and My Father is the vinedresser. Every branch in Me that does not bear fruit He takes away; and every branch that bears fruit He prunes, that it may bear more fruit.
John 15:1-2 (NKJV)

He was giving His disciples a glimpse into authenticity and imitation. He was trying to show them that there are many vines and many people who will come claiming to be the real deal, but I am the real deal, I am the only begotten Son of God, I am the "only" way to the Father! I am the truth and the life! Beloved, having a quiet personality does not validate the right principles or reality of living a quiet life. This is something that is inspired by the Holy Spirit and founded on the Word of God!

The Bible reminds us of the principles of minding your own business and living a quiet life, as it is written, "aspire"! Aspire! ASPIRE to live a quiet life!

"...But we urge you, brethren, that you increase more and more; that you also aspire to lead a quiet life, to mind your own business, and to work with your own hands, as we commanded you..."
1 Thessalonians 4:10-11 (NKJV)

Beloved, being private is a posture and attitude birthed in your heart and mind. It's something that all believers in Christ, whether an introvert or extrovert, whether mature or childish, whether male or female; are called to aspire to. When your mind and heart seeks to live a quiet life, that will be the beginning of that creditable reality in our thoughts, words and actions!

LIVING A QUIET LIFE

Every one of us who wants to create quietness out of life will need to start somewhere. You will have to decide the paintbrushes, the type of colours, the depth of colours, the stroke and movements that you will make as you paint the accurate and ideal picture of a quiet life that your life can accommodate. Beloved, a quiet life is something you will need to design for yourself! In the current social climate we live in, it takes some self-control (which is a fruit of the Holy Spirit) to design that kind of life.

The Word used for "quiet life" in the bible is originally written in Greek as **hēsychazō**, which means:

- to be silent,

- quiet

- acquiesce,

- to desist from the discussion

- to be still,

- at rest;

- to live peaceably,

Sometimes cultures, childhood, upbringing, family dysfunctions or your current lifestyle can imprint roots of chaos that curate drama, noise, distractions and turmoils; limiting you from desiring or experiencing the beauty and joys of quietness. Yet, glory be to Jesus Christ who came to heal us of every dysfunction and chaos that steals, kills and destroys the peace that is found in quietness! The Spirit of God longs to journey with us into territories of "living a quiet life" where we experience the strength of it, the peace of it, the freedom of it and no longer the pressure curated through unsolicited movements of noise or internal and external conflicts!

For instance, perhaps growing up in your family with your siblings, you always had to compete and pull each other down to survive and thrive? Are you carrying this same nature into your friendship and career relations? You cannot be happy for others and find yourself competing with friends, jealous or envious, pulling them down in your thoughts because you just don't know any better? Sibling rivalry can become a printed pattern of thinking and behaviour that can seep through into an individual's friendships and even marriage. Individuals who always competed with their siblings may end up in their adult life competing with their friends or their spouses. It's a miserable mindset that feeds and thrives on competing, low self-esteem, pride, envy and jealousy. The world calls sibling rivalry normal, yet when you look at it with spiritual eyes, you can see it is a dangerous mindset that enables toxic thoughts and behaviour.

Beloved, perhaps the picture you had of living a quiet life was depicted as quietness demonstrated through a personality? The Spirit of God wants to help you to experience the mysteries and whimsical dimensions of living a quiet life according to His perspective and vision. A quiet life in your thoughts, meditations of the heart, speech, behaviour and general lifestyle. There is great peace in quietness! There is love, joy and happiness in living a quiet life. Indeed, a quiet life creates an internal drama-free life. The internal wars diminish and are pulled down as you anchor onto a new way of thinking that is inspired by God's Word and Spirit.

Therefore, beloved, are you ready to hewn this type of quietness into your lifestyle? The Bible gives a footpath on how to begin to incorporate this into your daily life by urging you to make it a goal, an ambition, an objective to "live quiet life"! This means that you must make the active choice of deducing anything that is like noise in your life. Noise can be interpreted differently for everyone. For example, to me personally, in the area of friendships, noise is a friend who gossips, is envious, cynical, continually bickering or is a backbiter. That may not be the case for everyone. Hence, you have to figure out for yourself what noise looks like to your life and destiny. What are the things that distract you from your day to day progression, career, ministry, brand, family life and love life? If they take away from God's glory and His will for you, that my friend, could be noise that you need to retune.

DEFINING MINDING YOUR OWN BUSINESS

We live in a culture where human rights, equality, discrimination acts, technology, trends and perspectives are so advanced that there is a sense of entitlement that can make it difficult for the average person to establish boundaries that define "minding one's business". Take, for example, when you sign up to open a Facebook account, they will ask you your date of birth, your country of residence, your relationship status moreover access to Facebook will require access to your microphone, photographs and phone number. Beloved, technology has made your business its own business!

Another illustration is posting life events on social media. If you were to post your new engagement ring, instead of being merely congratulated, one or more onlookers may use this life update to find out details beyond your new engagement by enquiring from you when you are going to get married. Should your life updates give people the warrant to know more? Certainly not! Undoubtedly, our generation has lost the art and essence of minding its own business due to being entitled! How then can we define minding our own business in such a generation?

Minding your own business is described by society as "not asking questions about a situation that does not involve you or simply to stop meddling in what does not concern you". However, in the Bible, the original Greek words used for minding your own business are a clue to the mind of Christ concerning this.

Mind - the Greek word used is **prassō**, which means:

- to exercise,

- practise,

- to be busy with,

- carry on

- to undertake

- to do

- to accomplish and perform

- to commit and perpetrate

- to act

Your own business - the Greek word used is **idios**, which means:

- pertaining to one's self, one's own, belonging to one's self

- his (own, proper, several),

- home, (her, our, thine, your)

- own (business),

- private

The Bible is looking beyond the surface and urging us all to practice, exercise, accomplish and commit ourselves to the things that belong to us, ourselves, our homes and private affairs. The Bible is teaching us that it is improper and intrusive to commit ourselves to other people's private matters, belongings and homes.

As an illustration, social media can disguise such biblical boundaries, and if you are not careful, you may end up studying someone that you follow on social media by busying yourself with their life, home and belongings. Some who were studying other people's lives soon got taken advantage of by Satan when he saw how they were abusing their time. Satan began to plant thoughts of jealousy, envy and comparison. There's a saying that goes, "the devil finds work for idle hands".

Child of God, sometimes minding your own business can eliminate certain kind of attitudes and behaviours towards others. Attitudes and practices of gossiping about others, contentions with others, jealousy and envying towards others. You certainly can't control what people share about their lives, but you can control how you manage your time, what you commit your 24 hours to, what you practise when on social media or around people who are sharing information about their lives. Lastly, you can control how you accomplish your own life goals and private matters rather than other people's lives. Practising to be busy with your own life can keep your soul from troubles and aide productivity in your personal life!

SMALL STEPS OF MINDING YOUR BUSINESS

Social media

Look at the list of people you are following and those on your friend list. From these lists, are there people you are currently studying to the point of being consumed by their life? Their pictures and statuses move your heart more than the scriptures you read in the Bible in your own time? Child of God, there is nothing wrong with being inspired by an individual because we all have someone who inspires us, but there is something wrong with going on a person's profile 5 - 10+ times a day! Do you agree that that may be a sign of a form of obsession? Look again on all platforms of your social media, are there individuals that you have now busied yourself with more than you busy yourself with your own life? It may be time to limit how many times you visit people's profiles, perhaps cut down to once or twice and if this is a hard thing, it may be a sign that you have made an idol out of these individuals. Otherwise, it may be time to unfollow these people for the sake of your soul?

People you admire

Are you vivaciously living through other people? Be honest with yourself, are you morphing into your friend, a relative, a public figure or a celebrity? Have you lost sense of the authentic you, your gifts, talents, hobbies, likes and dislikes; studying this person's life? It may be time to take a step back and discover who you are. It's easy to get caught up in another person, but facing your reality can help put the real picture of your life into perspective.

One-upmanship

One of the characters of minding your own business is contentment in yourself and possessions; keeping you from the attitude and behaviour of one-upmanship. Such an attitude and mindset is very unwholesome and toxic, fuelled by a pre-occupation with out-doing another individual, to feel superior. If one is not careful, they may tumble into delusions, worry and fear; manifesting as anger, inferiority complex, superiority complex, anxiety, fits of rage, bitterness, feelings of depression, jealousy, envy and low self-esteem. One-upmanship is very prevalent in workplaces, in neighbourhoods, in family meetings, in church gatherings, within sibling relations, on social media platforms; somehow, somewhere there is a fearfully and wonderfully made individual who is not content and happy with who they are and what they have until they out-do their opponent. Cambridge dictionary defines it as, *"the art of achieving, demonstrating or assuming superiority in one's rivalry with a friend or opponent by obtaining privilege, status, status symbols."*

Beloved, what is the motive behind your achievements? Your drive? Your vision? Does your confidence come from being better than your rivals, or does it come from the Word of God? Are your achievements, assets, possessions, titles and status symbols concealing a small print of how you "don't mind your own business" but instead how you've made the belongings and lives of other people, your business? Child of God, can you see how minding your own business can begin to invite an atmosphere of peace, contentment and grace to grow? Do you perceive how not minding your own business can fuel an ambition to know the belongings of another person for the motive of competing and out-doing them so that you feel outstanding and superior?

Do you carry an attitude of wanting to know what other people are planning, wearing and achieving, to out-do them? If they buy a new coat, you have to get three new coats? If they move into a new house, you suddenly feel you need to move into a bigger house with a swimming pool? They bought a car, and now you are online shopping for a new car? The single acquaintance who is expressing her desire to take her future kids to private school and you being a mother, homeschooling yours but you suddenly have a change of mind to enrol your kids in a top private school? Your best friend gets engaged, and now you want to buy a promise ring with a diamond bigger than hers. These are all attitudes that the Holy Spirit wants to deal with, in each of us. The Spirit of God wants to work with you to uproot this toxic way of thinking, and it starts by taking small steps of minding your own business. Child of God, will you begin to work with the Holy Spirit today, to mind your own business?

Not Wasting Time

How much time do you spend on bettering your mind, faith walk and physical life? Be honest, do you spend 2-3 hours looking at what so and so is doing and then you only manage to squeeze in 1.5 hours a day on bible-study, prayer, therapy, business goals and your life in general? Minding your own business may free up more time to concentrate on building your present and future to leave a legacy. For example, 3 hours of researching and examining another person's life may not seem vapid in the short term perspective of 1 day, but when added together on a longer-term of 48 months, that's 4380 hours out of 35040 hours wasted! You've spent 182 days, that is half of a year focused on somebody else's life! Could you start looking at managing your time better daily? Concentrate on your growth, faith, career, family, goals, ideas and plans to add value into these. This will prove more fruitful for you in the big picture of life.

Entitlement

Part of minding your own business is resisting the urge to know what so and so has done, is doing and will be doing. Do you feel entitled to know what other people are doing, what they think and what their goals are? Here's a secret that can serve you well if you apply it - **never "feel" that you have the right to know more than what is presented at the table by anyone who is not your spouse** unless it has to do with the Word of God or is educative. As Christians, we are encouraged to study, research, seek and find the hidden mysteries of God's Word, but we are not encouraged to study and research acquittances, neighbours and brethren in Christ. Child of God, be polite, be content and be grateful that that individual has shared a facet of their life with you, beyond that, wanting to know more is prying and unprecedented curiosity which is improper according to God's Word.

There is a danger of entitlement and inability to mind one's business that has driven some Christians to trespass into witchcraft without even realising it! Witchcraft through false visions, false words of knowledge, false prophecy and false dreams because of fake prayers built on intrusion rather than love. They were praying with evil motives, and Satan took advantage of their hypocrisy. Child of God, do you use prayer as a weapon to monitor people? Instead of edifying through prayer, you have become a monitoring spirit? Before you pray for them, is your motive genuine or intrusive? Prayer has to have the ingredient of love! In the spirit realm, we cannot hide because our motives and hearts are laid bare. Do you often feel entitled to know more than what is being said or shown by someone? Is this sense of self-entitlement due to your upbringing? Is it a cultural behaviour? A church tradition? Is it due to being bored with your own life? Is it because of pride? Is it based on your position in society or ministry? Today, you can choose to start taking the steps of minding your own business by being aware of your feelings and way of thinking. Have the mind of Christ. You can begin to put a new foundation that aligns to God's Word in how you respond to people's information by conducting yourself according to God's Word in 1 Thessalonians 4:10-11.

Not controlling the narrative

Do you busy yourself with other people, in this case, namely haters, to the point that you worry about what they are saying and thinking about you?

Do you spend time trying to control the narrative of how people will perceive you? Child of God, do you busy yourself with trying to know what people think of you, if they like you, why they hate you, what they are planning about you? If people are speaking, feeling and thinking bad or wrong things about you, is that the end of your world?

Well, minding your own business is like an inner and outer job. The inside job creates an atmosphere for you. An atmosphere and mindset of peace, joy and contentment. Whereby you do not try to control people's thoughts, reactions and words about you. Here's a secret that can serve you well if you apply it in your life - **what other people think of you is none of your business, but what God thinks of you is what counts!** The moment you begin to understand and apply this, is the moment you will be freed from people bondage which can manifest itself as worry, second-guessing, paranoia and doubts. The Bible says:

Also do not take to heart everything people say, Lest you hear your servant cursing you. For many times, also, your own heart has known that even you have cursed others.
Ecclesiastes 7:21-22 (NKJV)

Making yourself of no reputation

Having a good reputation is excellent. However, we become ensnared when the opinions of what people have about us start to preside above God's view and Words; enslaving us. When your reputation lays in the hands of people's beliefs, admiration, respect, you will soon be in trouble if you don't live up to the laws and expectations of that reputation! Indeed, reputation in the hands of man is fragile, inevitable to shame, rejection, loss and degrading but your reputation in the hands of God is indicative of fruitfulness and multiplication. The Lord Jesus gives us an example of being free from the slavery of reputation. He lived below the expectations of what His form is associated with! The Lord Jesus is the Word of God that became flesh, yet He decided to take the form of a servant, losing Himself from the obscured expectations of man.

> Let this mind be in you which was also in Christ Jesus, who, being in the form of God, did not consider it robbery to be equal with God, but made Himself of no reputation, taking the form of a bondservant, and coming in the likeness of men. And being found in appearance as a man, He humbled Himself and became obedient to the point of death, even the death of the cross. Therefore God also has highly exalted Him and given Him the name which is above every name…
> **Philippians 2:5-9 (NKJV)**

Peace begins when you seize from trying to prove yourself to people. Many fall into the ditches of derision trying to prove their reputation's worth and value. It is tragic when all of one's years, months or days of trying to maintain or keep a reputation are suddenly lost because someone no longer sees them as the image they were trying to manage and preserve. Beloved, your worth is not confined to a reputation. Whether you have one or not, you are the express image of God, beautifully and wonderfully made, unique from any other human being on earth and you have greatness within you! Stop striving to keep an image that can easily be lost when you say the wrong things, do the wrong thing or even think the wrong thing. What reputation are you driving yourself to keep? Is it worth your mental health? Is it worth your financial health? For example, you are living hand to mouth, but you purchase clothing items or products to make you look like you are rich or better than your opponent or frenemy? Are you in intentional debt because you are trying to keep up an image?

Rumours and Stories

When you hear a scandal or a story circulating, do you just join in quickly by making small talk, sharing the story or partaking in those discussions? Did you know that sometimes when you do not mind your own business, this can attract plagues in your life? Never engage and conclude on rumours, stories and heralds of people whom you have not directly discussed the matter with and come to a place of transparency. For instance, Moses in the Bible married a black woman, but his sister Miriam and his nephew Aaron didn't understand his decision and felt that he was wrong to do that. They were so sure of their own opinions, perspectives and theories. They thought that they knew better than him and began to make small talk about his marriage and decisions; until God stepped in. Sadly, there was an unfortunate turn of events because Miriam ended up with leprosy.

The key focus scriptures are underlined

<u>Then Miriam and Aaron spoke against Moses because of the Ethiopian woman whom he had married</u>; for he had married an Ethiopian woman. So they said, "Has the Lord indeed spoken only through Moses? Has He not spoken through us also?" And the Lord heard it. (Now the man Moses was very humble, more than all men who were on the face of the earth.) <u>Suddenly the Lord said to Moses, Aaron, and Miriam, "Come out, you three, to the tabernacle of meeting!"</u> So the three came out. Then the Lord came down in the pillar of cloud and stood in the door of the tabernacle, and called Aaron and Miriam. And they both went forward. Then He said, "Hear now My words: If there is a prophet among you, I, the Lord, make Myself known to him in a vision; I speak to him in a dream. Not so with My servant Moses; He is faithful in all My house. I speak with him face to face, Even plainly, and not in dark sayings; And he sees the form of the Lord. Why then were you not afraid to speak against My servant Moses?" <u>So the anger of the Lord was aroused against them</u>, and He departed. And when the cloud departed from above the tabernacle, suddenly Miriam became leprous, as white as snow. Then Aaron turned toward Miriam, and there she was, a leper.

Numbers 12:1-10 (NKJV)

Therefore, child of God, be careful about joining in fruitless debates and conversation, regardless of how sincere, engaging and convincing it sounds, learn to mind your own business!

PRAYER

Holy Father, forgive me for making idols out of people and for making an idol out of myself. LORD Jesus be the Master of my life from this day. I surrender my heart, mind, soul and strength to You! God, teach me by Your Spirit how to practice minding my own business and living a quiet life from within so that it overflows out into all areas of my life. Reveal to me how to apply this wisdom in my daily life, empower me by Your Spirit to practice this wisdom for without You, I can do nothing. Reveal the Truth of living a quiet life and minding my own business according to Your good, acceptable and perfect will for me. This I pray in Jesus name, amen!

CHAPTER 7

Conclusion

What have you learnt about yourself and about God ways and plans, from the 6 chapters in this book? What tools of encouragement have you taken with you to begin a new journey as you apply these principles of being private? Take it one step at a time and be consistent as the Holy Spirit continues to reveal to you the art of being private according to God's will for you!

I pray that every form of blindness that you had before reading this book was removed through the Blood of Jesus Christ and that daily you will fill yourself with Jesus through His WORD, which sets you free. I pray that every chain of imprisonment that was entangling you was broken by the anointing of God, the Holy Spirit.

Beloved, if you have not yet given your life to Jesus the Christ, you are missing out on real love, hope and peace that transcends all understanding. It's written:

"If you confess with your mouth, "Jesus is LORD," and believe in your heart that God raised him from the dead, you will be saved."
Romans 10.9 (NKJV)

Just believe in your heart today that Jesus is the Son of God and confess it with your mouth. Say "Jesus I believe You are the Son of the living God, today be the

Lord and God of my life and teach me Your ways daily by Your Spirit, fill me right now with Your Holy Spirit in Jesus name, Amen."

You are now a new person in Christ, forgiven and sanctified! Now purchase a Bible in the NKJV or a version you understand better. If you don't already have one, beginning with the book of John read all through it. Read also Luke, Mark and Matthew and all the way to Revelations. Afterwards, you can then read from the book of Genesis back up to the book of Matthew.

Begin to study your Bible daily to know who Jesus is and who you are in Him. Even if it means being secluded from the world and from your friends for a time, even if they mock you, believe me, knowing who you are first through knowing who Jesus is, is more important than anything in the world. Lastly, although there are many online Bible teachings including Bible study teachings that I personally do every Wednesday (via my youtube channel titled Dephne Aviyah), I, however, strongly recommend that you find a bible teaching local church that practices the love of God, ask your relatives or friends where they attend church and then start attending church services, Bible studies and prayer meetings so that you can grow as you fellowship with others.

The grace of our LORD Jesus Christ, the love of God and fellowship of the Holy Spirit be with you today and forever. Amen. God bless you.

In His service

Dephne Victorious Aviyah

Acknowledgements

To my beloved husband Lloyd, I love you so deep. Thank you for your encouragement, prayers, mentorship, wisdom and love. You continue to inspire me to be the Dephne that God has called me to be.

To my parents, you are the best supporters a daughter could ever pray for. Thank you for helping me choose the book cover and for your continued support.

To my Pastors, faithful servants of God, thank you for your leadership, spiritual covering, direction and wisdom. May God continue empowering and watering you just as you empower and water me and all those under you.

References

www.biblegateway.com

http://www.blueletterbible.org/

http://www.dictionary.com

http://www.merriam-webster.com/

https://dictionary.cambridge.org/dictionary/

Contact Author

Website: www.dephneaviyah.com

Twitter: twitter.com/dephneaviyah

Instagram: instagram.com/dephneaviyah/

Facebook: https://www.facebook.com/dephneaviyah

Youtube: https://www.youtube.com/c/DephneAviyah/

Printed by Amazon Italia Logistica S.r.l.
Torrazza Piemonte (TO), Italy

28127605R00075